How to Get the Most Profit From Your COLLECTIBLES

A.J. KOCH

ARCO PUBLISHING, INC.
NEW YORK

Published by Arco Publishing, Inc.
219 Park Avenue South, New York, N.Y. 10003

Library of Congress Cataloging in Publication Data
Koch, A. J.
  How to get the most profit from your collectibles.
  Includes index.
  1. Collectibles as an investment.   I. Title.
AM237.K62   332.6'3   81-10896
ISBN 0-668-05119-1 (Cloth edition) AACR2
ISBN 0-668-05121-3 (Paper edition)

Printed in the United States of America

10 9 8 7 6 5 4 3 2 1

Contents

CONTENTS

CONTENTS

Acknowledgments

Illustrations and cartoons by Pascal Golay and Mary Miller. Photographs are courtesy of Christie's, Phillips Fine Art Auctioneers, William Doyle Galleries, Inc., Gem Antiques, J. P. Bittner, and the National Association of Watch and Clock Collectors. Useful information and guidance came from Carousel Art, New Orleans Jazz Club, the Pen Fanciers' Club, International Netsuke Collectors, Lillian B. Gottschalk, Classic Car Club of America, and The Society of Early American Decoration. Cover photo by Daniel Entino.

Preface

Collectibles have been a part of almost every culture since antiquity. Some objects have been collected for their usefulness, others for their beauty. Today, the range of objects considered collectible has expanded from such venerable and valuable standards as stamps, coins and art to more popular and useful items, such as pottery, glassware, old tools and all kinds of purely decorative objects.

Interest in collectibles has increased enormously during the past decade in the United States. It has been stimulated in part because some collectibles have proven a good investment and in part because there is a groundswell of interest in collectibles as home decorations, particularly when they have historical and aesthetic interest.

Most collectors and dealers will rightly advise you to buy an individual collectible because you like it or "fall in love with it" rather than because it is likely to gain in value over the years. The point of this book is to combine these motives. Many highly attractive collectibles cost considerable money to accumulate, insure, care for and display. Your primary benefit may very well be your enjoyment of the collecting process. But in our contemporary climate of inflation, there is no point in collecting something that is likely to stand still in value, or part of an overpriced fad, or of little intrinsic value to begin with. Following the principles of this book, you should find yourself collecting with greater financial reward as well as with greater personal satisfaction.

The lore of individual collectibles often grows and changes greatly within the course of each year, as new collector clubs form, as newsletters and magazines spring up—or die. New value-records are set; new prized objects emerge from obscure corners throughout the world. The information in this brief, quickly-read handbook was obtained from many sources and was accurate at the time it was written; readers are referred to many books, newsletters and magazines through which they can keep up-to-date on their chosen collectible.

Because the author continues to write articles in this field and will revise later editions of this book, collectors and readers are invited to relay new information about what is happening in the market of their favorite collectible.

Bibliography

In addition to the many books already listed in the text, the following books, magazines and newsletters are useful to collectors in pursuit of their prizes . . .

Art & Antique Auction Review, a newsletter published monthly by University Arts, Inc., IFM Building, Old Saybrook, CT 06475. It reviews, with many black-and-white pictures, the recent hammer prices at major international and regional auctions. Reading it is a fine way to monitor special auctions of your favorite collectible.

Antiques World, a magazine published monthly by Antiques News Associates, 122 East 42 Street, New York, NY 10168. Handsome illustrations in four colors aid the collector in keeping up-to-date on a wide variety of the top collectibles and their care.

The Encyclopedia of Collectibles, Time-Life Books, Alexandria, VA 1978. This is a fine source for pictures of many popular collectibles in color, from advertising giveaways to world war memorabilia. Comes in 16 volumes on a serial-purchase basis. It is available in some libraries.

Kovels on Antiques and Collectibles, a highly readable monthly newsletter for dealers and collectors. Address is P. O. Box 22200, Beachwood, OH 44122. It comments on a wide range of collectibles in the news and includes both prices and ways to determine authenticity or identification.

The Official Sotheby Parke Bernet Price Guide to Antiques & Decorative Arts, edited by Charles C. Colt, Jr., Simon and Schuster, New York, NY 1980. This volume includes about 33,000 entries and 1,300 black-and-white photographs of items that were actually sold at Sotheby's recent auctions.

Spinning Wheel, a bimonthly magazine of antiques and early crafts published by the American Antiques and Crafts Society, Fame Avenue, Hanover, PA 17331. Fine for popular craft items and collectibles of U. S. origin.

1

Profits from Your Collectibles

Why the rush to collectibles, or tangibles as the professional economists call them? The answer, in a word, is *inflation*, galloping inflation and the tough times investors face in trying to stay ahead of it.

Virulent inflation is something new to the United States investor. True, some inflation throughout our history (for those who take the trouble to study it) is an occasional fact of life. But such a wave of persistent inflation as this country had endured recently has not been part of the United States experience for generations.

How Previous Waves of Inflation Affected Collectibles

A recent article in *Forbes* magazine pointed out that during the past 1,000 years, until 1940 or so, there had been only three major periods of inflation in the English-speaking world. The first occurred around 1200 as England, conquered by the Normans in 1066, settled down to a feudal society dominated by rich and powerful local rulers with fealty to the King. The country prospered and foodstuffs, shelter and tangibles were in demand.

The second great inflationary upsurge occurred about 1600 at the time of the late Renaissance and its explorations. The middle-class capitalists began to assert themselves and, in turn, prospered. The fortuitous discovery of gold in the New World brought treasures and natural resources that increased enormously the wealth of the colonizing countries.

Again, at the beginning of the 1800's, there was an upsurge coincident with the Industrial Revolution as entrepreneurs, businessmen and shareholders in their enterprises prospered and swelled the demand for the material abundance of this world.

1

"But Mom, I'm saving for college!"

On each wave of inflation new groups of people came to enjoy wealth. Like the early powerful lords after the Norman invasion, they showed their wealth and their place of power through their furnishings, castles, country places, and city mansions. Artists and craftsmen flourished. All manner of collectibles were created to please the newly rich—those who had recently arrived at a station in life where they had the leisure and the money to accumulate objects of beauty or of interest.

The fourth period of great inflation, into which the Western world moved after the reconstruction period of World War II, might be termed the post-industrial society with its expanding government bureaucracy, expanded business administration, "information" service business, increasing leisure time, and also, since 1973, rapid increase in the price of oil and of the sources of energy. The emphasis, in this era, is on producing services, diversions and space exploration rather than goods. For the first time, the average person has an opportunity—the time and the means—to become a collector of sorts.

With each wave of inflation the market for collectibles has expanded further. Auction houses were born in the 18th century to handle goods and furnishings accumulated in England and else-where at the time of the Renaissance and recognized and written about by the enlightened pens of that time. The modern breed of intelligent collector was born in such trend setters as Horace Wal-pole, son of the great Whig politician of Queen Anne's time (1702–1714), Sir Robert Walpole.

The experience of the very early collectors taught the people who had newly found leisure and wealth that collections had a practical purpose as well as an ability to provide a deep-seated pleasure. The value of collectibles—good collectibles—persisted despite the political ups and downs of princes and their merchant allies, who occasionally went bankrupt in business. The collector, adapting to such failures, could often maintain his family and his home quite well on the proceeds of the sale of a collection. Many of Europe's titled and/or wealthy families and many affluent people in the United States manage this same graceful transfer of value *to this day.*

Effects of the Present Inflationary Wave on Collectibles

What the Europeans have known for centuries, the U.S. citizen has begun to learn since the 1950s, when the fourth great inflationary trend set in.

With inflation sapping the national power and causing a radi-cal revision of family and living style, there has come a new rise in values for tangibles, as the U.S. collector ransacks attics for any-thing that might be sold. The auction houses have repeatedly broken records for prices, now for this type of art or furnishing, now for that. *Not all periods, not all artists,* have appreciated equally but, given time and continuing inflation and the expanding markets for collectibles, prices for all *periods* will even out *upon new high ground.*

While it is true that some collectibles, such as Art Nouveau and Art Deco furniture, posters, bronzes and glass, hitherto ne-glected (Art Nouveau and Art Deco paintings and drawings still are), have appreciated more swiftly in recent years than such ven-erable collectibles as old masters, coins and stamps, this is mostly a matter of galloping percentages from a low base. Once a collect-ible has had its day of play, it settles down to appreciate at a fairly steady rate, supported by the enthusiasm of a growing horde of collectors competing for a limited supply.

Which Collectibles Will Furnish the Best Profit

In general, the most traditional collectibles, listed in group 1 below, will get premium play as profit makers because they have proven themselves as preservers of value over the years. There is an organized auction market for them and long-established dealers handle them. Their liquidity and marketability as collectibles make them increasingly buyable via credit cards or lines of credit granted by a bank.

In group 2 are brash new collectibles, sought out because they have intrinsic value, an aura of nostalgia or historical value, but that have not yet been bid out of sight by collectors and institutions, even though they have been rising at a good rate.

Then there are the collectibles of group 3—those that some individuals collect fanatically but that have relatively little popular appeal to a broad group of collectors, have limited liquidity and a thin market, and are thus probably going to stand still in value for a few more years until they break out and join the second rank.

THREE GROUPS OF COLLECTIBLES

1. Old masters, Chinese ceramics, stamps, coins, rare books, antique jewelry, silverware, export porcelain, paintings of all periods, sculpture, period furniture, American Indian art, pre-Columbian art, professional photographs, watercolors, drawings, and graphics of well-known artists, snuff bottles, autographs, historical prints

2. Paperweights, antique marbles, antique bottles, comic books and comic-strip art, Disney cels, dolls, dollhouses, decoys, classic cars, antique tools, paintings, watercolors, and drawings of lesser-known artists, domestic furniture and furnishings of recent years, art pottery, art glass, popular ceramics, beer cans, baseball cards, postcards, phonograph records of certain "stars" or of historical performances

3. Advertising art, bottle caps, match covers, barbed wire, contemporary containers in all materials, architectural decorations, amateur photographs, old mass-circulation magazines, most old phonograph records

Professional Investors Are Turning to Collectibles for Enriched Return

The plain fact of the matter is this: Even the professional financial community is getting into tangibles or collectibles as a more rewarding investment, at least for the time being, rather than their traditional media such as stocks and bonds or government paper.

As John Marion, President of Sotheby Parke Bernet, said about the new service announced by this auction house and Citibank to assist new investors in the acquisition and maintenance of fine art, antiques and similar property, "Citibank and Sotheby Parke Bernet are responding to the public's increasing awareness of the importance placed on the ownership of tangible property." With college funds, pension funds and major investors feeling their way into these hitherto unfamiliar markets, there is a rapidly expanding attempt to educate the public about items seldom bought for investment because the ordinary investor, and even the expert financial advisor, knew little or nothing about them. To an extent, it is a case of the eager blind leading the desperate blind. And of course, both are in for some disillusion. Nonetheless, the rush to collectibles is on and your best protection is the protection all true collectors have: *actual and extensive knowledge of your collectibles.*

The Difference Between a Collector and an Investor

For the purpose of differentiating a collector from an investor, assume that a collector is a person who collects something, either of value or not. He/she accumulates beloved objects, sometimes willy-nilly, sometimes with great knowledge and with cultural repercussions, as did Horace Walpole in the 18th century. He wrote knowledgeably about art, built Strawberry Hill, a model of quaint rusticity near London, ran a private printing press and generally, through example and writing, generated the Gothic revival in English and American architecture. He also popularized collecting among literate people.

To cite a more recent example, there is Sheldon Wilmarth Lewis, who died recently. He collected Horace Walpole letters and memorabilia, wrote about them all his life and left his home and library in Farmington, Connecticut, to his alma mater, Yale. Neither of these men considered their collections an investment but both, particularly Lewis, knew that their collections had an increasing value. For today's communication networks magnify the ramifications of provenance and attribution and thus the publicity hedging items that were once part of a collection of a famous or extremely discriminating collector.

An investor, on the other hand, by definition entrusts his money directly, or through a broker/advisor, *to someone else's judgment* in the hope of income or a profit. By custom, these days, the investor can, but is unlikely to, retain managerial control of the invested capital; most investment media provide for inside management with the shareholder or investor rather remote, though not always, from the action of the enterprise. With the collector, the success or failure of his or her enterprise rests squarely on the collector's acumen and ability to acquire a superior and meaningful collection. At the same time, with established collectibles—unlike investment in 1,000 shares of General Electric—the sum of the whole of a superior collection is worth far more than the sum of its parts.

For example, the John N. Luff collection of stamps through the year 1940, when John Luff retired from collecting, is unique in the world. Mr. Luff was editor of Scott's catalogs and he attempted, in

"It's that lawyer of your Uncle Milton's estate, dear. More delays, more excuses. With this inflation, aren't you glad Uncle Milton left you his collection of rare stamps rather than his money?"

order to evaluate and describe the stamps in the annual catalogs accurately, to have on hand an example of each and every stamp printed for every country of the world since stamps were originated by Sir Rowland Hill in England, in 1840. That meant a century of stamps. His incomparable and practically priceless collection is now used by the Philatelic Foundation, a nonprofit research and educational institution located in New York City, as a touchstone against which can be measured the authenticity of stamps submitted to its Expert Committee for an opinion. The foundation was organized for the benefit of stamp collectors in 1945. Needless to say, the Luff and other collections used for the same purpose of verification are kept in a vault and treated as a rare treasure.

As it happens, stamps, like rare coins and books, are mature collectibles with well-established clubs for collectors and stable markets. All three have rewarded collectors financially during the past years, particularly stamps, which rose in value, according to Scott's index, 61 percent in a recent twelve month period. And the sale of the Marc Haas collection of U.S. stamps and covers in September of 1979 caused a new high record for any collection of stamps. About 3,200 items went for a total in excess of $10 million. Mr. Haas was a New York businessman and a devoted collector over a period of about 35 years. He was an investor in more conventional media, too, but he will probably be remembered above all for the quality and value of his stamp collection.

Performance of Collectibles in Recent Markets

Collectibles have fascinated professional financial advisors for only a few years now, since they began to realize that there was more money made in these tangibles than in traditional stocks, bonds and foreign exchange. In fact, the traditional media could not keep up with the rapidly inflating Consumer Price Index (CPI).

For four years now, the underwriting and stock brokerage firm of Salomon Brothers has been comparing the performance of tangibles with traditional financial assets. For the year ending June 1, 1979, they added rare books to their rankings for the first time. Why? Because rare books, over a ten-year period, had appreciated on average 15.7 percent a year.

The following table breaks out a number of traditional investment media and compares them with a number of collectibles and commodities and two forms of real estate.

**COMPARATIVE PERFORMANCES OF SELECTED
INVESTMENT MEDIA AND COLLECTIBLES**

Compound Annual Rates of Return

	10 years	Rank	5 years	Rank	1 year	Rank
Oil	30.8%	1	20.9%	5	14.3%	6
Gold	28.0	2	30.7	3	−13.9	14
Oriental Carpets	27.3	3	20.9	6	−0.2	11
U.S. Coins	27.1	4	29.7	4	−8.0	12
U.S. Stamps	23.5	5	32.9	1	18.0	4
Chinese Ceramics	22.9	6	30.7	2	36.5	1
Silver	21.5	7	20.1	7	−26.6	16
Rare Books	16.8	8	13.8	11	18.0	5
Old Masters	15.4	9	16.8	9	22.9	3
Farmland	14.6	10	14.8	10	9.7	8
Diamonds	14.5	11	16.9	8	0.0	10
Housing	10.3	12	11.6	12	8.1	9
CPI	8.3	13	9.7	14	10.0	7
Stocks	5.8	14	9.8	13	25.3	2
Foreign Exchange	5.3	15	3.1	15	−17.3	15
Bonds	3.8	16	1.1	16	−9.6	13

Source: Salomon Brothers.

Salomon Brothers' analyst notes that the tangibles, or collectibles, have demonstrated over the past ten years a price growth well in excess of inflation rates, whereas traditional investment media *have not.* And even though the analyst (with a natural bias toward his familiar stocks and bonds) believes collectibles are highly priced in relationship to underpriced stocks and bonds, *he is not willing to say that tangibles have no further to go.* And he is probably right. Tangibles will tend to maintain a steady upward trend, for there are factors at work that make them behave differently than gold or silver, or other volatile "collectible" commodities. Commodities via paper certificates of ownership have a common unit value; collectibles do not; each unit tends to be unique, with its own flaws, age, color, scratches, authenticity, provenance and the like. A Krugerrand—the contemporary currency of the Republic of South Africa—is a Krugerrand and contains exactly one ounce of fine gold; there are so many in circulation that it has hardly any *numismatic* value. Its actual value fluctuates with the daily price of an ounce of gold. This may be up or down. A gold piece with numismatic value, such as the U.S. St. Gaudens $20 gold piece, has scarcity, condition and aesthetic value, which give it a price of about $2,000–many times its value in ounces of gold. These are qualities a collector of coins, or numismatist, will know intimately, a knowledge beyond the capability or interest of most investors or the usual sort of investment advisory service.

Traditional Investment Advisors
Get into the Act

Reliable advisory services and banks that want to attract investment money know and feel this gap in knowledge. As they start to put together portfolios of stamps, coins and art, they usually employ or tie in with an expert. Citibank, in announcing a new art-investment plan for investors with $1 million or more, has retained the services of a former vice president of Sotheby Parke Bernet, the auction house. The expert is a man who knows paintings and their markets thoroughly and presumably will collect art on behalf of the millionaire investors. Citibank will charge an annual management fee of 1 percent of the portfolio's value. Many of these sponsored plans begin with high minimums until the bugs are worked out; then they are opened to the smaller investors with, say, $25,000 to put in. You pay a fee for the expertise and you can switch if the chosen portfolio does not perform as you expected. Citibank, down the road, is undoubtedly anticipating business from college endowments, various trusts and pension plans—the really big money that is dangerously hurting from low returns on bonds and stocks. You can expect other such plans to appear in the next few years as institutions, with millions of dollars to invest, enter the collectibles market and actively choose relatively few objects. In the case of distinctive, one-of-a-kind collectibles of highest quality, the prices can only go one way—up sharply.

The new collection scene has made the Madison Avenue auction houses an unexpected rival of Wall Street for attracting new money from investors. When you used to say Madison Avenue, you meant "advertising." The new "Madison Avenue" means art galleries and collectibles, both in shops and auction houses such as the pioneering Sotheby Parke Bernet with its bustling rooms on Madison and its sibling on York Avenue for decorative objects; the Phillips Gallery, on Madison Avenue and at 501 East 72nd Street; Christie's on Park Avenue and 805 East End Avenue; and the innumerable shops specializing in all manner of collectibles up and down the avenue between the fifties and the nineties. The William Doyle Galleries and the Manhattan Galleries are just a few blocks off Madison, on the upper east side. From this hub of activity, these firms have branched throughout the United States and competitive auction houses in many cities now take their marketing cues from the "Madison Avenue" leaders.

Characteristics of a Collectible with Profit Potential

There is purely personal psychic pleasure in chasing and accumulating collectibles of various sorts for decoration and the sheer power of accumulation—Freud knew this—but if you want to make a *significant profit* you must as soon as possible become an expert in the objects you collect. You may have no one to tell you anything. In that case you will have to fall back on your native wit, curiosity and self-education through mistakes. That is an extreme situation, however, since most worthwhile objects—those that have intrinsic value such as gold coins and sterling silverware, or have aesthetic value such as oil paintings, or have both such as jewelry—have already attracted thousands of collectors who have organized the market and written books; they are serviced by dealers and, in short, are simply waiting for you to get your feet wet and join them in a most profitable pleasure. For sheer fun, you may want to collect tin-can labels, plastic detergent bottles made since World War II, candy-bar wrappers (all the Baby Ruth wrappers since the bar went on the market in the 1920's!) or old radio sets— a fascinating collection of electronic devices as well as furniture; some radio cabinetry was fairly good Art Deco. You may even create a new craze for low-tech items of modern design to succeed the rage for high-tech decor. Well, these collectibles are intriguing and may attract some publicity in design magazines overanxious to observe new trends and the decline of old ones—although the latter may just recently have left their cradles. The frenetic futurists do serve a purpose, however; they virtually assure that every collectible will have its day. So, if you really must collect folk-protest epigraphy from the late 20th century (anti-nuke posters, etc.), do it as your *second* collectible and let out fully the manic stops of your psyche. *But to assure yourself of profit,* make your first choice from the many established collectibles with these characteristics:

1. *A generous supply* in the hands of many collectors who can be persuaded to trade, who are willing to form a market in which there are reliable dealers who know what they are handling and will vouch for the authenticity of what they are selling.

As already mentioned, the value of things collected totals more than the sum of the several parts. Your significant collection will be worth more as a whole than will be the sum of its valuable parts. When other investment media tail off to indifferent rewards, investors will naturally look to alternatives that seem to have preserved value, even increased it against the challenge of inflation. And when substantial and essentially untutored wealth enters the market of collectibles, the prices will naturally rise: There are limited numbers of most traditional collectibles available, just so many stamps, coins, antique paperweights. And some investors, switching to collectibles, have a lot of capital they can use in competing for prize collections and collectibles.

2. *A network of collectors,* joined by researchers, dealers and auction representatives who act as winnowers and sifters of what are really important specimens in your field. Many popular collectibles have a membership association that educates the public, does research and to a certain extent tries to act as a board of appeal in matters of authenticity. Dealers and auction house experts usually maintain close touch with these associations. Some collectibles with not enough enthusiasts to maintain an association may have informal clubs scattered throughout the country. These clubs also serve as market outposts and centers of expertise.

3. *A means of communication:* coverage in a newspaper, newsletter, perhaps discussion on a radio program or a TV show. It helps when the collectible is regularly offered at auction, either locally or in New York, because newspapers covering the auction will talk about the collectible; ads will mention and picture it. It helps even more to have an auction house somewhere in the United States that *specializes* in your collectible. You will feel better if the auction occurs near you. But lacking that, be sure that there is market action *someplace,* where you might go once a year for a firsthand view of the specimens coming up for sale, where you might ship your seconds or duplicates for sale and where you might mail or telephone a buy/bid.

4. *Aesthetic, historical or practical* value: A good collectible will have one or more of these values, sometimes all three, such as an Art Deco chair from the liner Normandie on which one can still sit, which has its position in the history of furniture and which is highly attractive with its upholstery intact, or perhaps in a less valuable sample, which has its fabric replaced by one duplicated in modern thread. A less important collectible, such as postcards with stamps intact, may come from significant commercial studios in individual countries. Some of these featured artists or photographers who later became famous. Some have historical significance, such as French postcards depicting the Paris Exposition Universelle des Arts Decoratifs in 1925, which had a lasting influence on the Art Deco movement.

Much of the pleasure and fun of collecting emerge from your contact with fellow collectors, the immense delight in whisking a prime specimen from under the itching fingers of a competitor intent on possession. Sometimes, another collector happens to focus on an area complementary rather than competitive with your own; with such a person a lasting relationship may prove rewarding.

Collecting is an infinitely more human, more intelligent and more civilizing experience for the individual who participates than is most investing. The passionate collector accumulates a meaningful group of specimens, learns their significance, communicates with others about them and often adds to the sum of human knowledge. That is what collecting is when practiced on its highest level, as with Horace Walpole; or J. Pierpont Morgan, whose books resulted in the Pierpont Morgan Library; or Henry Frick, whose painting and sculpture collection is now in his own splendid mansion on Fifth Avenue in New York; or J. Paul Getty, whose accumulation of art inhabits a recreated Roman villa near Los Angeles.

The Exception of Mail Order "Limited" Edition Collectibles

Various manufacturers and merchandisers are today capitalizing on the popularity of collectibles by deliberately creating contemporary plates, medals, commemorative coins, figurines, glass, signed prints of well-known artists, fine-edition books and other objects where the supply is flexible. The offering is usually so structured that the sponsor is assured of a good profit immediately and the quantity of plates, medals or books published is directly related to the number of those who order. If about 100,00 persons order a plate, that number is manufactured and then the mold is destroyed. Special graphics are run on the volume principle. The sponsor is guaranteed a profit with a *few* or *no leftovers.* Or you may be offered a portfolio of prints from a famous living artist, *each limited to 500 signed and approved by the artist.* Here, while it is true that the particular print is limited to 500, the artist is still living and presumably agreeable to making 500 new prints of *another of his paintings.* Thus the artist himself becomes a nearly inexhaustible supply of new material to satisfy the market. In so doing, he enriches himself and his sponsor, but the collector holding the merchandise may be chagrined to find it does not sell very well on the after-market.

These schemes are convenient for passive collectors. The sponsors often hedge their promises of increased value by mentioning that prints have been known to double in value after a certain number of years. But in most cases the basis for this claim will turn out to be in other *supply/demand circumstances*—an older print or plate, or a fine-edition book that had a truly limited edition of less than 500 and was sought after by discriminating collectors.

Importance—and Rewards—of Expertise

The true collector, in distinction of the passive collector, or the collector/investor, knows all these supply/demand facts and has a good idea of the actual quality and supply of the object and of what is available to the market. To make money in your collectible, you simply have to know as much as possible about it, aesthetically, historically and economically. You combine the work of a scholar with that of a detective and intuitive financier. You can, of course, employ the services of an expert—many great collectors of art have done so and both collector and consultant have profited handsomely. Bernard Berenson, the immensely intelligent and brillant collector and art critic, helped several wealthy U.S. patrons to amass collections of enormous distinction and beauty. The commissions enabled Berenson to pursue his own research for about six decades of his mature life. This is something you could aim to do, too, as your collector's skills increase. Collecting—buying better pieces, selling duplicates or inferior pieces to build up your main collection and collecting fees as an appraiser or consultant—can soon furnish a second income and certainly give you plenty to do during retirement years from a previous profession.

Collecting can very well run in the family; it is not unusual at all for a stamp collection to be passed down from father/mother to son/daughter; for coins to accumulate over several generations; and for paintings gathered by one generation to be pared in quantity and refreshed in quality by the next with the best of each generation's enthusiasm preserved. Sometimes the collection passes to an institution that will appreciate this tangible wealth if there are no strings attached to the gift. Sometimes it goes to the wrong institution, which sensibly realizes the mismatch, takes the financial benefit and releases the care and feeding of the collection to a private collector or to another institution more capable of giving it meaningful support and protection.

A Collection in the Family: The Story of the John Work Garrett Coin Collection

The John Work Garrett Collection of coins is a case in point. Its auction in four parts began at the end of November 1979 and brought record prices for a coin collection as a whole and for individual pieces. It included two Brasher doubloons, one in mint state and of the finest quality known, which in itself exceeded a pre-auction estimate of $500,000. It went for $750,000.

The collection was actually begun in the 1860's by T. Harrison Garrett, later president of the Baltimore & Ohio Railroad. By the time he died in 1888, he had built it into one of the finest collections specializing in U.S. coinage. Two of his sons, Robert and John Work Garrett, maintained and improved the collection after their father's death. John Work Garrett added unusual rarities, including very rare silver Nova Constellation pattern coins of 1783, the only surving examples of the first coins minted by the U.S. government.

For about two decades, while under Robert Garrett's care, the collection was kept at Princeton University and was available on loan for public display. At length it became the property of John Work Garrett and his wife. He was a U.S. diplomat whose ties were with Johns Hopkins University, where he served as trustee following his retirement. After his death and the later death of his widow, the coins were left to Johns Hopkins. A sale of 678 lots of duplicate coins in 1976 brought $2.3 million at an auction by Stacks in New York. Johns Hopkins University subsequently decided to sell the remainder of the collection when it weighed its monetary value against the maintenance cost and lack of proper facilities to display it or make it available to scholars, or to provide any sort of educational environment for it. So it consigned the entire collection for sale by Q. David Bowers, of Bowers & Ruddy Galleries of Los Angeles, which held the sale in New York in four parts. In preparation for the sale, M. W. David Bowers of the auction concern, himself a collector and writer on coins, put together a 600-page book, *The History of United States Coinage as Illustrated by the Garrett Collection*, with 40 full-color plates, a highly readable text and a generous selection of intriguing correspondence that gives the reader an inside view of numismatic happenings as seen through the eyes of leading collectors and dealers. It is entirely likely that this book itself, retailing now for $29.95, will become a collectors' item among coin people as well as collectors of rare books. As often happens, leading collectors and experts do their books as a labor of lavish love, with relatively few copies printed or sold—an ideal collecting situation: high quality and limited supply.

Not all collections after a century have such a splendid ending. More or less immortalized in the book, the Garrett Collection is now dispersed to fill out gaps in rival collections; some rarities went to numismatic museums.

When To Throw Back
What You Do Not Need

With many collectibles there are enough items available so that several institutions throughout the country can have a representative or nearly complete collection—just as many private collectors can logically expect to accumulate a complete collection of Indian Head pennies over the period of a lifetime, provided enough diligence and financial support are forthcoming. The institutional competition eventually tapers off; there is no need to have complete collections of the same object duplicated incessantly in too many places. A few top collections, displayed and sent on the road, are sufficient if well documented. Museums offer for sale their duplicates and unwanted lesser works. These remainders form a market of limited number and—under current circumstances—ever increasing demand as private investors abandon inflated paper and turn to the fascinating world of collectibles.

In this sense, collecting is like fishing; you catch and keep what you really need to upgrade your reputation as a fisherman, and throw back the rest for someone else to catch. With collectibles, however, the timing of the throw-back can mean extra profits. Most collectors allow their seconds and duplicates to accumulate until a significant sale takes place where they can ride on the tide of publicity then generated. One spectacular sale will help all

"All right, lady, I give up—just don't shoot!"

collectibles of its kind, whether good or bad. For example, the Charles Gardner sale of antique bottles by the Skinner Auction Gallery of Bolton, Massachusetts, in 1974, offered such a fine collection of antique bottles and brought such high prices—$40,000 for a rare flask-shaped bottle—that it set new milestones. Along with the publications of definitive books on the subject by George McKearin and his daughter, Helen, it showed that U.S antique bottle collecting had reached full maturity and could be highly profitable. It is not at all unusual for dealers today to state that "a bottle like that from the Gardner sale cost $——" (usually less than what today's dealers are offering, *but not always,* because the bottles of the Gardner collection had such rarity and quality that duplicates are not available in today's markets). With bottles, of course, the supply tends to shrink because of breakage, chemical aging of the glass which may cause frosting, scratches, chips, cracks and other flaws that diminish value or eliminate it entirely.

Because the most profitable collectibles are not standardized and require intelligent analysis of details to determine their number, quality and condition, and where they fit into their fields, *the collector who is most alert and intelligent can expect the greatest rewards; the more passive collector can tag along behind, pick up the leavings and probably sell them for a modest profit later depending on the strength of the lead established by front-running collectors.*

Most of the time, however, the excitement of collecting tends to make it a highly competitive, highly civilized race in which the greatest profits go to the person who is the most alert, dedicated and discriminating, the fellow who knows what he is doing in a competitive and demanding field.

If this situation intrigues you, collectibles are your scene, and you will make a good profit with them.

2

Getting a Good Start on a Collection

Most collectors begin with what they have on hand, what they have inherited, what they began to collect as a child's hobby. Some of the fervor of collecting may be in the family. You may inherit, along with stamps, coins or furniture, a gene that will not let you rest until you are busy collecting something.

A Healthy Process

Now, of course, one can overdo this and become almost a miser with "things." Every now and then you read in the obituary pages a feature on an eccentric who was known to be wealthy but lived in a chaos of his collectibles. Depending on the balance of mind of said collector, the collectibles may be valuable, even if in disorder. Sometimes they amount to old newspapers, empty tin cans, a plethora of cats or turtles, or a weedy, gothic garden of green, blooming personalities, all of whom seem to have been the worse for conversation each day with their patron. Frankly, there probably is some of this eccentric lust in any devoted collector. A little of it is a good thing, a bit of it is still healthy: You have to love your "things" in order to do right by them and enable them to do right by you. But you do have to watch out for an unhealthy retention of "everything" simply for the sake of squirreling it away.

You will have more joy from the activity if you let much of the material flow through, if you define your goals and work toward them over years. You will always come across duplicates; you decide which is best to keep for yourself and cast the other back for catching by another collector. One of the pleasures of acquiring a thematic group of a mature collectible is the sane social pleasure you will find in showing your collection and talking about it with others. This can lead to trading, barter, friendly leads of where-to-buy, where-to-sell information. Thus you subtract a few items and add a few items to your collection until, eventually, it takes on significant shape and meaning, and greatly increased value. In the process you will enjoy a most civilized and educational experience. You will dip into the history of culture and taste, you will know intimately how your chosen collectible was or is made; you will inevitably come to grips with the economic history of the United States and its trends in investment media. In other words, the true collector may overindulge from time to time, but basically he or she is part of a humanistic process that broadens minds, increases knowledge and very often makes possible a new aesthetic, life-enriching experience for collectors as well as for their families, and sometimes for the world at large when a superbly representative collection winds up in a museum (at a tax deduction) where posterity can admire it and the collectors' acumen.

When to Start

The best time to start collecting is *now*, no matter how old you are. If you begin as a very young person, so much the better; you will grow up with your collection and find it a pleasant hobby, a natural way to attract new friends and a splendid way to start accumulating capital that can eventually support family activities, business and even later retirement, with something personal to leave to your heirs. Perhaps it seems a bit unrealistic in light of the demonstrated independence of one generation from another, but every young person ought to begin collecting something, first as a hobby, then as a dedicated pursuit. Most collectors will tell you that they wish they had paid more attention to collecting when they were young. Then, there were many more possibilities to acquire a significant collection, more chances to learn from older relatives. Actually, this has been the lament of every generation of collectors since antiquity and particularly since the 18th century when collecting became popular among the middle class.

It is said that the 1980's will be the decade of collectibles—they will emerge on the investment scene as a sensible way to accumulate capital in the form of material objects whose value will stay ahead of or even smartly outpace continuing inflation. Unfortunately, inflation is also likely to be a characteristic of this transitional decade during which energy sources, extraordinary expenditures for defense and gearing up for the colonizing of outer space will keep the money paper presses going strong in all industrial countries.

This popularity of collectibles is a fun thing as well as a way to make money; it will spread just as buying a house became the motive of most U.S. families in the decades since World War II. In a way, the collectibles craze has multiple relevance to the "nesting" craze. Collectibles frequently are objects of beauty and utility and can spruce up a nest. Collecting is an entirely healthy and freedom-preserving trend in an era when the federal government is only beginning to realize it cannot guarantee prosperity and happiness for the individual. So more than ever, the time is *now* to begin collecting. If you have already started and have the kernel of a collection in the attic, dust it off, weed it out and build on it aggressively.

Collectibles That Will Furnish You the Greatest Profit

Any shrewd investor's slogan can apply to collectibles, too. "Buy cheap and sell dear." "Buy before the crowd knows about your collection; sell when the crowd begins to buy." But the ancient question remains, "Buy what? Sell what? And when?" The market for collectibles is very much like the stock market was during the Great Bull Market of the twenties, or to a lesser extent, the sixties. It really does not matter so much which one of the collectibles mentioned in this book you choose—there are probably *some not mentioned* that you can collect and do well with—but the important thing is to choose the one or two that are for you and then plunge in. You will find yourself in an inefficient market, but a market growing more efficient by the week. The collectibles mentioned in this book, and others related to them, are pretty sure to appreciate in value in the years ahead. They will shoot up if inflation accelerates; they will move up more gradually if inflation moderates throughout the world. But you will make money if you follow the collection principles outlined in this book.

Remember, collectibles are something that the mass of U.S. citizens have only recently discovered. Affluent Europeans have been collecting valuable antiques for centuries. As with U.S. land that they are now buying avidly, Europeans know a good thing when they see it; they are also into U.S. collectibles as they consider them a fairly virgin territory whereas antiques in Europe have not much further to go before they can be bought by only a few very wealthy people and institutions. As U.S. collectibles are beginning to get recognition, the roots for many budding collections are to be found in the attics of U.S. families.

Because of this hoard now coming out of houses that are being sold to settle estates, the action has swung across the Atlantic to the United States for both domestic and foreign collectors. Some important and valuable U.S. collectibles are actually foreign material, such as Chinese Export porcelain, and 18th century English and French furniture. They were imported in this country by well-to-do families because they could not yet find elegance among the local craftsmen and sometimes for reasons of sheer snobbery. These emotions are still very much a part of the U.S. collectible scene today.

Of course, you will want to avoid fad items such as barbed wire, pet rocks, perishable plants, circus calliopes, white elephants that take more trouble in restoration, maintenance, care and insurance than they can possible return in profit. Above all avoid collecting what nobody else wants to collect. Always look for things for which there is a fairly liquid market, even if it is only next year's version of the rummage, attic or garage sale where you bought the item. It is hard to say exactly what objects to avoid. Tomorrow you may discover another collector of them, then another, and before you know it you will have a local market. In fact, if you have the energy and the enthusiasm, you can take up an off-beat collectible and make an eventual market for it.

But why not be *practical* about this and hedge your bets. Select first of all a collectible that already has an identifiable market, has regular sales, has several dealers in the United States and regularly appears at auctions. Then if you have a yen for barbed wire . . . or something bizarre or original or that has a quirky fascination for you, collect it lightheartedly, not too aggressively, as a second or third collectible in your program. Sometimes intuition proves a better guide than objective analysis. So if you have a hunch about a certain thing, indulge in it, but only lightly until further evidence shows that you have blustered into a good thing well before the crowd begins to discover it and comes roaring in.

Who would have thought, for example, that Depression Glass, the kind you used to get free at "dish night" at the movies in the thirties and could buy for a nickel a piece at the five and dime would now be worth several dollars a piece? Or that decoys that used to lie around in the boathouse, barn, woodshed or garage attic most of the year now are bringing hundreds, even thousands of dollars apiece at regular auctions?

Boning Up on Your Chosen Collectible

The odd thing about most collectibles, except the most mature ones such as coins, Oriental ceramics, stamps, rare books, and master paintings, drawings and prints—all of which have established international markets and have reputable dealers, collectors' associations and museum experts authenticating them, upgrading them and guiding collectors—is the helter-skelter and inefficient way in which their markets work.

For most of the collectibles sketched in this book, except where noted otherwise, you will find auctions and dealers somewhere in the United States—if not in the large city near which you live, then at the country auction that specializes in collectibles emerging from the attics of your region. The point is that very few people know the value of the incidental collectibles they have inherited or accumulated over the years. An object might be considered "that old chair from Grandma's parlor," but you, if you are a thoroughgoing collector, will know that it is a Belter or a Gustav Stickley and worth about $5,500. You have a special knowledge; you know what it is actually worth and you know where it is located—something the dealer and auction gallery expert may not know. So you try to buy Grandma's chair for $75 and then later sell it to a dealer or better still at auction for the $5,500. That is how you make money with your special knowledge: Buy, knowing something that the rest of the market does not; sell when and where you can get a much better price. In highly efficient markets such as stocks traded in the various exchanges as well as over the counter, you could never do this because each certificate is plainly identified and registered. Its value in one part of the country is roughly what it is in another part and people who come across a stock certificate in the attic know what to do with it: They will take it to a stockbroker or banker and try to see if it is still worth something. Today, it is still not commonplace to take a chair, or a vase, to an appraiser or to an auction house during one of its heirloom discovery days. The majority of the U.S. populace still could not care less about antiques they still call "old things" or "junk." But within the next decade, watch out! There will be much media publicity about attic treasures—not always the multi-thousand-dollar discoveries but discoveries of several objects worth a few hundred dollars each, enough to finance a family vacation perhaps. Or they may become the core of your expanding collection.

Each collectible sketched in the second section of this book suggests sources of further information. Museums are listed where you can see your collectible and often buy an informative book about the special collection you see on display. Then there are clubs and organizations that have educational meetings and sometimes publish a newsletter that can keep you up-to-date and serve as a bulletin board of items available for purchase and at what price. Also, the leading books in the field are listed. Some of these books are available at libraries, particularly at big-city libraries.

They are usually indexed under the name of the collectible and sometimes are cross-indexed under "antiques" or "collectibles" and by the author's name. If you have trouble finding them, ask the librarian and be ready to give the name of the book and of its author. You can often find books on your collectible in a big bookstore such as B. Dalton, Walden, Brentano's or Barnes & Noble. Look for the shelves marked "Antiques" or "Collectibles." Then page through the books available on your subject and decide which one or more you may eventually want to buy.

You will not find a uniform level of excellence in these books. In general, each mature collectible, such as coins and stamps, Oriental ceramics or American glass bottles, has one or more definitive books complete with pictures that will give you a feeling for the whole collectible. The Time-Life *Encyclopedia of Collectibles* does this quickly for many collectibles and its excellent pictures at least show you what a typical piece might look like. For the most part, the pictures were taken of pieces from significant collections.

But on the whole, once you have seen a collection or two in a museum, have plunged into the organization and newsletter or magazine network that puts collectors in touch with dealers and auctions, and have access to the books in your field, you have to use your feet, your eyes and your head. Seeing and handling the collectible itself, looking for identifying marks, discerning chips, cracks, clever restorations or substitutions, realizing that a part is missing—all these skills come with experience in actual knowing and sensing a collectible. You learn to size it up for authenticity, beauty and provenance (in the collection of what significant and/or famous collectors it has been a previous part).

Becoming an Expert in Your Collectible

As you bone up on your collectible as a beginner, you will sooner or later run into the experts in your field, read their books, hear about them through dealers, perhaps meet them at auctions, at seminars or at collectors' club meetings. Perhaps you envy them their knowledge and the way people turn to them for authoritative answers. And you may suspect they are often paid for their advice. They are, and often well paid, too. Some of them become art appraisers; some buy for wealthy clients (as did Bernard Berenson for Mrs. Gardner) and literally make their living through commissions, doing what they most enjoy.

If you also have a flair for self-promotion and management, you may very well wind up in the business as a dealer, decorator, columnist, journalist or free-lance trader. Then you will be making added spin-off profits from your collectibles and the expertise you have acquired in accumulating your collection.

Along the way to your expertise you may have taken courses in antiquities, in art history and in the contemporary marketing of antiques. You may have apprenticed yourself to one of the leading dealers in your field or to an auction house that specializes in your collectible. The degree to which you go into professionalism is, of course, up to you. Some people prefer to accumulate a fine collection and to appreciate its beauty but want nonetheless to know that it has increased handsomely in value.

No one is going to teach you all you need to know to become an expert in your field. You may find some courses and seminars, particularly those sponsored by museums and auction houses, that can give you a good foundation of knowledge. But then you will be on your own and the degree of expertise you develop can pay you handsomely in the future. For if you really want *to make money* in collectibles, you will see to it that you know as much as anybody in the world about your specialty—and a good deal more. With the growing popularity of collectibles and the full light of publicity the media will give them, you will have to depend more and more on your wits to get the better of situations. For the moment, collectibles still offer a rare marketplace where legitimate use of wits will bring you more than patience or planning. Prizes will surface that need quick action lest they be lost forever. The game is still played secretively, confidentially—the auction houses rarely identify a buyer or even a consignee unless, for some reason, either of the parties prefer to be identified. If they prefer not, it is part of the honor of the house not to mention names. The seller, preferring anonymity, can be listed as "private owner." And of course, the buyer who wants double insurance of anonymity will have a friend or agent do the bidding for him as a stand-in.

A Case Where Knowing a Bit More than the Competition Paid Off

Perhaps true collectors are littered under Mercury, as was the amiable Shakespearean rogue Autolycus, "a snapper-up of unconsidered trifles." Certainly the successful collector has to be alert to the worth of things and be ready to snap up bargains when they appear.

Such was the case when Richard Feigen, a Manhattan art dealer and collector, beat out many supposedly savvy competitors for a landscape thought by everyone else to be the work of a *pupil* of Claude Lorrain, the French painter, so famous that he was usually known simply as "Claude." The bidding at the Christie auction went as high as $2,500 and Feigen snapped up the prize. For he had a sharper eye even than Christie's experts (who stand behind their qualifications of authenticity for years and are thus cautious). He suspected that the landscape was by Claude himself. Feigen made a few low-key and indirect inquiries before the auction to bolster his hunch. (Note he was not risking much money at an auction of important paintings!) But after he bought it, the world's leading expert on Claude Lorrain confirmed that the painting *was an original* by Claude and that its true value was about $350,000 to $375,000, about 150 times what Feigen had paid for it. This was a superb collector at work. Even if the expert had not provided the ultimate authenticity, Feigen still would have bought an attractive painting, considered the work of a pupil of Claude, at its going market value. By bidding $2,500 he had little to lose and literally a small fortune to gain. Now, it is entirely possible that yet another expert will call into question the authenticity of this particular painting. Yet, even though a controversy might continue for decades, it will be worth a lot more than the $2,500. You (and Mr. Feigen) can be sure of that! The painting's continuing fame and value are now in the hands of the media. Who knows what additional hundreds of thousands that Claude may be worth in the years to come!

Or take the example where the sum of money was not so large but the multiplier even higher. A housewife in Claremont, California, bought a pretty dish at a garage sale for $1.00. Her later research proved it to be a Goebel Hummel plate worth about $1,200. That is twelve hundred times as much. These surprise rewards occasionally rejoice an amateur's heart; they happen more frequently to professional collectors who know very well what they see and buy. But they are usually quiet about it until they have nailed down what they want to purchase.

Lack of Government Regulations

Unlike the cases of the stock, bond, commodity and real estate markets, there is no regulatory body such as the SEC, the CFTC, the Attorney General of a state or even the IRS that takes much of an interest in collectibles unless there are repeated complaints of fraud. As a result, the collectibles market is unusually lucrative and curiously unregulated at present. Newspapers only recently began to publish results of sales and seldom identify buyers or sellers. That is why considerable profit can be made in it by the collector who has the will and a keen knowledge of values and of "what is going on."

Undoubtedly the government will take a firmer stand as the public gets more involved in these markets, if abuses emerge and complaints multiply. But for the next few years the market is open and free-wheeling to those who are willing to use their wits to make a profit.

As of the writing of this book, the combined annual sales of all the major auction houses (Sotheby's, Christie's, Phillips, and William Doyle in the United States) amount to only about $300,000,000. As industries go, this is small potatoes, *even though* it represents a 30-percent increase over 1979 and a tripling in volume over only five years ago. Clearly *this is a growth market* and the prospects for continuing high growth are good for the next decade or so as the U.S. public plunges into tangibles as a hedge against inflation and a stimulating, exciting activity as well.

Ask any friend or relative what he/she collects and you will be surprised to learn how many people collect *something,* even if they seem shy or diffident to say so. Reflect on what you have already collected. Perhaps it is a miscellaneous amount of things kept from childhood; perhaps it is a small collection of dishes or jewelry inherited from a parent or grandparent. Of course, some lucky folks even inherit a significant collection of stamps, coins, spoons, paintings or Rose Medallion Chinese Export Porcelain. Ten years ago these inheritances may not have seemed very much. Today they might very well be a worthwhile windfall on which to add, or perhaps to sell at auction so that you can send a child through college, build a house—or start a new collection of objects more to your liking.

The time to get started was yesterday but if you missed the boat then, start now. If you have a good reason for starting tomorrow, OK; a day or two of delay in this massive, unwieldy growth market does not make much difference at the moment. It may later, when the market gets better organized. That may be the time for you to cash in, pare down, upgrade, take your profits and shift at least some of your investments to a collectible (if any) that is still *undervalued.*

If you do this and you do become an expert in your chosen collectible, it is likely that you will look back on the 1980's as the decade in which you accumulated a fortune in collectibles and had a lot of legitimate, legal and cultural pleasure in doing so.

Experts Who Can Help You at Minimum Cost

As with any popular investment medium—stocks, bonds, commodities, government paper, real estate—those who deal in the medium find a business advantage and profit in talking about the medium, in making its profits and pitfalls evident to the public. This has a way of attracting bidders and expanding the market.

So it is, too, with collectibles. Each collector/enthusiast has a thirst for knowledge; people with a financial stake in that commodity find that an educated public forms the best market with fewer complaints and cries of "cheating." Satisfied collectors tell friends and buy more; dissatisfied collectors bad-mouth the process and tend to limit market expansion and, in extreme cases, enter suits for fraud with unsavory publicity. Almost all of these dissatisfactions stem from a lack of knowledge that encourages a collector to have wrong expectations and/or opens the door to paying too much for a legitimate piece, and to paying a relatively small sum for a bargain piece that turns out to be a fake and nearly worthless. These negative experiences work against the growth of a liquid, confident market and the mutual profit of all those concerned with it.

That is why you will find honest dealers, appraisers, auction houses, collectors' associations and consumer shows quite willing and able to educate you. And they will charge you little or nothing for their trouble.

For the collectibles market sketched in the second half of this book, you will find certain museums mentioned, certain publications identified and (most valuable for you) names of collectors' associations. These are organized for the sake of collectors like yourself who want more information and reliable access to a market that may seem strange at first. Here is how to go about using the various sources of information.

Collectors' Associations

Start with your collectors' association (if there is one). Identify yourself as a collector with specific interests and apply for membership. Ask that association's secretary for:

1. The name, address and telephone number of reliable dealers near your home.

2. A subscription to a newsletter the association might publish (this will keep you up to date on interesting

current sales and discoveries, and it may even list, as a courtesy to members, items that are available for purchase or that are wanted to buy).

3. A list of books, magazines or other publications recommended by the association. These change from time to time but the association will probably know what is being published where.

4. Identification of auctions taking place in your vicinity.

Some associations publish form letters that give some or all of this information. Most will answer your personal questions. *You can rely on your association to bring you up to date on changes that may have taken place since the preparation of the current edition of this guide.*

Museums

Not every collectible has yet made it to a museum. But many of the collectibles in this guide have. You can identify where you can view, often examine closely, a significant collection. You will often find that such a museum has published one or more books or pamphlets on the collection. It may also have guided tours through the collection and may have developed, too, as part of its education program, a lecture or series of lectures on the subject of its special collection.

The advantage of such programs is that they are authoritative, are disinterested in market fluctuations or in promoting the market and are available at little or no cost—perhaps the price of admission or the cost of a book.

When museums have a special collection, that very fact attracts more of the same collectible to them and there may come a time when the curator and board of trustees decide to sell off through a dealer or at auction the duplicate or inferior pieces. Other things being equal, a collectible that has been a part of a major museum collection (or part of the hoard of a prominent private collector, for that matter) is worth more on the market than an identical item without such a distinguished provenance. This may seem a bit irrational; it is part of the mystique of collecting. The fame of a collector or museum rubs off on collectibles. That is why you will want to know when a celebrated museum, or perhaps a well-known specialty dealer, is planning to weed a collection.

Dealers

Dealers have a selfish interest in a collectible. But a dealer is an expert who makes a living from handling your collectible among others. It pays a dealer to make a certain amount of information available to enthusiasts like yourself. Usually this will be in the form of personal answers to your questions.

By all means visit personally the leading dealers in your collectible, both where you live and work and on your travels. Ask questions, learn from the answers. Naturally, if you buy something—it need not be a major purchase—that dealer will feel a conversation with you is not a waste of time. But some dealers, simply because they like to talk on the subject they know so well, will go on for quite a while and provide a wealth of entirely gratuitous information as well as pertinent answers to your questions. Accept the froth with the facts for the time being. The froth may be laden with all kinds of factual bits and pieces that could serve you later when you are a more sophisticated collector. Then, too, a ready and ever-accepting ear is the price you must sometimes pay for the facts you might want at the moment. Never slam shut a walking encyclopedia—it is usually an educational opportunity knocking.

As you learn more from your dealer-friend, you will undoubtedly consider buying something from him. Presumably you now have confidence in his advice and perhaps he comes recommended to you by another collector or a collector's association. As always in collectibles, especially when you are obviously a beginner, *let the buyer beware!* must be your rule of thumb, both in accepting advice or in buying. You cannot be told too many times that your own experience and knowledge in this largely unregulated market is your best protection as well as your best advantage for making a profit. In Chapter 3 you will find additional guidelines to use when establishing a buying relationship with a dealer. As a beginner seeking information, be very glad when you find a dealer whom you consider reputable and who is willing to give you free information.

Auction Houses

The major auction companies in the United States all had their beginnings in England—Sotheby's, Christie's and Phillips. Through branches and affiliates they provide an international network of sales and of purchase opportunities, and a valuable part of these networks is their pricing information. Even independent appraisers will look up auction records of a particular collectible as one of the first steps in putting a value on it. Current auction prices are more meaningful than isolated local sales or sales through dealers, which may or may not be accurately recorded. The auction houses are the great record keepers of the prices of collectibles. The auction price is public knowledge; there are witnesses to the bidding. Thus there is no opportunity to bluff a price for the purpose of exciting the market.

There is one caution when weighing auction prices; that is the matter of reserves, minimum prices set by the seller that cause the auction house to "buy in" if that amount or a higher amount is not bid. In a sense, the seller "buys" his own merchandise to prevent it from going at a lower price. Owners of a particular collectible, particularly dealers with a stake in the level of price for it, have been known to set a high reserve and/or organize the bidding so that it will go to an artificial high simply to have this figure (usually a record high) become part of the record or archive of a collectible. Supposedly this will cause the next offering of a similar item to go for a similar amount. Sometimes this works in the dealer's favor. Other times, it does not. The media often manage to find out whether a real sale was made or whether the bidding ended in a buy-in to meet a reserve. Some auction houses, in order not to get caught in this game, indicate when a reserve has been set and for how much. Others warn buyers to assume a reserve has been set that more or less falls within the estimated price range. When an item reappears at another sale at about the same or lower price than at a previous sale, you can be pretty sure it did not sell at the earlier sale. These are matters that dealers and auction houses are loath to discuss openly. Be assured that they occur, however, and calculate your bid accordingly.

The advantage of following your collectible via review of the price at the largest auction house that handles it in the greatest volume is simply the fact that a great volume of transactions tends to smooth out the price curve and eliminate the occasional artificial prices that may slip in.

To promote interest in and understanding of many collectibles, auction houses such as Sotheby's, Phillips and Christie's conduct seminars. These seminars may not be free. Phillips, for example, has certain prestigious three-day seminars for which he charges $300. But then you are in the hands of experts who can tell you all you could possibly want to know.

Another program that the auction houses have been encouraging lately is "heritage discovery days." These events, as in the case of Sotheby's, may take place in several metropolitan areas of the United States. Interested residents bring in their collectibles for identification and appraisal free of charge. You may discover you own a real treasure. Most of the time you will find you have something of modest value. But at least you will *know what it is and how much it is worth and where it might fit into a worthwhile collection.* Of course, the sponsor of the event will be glad to sell it for you if you decide to part with it.

Still another benefit of visits to an auction house (and to a lesser extent to a dealer) is the group of fellow collectors you are likely to meet. There is a certain fun and excitement in attending an auction. Even if you do not buy a thing, you will find a visit valuable if you make a habit of asking questions of any expert on hand and particularly of other collectors who appear to be talking knowledgeably. Provided you use your judgment and sense of tact, you can find out a lot at no cost and possibly win new friends in the process.

One of the perennial games at an auction exhibit of a certain collectible is the challenge to identify the values of objects and then compare what you would say with what the experts say in the brochure listing the object and its presale estimate. So haunt all important sales and auctions of your collectible whenever possible.

If you cannot follow auctions in person, you can often read reports on them in major metropolitan newspapers, such as *The New York Times* on Fridays or on Sundays in the *Arts and Leisure* section. You can also subscribe to selected presale brochures of auctions of your collectible, and also to lists of achieved prices.

Some collectors, in fact, who have developed sufficient knowledge of their collectible deal with the auction houses and their specialists almost entirely by mail or telephone. They obtain necessary presale information and then submit a mailed bid, naming the top price they are willing to pay for a specific item. In some very important sales, bidders follow and participate in the auction via TV screen or telephone from areas remote from the auction itself. Modern electronic communication, therefore, puts a bidder in New York on an equal footing with a bidder in San Francisco or Paris, even though the auction itself is taking place in London.

Appraisers

An appraiser is an expert consultant and is not likely to give his advice free. But as it happens, many appraisers are also dealers and as such will be as ready to give you answers to your questions as any other dealer interested in expanding his market.

For the moment, consider an appraiser as a source of free information—available if the appraiser wears other hats and considers it worthwhile to educate the collector who probably will later come forth for a paid appraisal.

Staff members of the major auction houses are often qualified appraisers who, as explained previously, give you certain kinds of information gratis.

Paid Information from an Appraiser

An appraiser also provides a valuable professional service. Such an appraiser carries legal and financial weight when you might want to obtain a loan with your collection as collateral or when, as an executor, you want to evaluate a collection for estate taxes and settlement, or simply when you want to get a handle on what you should ask for your collection before approaching a dealer or potential buyer. You cannot expect to get such a systematic and professional evaluation free.

Sometimes an appraiser will agree on a flat rate; sometimes the charge will be on a percentage basis—sometimes as high as 10 percent on small collections, often as low as 2 percent on larger, more valuable accumulations. Sometimes an appraiser will quote an hourly fee.

Appraisers will usually agree to examine your collection in your home and you can help in the task—and minimize the final charge—by having your items in order: receipts for prices paid; documentation, including provenance of as many objects as possible; records of previous appraisals; clippings of prestigious shows in which your collection, or parts of it, were displayed; and other relevant material of this sort. These documents make the appraiser's job shorter; thus he can lower his fee. You will find the process swift and agreeable unless you had sentimental illusions about the value of certain pieces. The appraiser is not out to flatter you or massage your emotions; an appraisal is a businesslike procedure based on what an expert knows about a specialty and its present market.

On the other hand, you should tell the appraiser the purpose of the appraisal—whether it is to get adequate insurance or whether it is to prepare to sell the collection, and whether the collection is to be bartered, auctioned or sold through a dealer. You, and perhaps your accountant, will want to view the event in the context of your financial and tax situation. Then tell the appraiser your goal. It is to your advantage to undervalue slightly in tax situations, such as the settlement of an estate, and to overvalue slightly objects you want to sell at an attractive (to you) asking price or objects you want to insure.

How To Find the Right Appraiser

Finding the right appraiser is like finding any professional consultant. You have to ask people who have already used one. You might, for example, ask your local bank, which has had experience in settling numerous estates. Your lawyer is another source. So is the association of collectors of which you are a member. A dealer in your collectible also ought to know a competent appraiser in that field.

If all else fails, you can consult your local Yellow Pages under Appraisers and call to see if any of them specialize in your collectible or in a related field. This is the starting-from-scratch way of smoking out an expert. Yet, in the last analysis, you will have to decide on the competence and suitability of any appraiser, regardless of his references.

As you proceed more deeply into collectibles you will find it worth your while to maintain continuing touch with an appraiser. A little time screening candidates at the start will pay off later as you need periodic updatings of values and evaluation of new items in your collection.

To get a professional opinion on the several local firms who are candidates, you might want to write or telephone one or both of the national association of appraisers: American Society of Appraisers, 60 East 42nd Street, New York, NY 10017 (212-687-6305) and Appraisers Association of America, 60 East 42nd Street, New York, NY 10017 (212-867-9775).

Your Relationship with an Appraiser

Once you have located an appraiser, talk fees with him so that you both know what is expected in the way of service and expenses. Decide how the appraiser will report to you and the time frame of his appraisal: when you can expect his final report.

When you have received this written and dated report, check it over immediately to be sure it covers the ground agreed on and that no item has been omitted. That means an actual verification of the appraisal with the inventory of your collectible. If anything has been overlooked or uncovered and added by you after the appraiser's visit, ask for a correction. Sometimes it can be done without an additional visit, sometimes it cannot. If evaluations seem too high or too low, ask the appraiser to justify the differential.

Once this is done and the appraiser has adjusted it with your approval, keep the original record in a safe place, probably your bank safe deposit box. You can have home copies made for ready reference and for distribution to whomever needs them. Update the figures when necessary. Your ongoing relationship with your appraiser can be fairly simple and inexpensive once the first comprehensive appraisal is made. Be sure the appraiser, too, has a file copy of his work so he can refer to it if you call him on the telephone for questions, additions and/or adjustment of any sort.

Shows

Specialized expositions including your collectible can be great places for picking up facts about it. Experts will be on hand to answer questions, conduct seminars and distribute explanatory literature.

Shows may take the form of exhibits in conjunction with conventions such as the Antiquarian Book Fair, which takes place every year with the annual convention of the Antiquarian Book Sellers Association. The show is open to the public—both exhibits and informative talks—but some of the keenest dealing goes on among the exhibitors themselves.

Most of these shows have a nominal admission charge, but your favorite dealer will usually have a fistful of complimentary tickets. Ask your dealer about this. If you are a regular customer, you can expect regular complimentary tickets to all such conventions or exhibits in your vicinity.

If you have not yet made friends with local dealers, perhaps your proven membership of a collectors' association will enable you to enter free. Generally you will hear about the exhibits and/or show through the newsletter of your association. It will give times of the show, the educational features planned and details about entrance fees.

3

Identifying the Market for Your Collectibles

Your collectible will furnish you with its greatest profit only if you identify and work with the market in that collectible. The items you own *do not progress in value in isolation* (although they may seem to do so). Rather, their value is a direct or indirect reflection on how similar items are valued and traded by collectors throughout the world.

This implies, of course, participation in the relative prosperity of the U.S. and international economies, the value of the U.S. dollar and the relative demand for your collectible either in other countries or in regions of the United States. The market for American Western paintings, for example, has been most active in the southwestern part of the United States, even though collectors who live out there buy these paintings through New York dealers or auction houses in Manhattan as well as from dealers in Texas and perhaps an auction or two in Los Angeles.

The market for U.S. antique bottles is more concentrated in the eastern part of the United States where backyard "bottling" is more rewarding and attics yield more vintage bottles simply because there are older attics in the East. Then, too, one of the most prominent specialty houses, the Skinner Auction Galleries of Bolton, Massachusetts, regularly has auctions featuring bottles. Its auction some years ago of the Charles Gardner collection, remarkable in scope and quality, set many price "highs" that are only now—with the U.S. dollar substantially more inflated—being exceeded. The major auction houses have yet to feature antique bottles in a special sale, although the quantities of bottles included in their Americana sales grow larger by the year.

Antique U.S. bottles are not avidly collected (yet) outside the United States, while painters of the American West such as Bierstadt, Moran and Church now attract more international bidders.

34

Active sales and auctions of these paintings still tend, however, to take place in the United States. That is natural; that is where the most collectors are—in quantity and in affluence.

These patterns will vary with individual collectibles. It is not so important that a market pattern be this or that; just be sure you know what the pattern is.

For example, if collecting antique bottles gradually becomes as popular in the Far West—in California and Arizona, for example—as it is in Connecticut, New York and Pennsylvania, the enterprising collector in the East can probably profit best by buying East and selling West. This takes advantage of the difference in supply and demand. The supply is still heavily in the East. The growing demand is in the West where eventually a dealer may serve as a major outlet and profit-maker for Eastern bottlers and collections. On both coasts, of course, collectors still dig for bottles and so replenish the supply.

With Navaho rugs, the regional advantage is reversed. The collector will profit most by buying at the Arizona source—both new and antique rugs (or as they were originally, blankets)—and selling to a Midwestern or Eastern market now more aware of the decorative quality and value of these Indian creations. As a collector of Navaho rugs, you will also recognize that the prices for new and old rugs may outrace one another. The Navaho blanket/rug is one of the relatively few collectibles that continue in production—still from the authentic Indian source; often the new creations have greater aesthetic value than the old specimens and may also exist in better condition.

These market characteristics, often so distinctive and surprising, are highly important for you, as a collector, to know. Otherwise you are likely to buy and collect willy-nilly. If you have any feel for your collectible, you are likely to make some profit, even in this helter-skelter manner. But you will make a maximum profit only if you know what you are doing. So often the lucky buy or sale comes to the person who is ready for it. That is, the opportunity arises; you recognize it as such and know what to do about it.

The previous chapter showed you how to educate yourself about your collectible. This chapter will tell you how to buy your collectibles at an advantage, setting yourself up to reap a maximum profit later when you might sell (as explained in Chapter 4).

There are five major sources for adding to your collection: (1) dealers, (2) major auctions, (3) shows, (4) local sales, such as flea markets and fairs, and (5) fellow collectors (either directly or through your collectors' association).

Sources of Collectibles—Dealers

Of all these sources, probably the most important is the dealer. A dealer has expertise and is in the business of supplying items to collectors. The dealer makes a profit through helping you make a profit as you build your collection. It is very important to select a dealer with whom you can do business with confidence. This is more than a matter of simple business honesty, although that is necessary as a basis for dealings. For the best relationship you will have to generate a more personal feeling between the two of you— a kind of business friendship wherein the dealer recognizes you as a serious and continuing customer. As such, you are due special consideration, perhaps a little extra effort in finding a piece that will significantly build up your collection. Perhaps there is a feeling on your part that the dealer is doing well on the searches and purchases he makes on your behalf but is not exactly getting rich at your expense.

These feelings can seldom be cultivated deliberately but nonetheless hover about the best of collector-dealer relationships. Until you sense them, settle for an honest dealer, reasonably diligent in his work for you.

Naturally you will check out your dealer through fellow collectors, possibly the executive secretary of your collectors' organization. In fact, the dealer probably is a member of that organization.

Try the dealer out on small purchases. Check performance. Have some of the items you bought appraised and compare the appraised market value with what you paid the dealer. Be careful and tactful in this second appraisal. If you suspect a dealer of overpricing, ask for the item "on approval" and have it appraised elsewhere. But do not tell the dealer this is what you intend to do. Telling him, of course, suggests that you do not have full trust in him.

The test appraisal, particularly if you are a neophyte collector and unduly skeptical of being taken in, should help to settle your doubts and pave the way to an ongoing, confident relationship.

You may wonder why a collector would need a dealer. The answer is simple! The collector needs the dealer's expertise and information/supply network. Because the dealer has a reputation in the market for your collectible, news of available pieces, even tentative feelers toward buying and selling, will come to his attention. The dealer, knowing your likes and dislikes, knowing the present shape and future plans for your collection, can act as your expert/agent as you embellish your collection. The dealer's fee or compensation comes through his markups from wholesale to retail or the price he charges you.

As you do more and more business with the chosen dealer, you might manage to agree on a flat fee, say 10 percent, of any buying or selling he does for you. Such an open-handed relationship will prevent wonder on your part as to whether this or that piece was marked up unusually high. In the long run, any honest dealer will welcome any agreement that simplifies transactions with a valued and repeat customer. Some dealers will extend credit to desirable customers, or at the very least allow you to charge purchases on one of the widely accepted credit cards. A better way is to settle on the price of a major purchase and then propose installment payment, possibly over six months to a year at no interest. This is, in effect, financing by the dealer. The dealer will be more willing to do this if he already owns the item as part of his inventory. He will be less likely to agree if he has to use his own money to buy into the market. But if you are a good customer, you can ask for and get accommodations from time to time.

Buying and Selling Services
You Can Expect from a Dealer

1. *Evaluation of Authenticity.* Relatively few collectibles have a provenance or guarantee attached. The most famous, of course, often do. With such attribution you know where you stand. A reputable dealer, however, should be able to fill in some of the gaps. That does not mean he can guarantee authenticity but he should be able to give you some kind of standard designation, such as "attributed to" such and such a maker, and he probably will cite the phrase used in a previous sale or a write-up on your item. Certain items of documentation may come with the piece. His reputation as an expert means much in the market. Get his opinion in writing, of course, and keep it with your records.

2. *Aggressive Search.* It is the dealer's business to know the market of the collectibles he handles. That does not only mean prices; it means source of supply, approximate quantity of supply and approximate quality of supply. Thus when the dealer finds you the item you are looking for, he should be able to tell you whether it is—or is not—about as good a specimen as you can expect to find. Unchipped chalkware, for example, would be very unusual, whereas an unchipped Rose Medallion plate in Export Porcelain would be fairly usual; it was much more durable and many more

plates were imported into the United States than examples of chalkware, which was largely regional folk art without manufacturing standards, was limited in volume to what an individual could create, is very breakable, and flakes easily.

3. *Credit and Willingness to Refund.* Once you have established a relationship with a dealer, you ought be able to get a reasonable amount of credit from him, particularly on major purchases that already are a part of the shop's inventory. This is simply retail credit payable in monthly installments or on whatever terms you can persuade the dealer to give you. As mentioned before, however, be sure you agree on price before you ask for terms. A hard-driving dealer may raise the price to cover the cost of carrying you if you ask to be carried before you agree on price.

Reputable dealers, more than other sources of collectibles, will generally stand behind their merchandise and refund purchases promptly if an item turns out not to be as represented. Sometimes these discrepancies in representation are not the fault of the dealer. Once in a while new facts come to light that invalidate previous attributions. At other times, the dealer may be proved wrong by another expert whose argument is more persuasive. The point is that good dealers will rectify the mistake, whether or not it is their fault.

Sources of Collectibles—Auctions

Because of the publicity given to auction sales and the public records kept by the major auction houses, market prices are dominated by this source of collectibles. Most of the goods they handle—antiques of all kinds, paintings, stamps, Oriental ceramics, rare books and lesser collectibles—are objects originally collected by private parties, dealers and museums. It is true that 80 percent of auction prices are less than $1000, 60 percent less than $500. Yet auction houses also handle very many of the highly publicized big-ticket items that set records, which seem to be exceeded each year as inflation and new waves of collectors cause prices to rise on a diminishing number of top-quality objects. For this reason, they have an image of dealing in very valuable and expensive collectibles. They do do this, but they furnish many a piece for modest collectors, too.

As an avid collector, you should make it a point to attend most auctions that include your collectible. And be sure you have a way of following auction prices achieved by your collectible, wherever it is auctioned. In the sketches of each collectible that form the second part of this book you will get some ideas on the communication sources available.

Auctions provide probably the greatest excitement in collecting, simply for sheer suspense. To an earlier generation brought up on American Tobacco's radio cry of the tobacco auctioneer, or to the country person familiar with a typical auction of livestock and farm equipment, an auctioneer's patter and singsong seem all part of the American grain. Yet the great interest in auctions in the United States featuring art, antiques and other collectibles that attract international bidders developed since World War II.

Auctions in other parts of the world have taken place at least as early as the time of the Romans, who used this method to dispose of trophies of war. In the 17th century, in Holland, auctions were instituted to dispose of perishable foods and prized bulbs, a factor that led to the making and breaking of astronomical prices during a period of tulip mania when collectors of rare bulbs went berserk. In the 18th century, auctions of art and household goods became firmly established in England, particularly in London. An advertised auction of a book collection in 1713 in Boston was perhaps the first of its kind in the United States.

Today most large cities in the United States have general auctions several times a year, and the category "auctioneer" is a standard one in most metropolitan Yellow Pages. To find out whether the auctioneers in your locality deal in your collectible, simply call and ask. The leading houses that feature your collectible will be identified by your collectors' association magazine or newsletter, or if there are neither of these, by the executive secretary of the association. If there is no association (a rare situation in the case of a collectible with an established market), you might try asking a fellow collector or the dealer from which you bought your specimens. Chances are he bought some of his merchandise at one auction or another, but he may have had to go to New York to do so.

An odd fact about the auction market—you are talking about the same price for wholesaler, dealer and consumer/collector like yourself. In this situation a knowledgeable collector has a distinct advantage. He can usually afford to pay more than the wholesaler, who must mark up the item in order to sell it at a profit. A collector, even if he expects to sell at a profit many years in the future, probably intends to hang on to an item and give it plenty of time to appreciate in value and survive more than one wave of collectors' interest. Thus the dealer/expert will usually drop out of the bidding when it reaches a point beyond which there is no resale profit to be expected. As a collector, then, you can usually get a specific piece for what amounts to the wholesale price. Of course, when you are after a really important piece and have a certain know-how gained from your self-education and experience, it is expected that you will probably know at least some of the dealers in the room, at least by sight, and know, too, that they are not likely to bid much more than the wholesale price for an item.

There is an exception to this likelihood. Sometimes a dealer may bid on behalf of a prominent collector who is determined to have the item even at an inflated cost. The last several thousand (or more!) dollars may not mean much to such a wealthy collector. What do they mean to you? That is a question you will have to answer for yourself. In such a situation, although you may think you are bidding against a recognized dealer, you are bidding against another collector. Have you set realistic limits for yourself?

General Auctions

Most collectibles are handled at general auctions, where you will find collectibles grouped together in kind but mostly lumped in a single session with others items not necessarily related. Thus you will have antique furniture, paintings, glass, decoys, paperweights and miscellaneous pieces from an estate all at one sale. This kind of sale is more likely to take place in a small town or in a rural area and simply to furnish an outlet for various pieces accumulated over a period of time. It is likely to be advertised accurately but sketchily, with only occasional attempts to characterize individual objects. In fact, some general auctions are little better than a flea market, run by a person who has a gift of gab making the sale more interesting by using auction methods. Because you are being offered something at this kind of auction rather than by price tag does not mean the goods offered are any more authentic or worthwhile than goods offered in other ways. Most auction sales will allow money returns within a specified time if the item purchased turns out not to be as represented. Of course, if a piece is given a general representation with no attempt at proving authenticity or provenance, such as, for instance, an "Oriental plate," it is what the words imply: a plate probably with an Oriental design on it that might have been made in Japan, China, the United States or Europe. The collector will buy such a plate if it is attractive or because he recognizes it as a particular kind of Oriental plate, perhaps an example of Rose Medallion Export Porcelain, collected for years and enjoying a revival today. On the other hand, if a plate is represented as Rose Medallion and turns out to be a cheap imitation made in Czechoslovakia between World War I and World War II and the collector can prove it, he has a case for a refund. In actuality, local managers of general auctions avoid getting caught in these traps by sidestepping specific identifications. They are out to move merchandise; let the buyer beware! The alert collector has to feel his or her way into such auctions by asking questions and observing the quality of merchandise that flows through the display rooms.

Specialized International Auction Houses

The marvelous art of staging an auction has been perfected by such firms as Sotheby Parke Bernet, known now mostly as Sotheby's; Christie, Manson & Woods, known as Christie's; and Phillips Ward-Price, known as Phillips. These international leaders, in competition with regional or one-location specialized auctions, are active in every large metropolitan area; they set the tone for auction standards. They have pioneered promotion and display techniques and authentication and educational programs that have upgraded enormously the reputable buying and selling of art, antiques and lesser collectibles. They have made auctions a vital channel for retailing this kind of merchandise. As it has been said, the leading auction houses establish the going price on most collectibles, for they attract the volume sales in any one collectible and quirks in the pricing tend to even out. Sometimes specialty dealers become a big factor in a particular collectible because they both buy and sell via auction as well as over their retail counter. They use auctions as a quick way of obtaining needed merchandise and of disposing of items they may want to throw back on the market for any number of reasons.

As a specific collectible becomes more prominent each year, you will find it featured at theme auctions, such as Sotheby's "Collectors' Carousel" or Christie's smaller auctions of specific collectibles such as toys, dolls, lead soldiers and other less-focused sales labeled "Americana".

Of course, the international auction houses have for a long time featured entire sales on periods and types of art and furniture and on popular and valuable collectibles such as coins, stamps, Oriental ceramics, books, pre-Columbian ceramics, jewelry, posters, prints and drawings. As an avid collector, you will probably know about these sales as they come up by following the columns that cover such things in most metropolitan newspapers and all specialized publications printed for collectors. In Chapter 6 of this book you will find many of these newsletters and magazines listed with addresses.

Another source of detailed news about auctions is the steady stream of catalogs that pour from the leading international auction houses. These bring photographs, often in four colors, of the most important pieces offered. Typical catalogs will also describe the item in some detail and tell its provenance, if known, and usually have a code for condition.

In every auction firm's catalog there is a definite terminology used in the description of objects as to authorship, period, culture, source or origin, and the auction house considers these statements qualified by its conditions of sale and terms of quarantee.

If the artist's or maker's name appears before the description, it usually means that the object is ascribed to the creator either by an outside expert or by the staff of the auction house. If the work is "attributed" to a creator, it is ascribed on the basis of style but with less certainty. Further gradations of authorship authenticity may be used, such as "circle of," "studio of," "school of," "follower of," "manner of" and "after," which would suggest a copy of a known work of the artist.

Work that has a signature thought in the best judgment of the auction house to be authentic is represented as "signed." If a work is dated, the date is thought by the auction house to be that of execution of the piece.

Customs vary with auction houses and it is worth the collector's while to study the way in which pieces of importance are represented. Such descriptions indicate previous owners, important exhibitions in which the piece appeared and indications of mention or illustration in a book or books on the subject. All of these intangible situations affect the price the object will achieve. If you happen to buy it, you will want to keep a copy of this information and the date of the sale within your collector's archives to help you in later valuation and in the possible sale of your collection.

Various auction houses have different wording for their condition of sale, the commission charged, returns and refunds, and guarantees of authenticity. You will find all of these terms spelled out in the individual catalogs that publicize the sale. Most collectors subscribe to catalogs that cover their specialty and thus are kept up-to-date on what is being offered and at what estimated prices. Catalogs characteristically include in rear pages or with each item a notation that gives an educated estimate of the probable knock-down price. This gives the collector an idea of where the bidding will focus.

Restricted or Unrestricted Sale

Most auctions, in addition to the terms of guarantee and the conditions of sale, will state whether the sale is "unrestricted." The reverse is seldom clearly indicated, however—a statement that the buyer can assume all items have "reserves" unless otherwise indicated. Reserves are a minimum amount agreed on by the seller and the auction house. If the bidding does not reach the reserve amount, the auction house bids in and the seller retains the property at the expense of a service charge. There is nothing illegal about this but collectors do not like the practice; they would prefer, naturally, to be able to pick up inexpensively those items that no one seems to want on that particular day. That is one of the reason reserves were instituted, to protect sellers from the poor results of a bad day or simply from a miscalculation of estimated value. The use of reserves varies with the auction houses. You will want to find out about the use of reserves on your kind of collectible. The best way is for you to offer a duplicate or unwanted item to auction and see what happens under what circumstances. Auction houses like sellers as well as buyers. But they are likely to approach a buyer differently than they would a seller and to tell the seller more about their manner of operations than they will a buyer.

Conditions of Sale

Frequent bidders at auction are known by the auction house and have no trouble in bidding, picking up merchandise and issuing checks to cover the purchase. They will usually receive a notification of a successful bid and an invoice, and will be expected to settle within ten days or so depending on the terms of the house. This they can do by check. For bidders unknown to the auction house, some sort of credit identification must be made before the sale. At some auctions, numbers on paddles are assigned to collectors and dealers who intend to bid. To get the paddle, you have to provide identification and whatever credit references the management considers necessary. This enables the auctioneer to accept bids with positive identification from many bidders and eliminates strangers that gum up an auction with bids that are later considered unacceptable, or that are not paid.

Most auction houses split the sales commission between the buyer and seller. Each customarily pays 10 percent of the amount of the successful bid. The buyer is also subject to sales taxes if the item is delivered in the state where the auction takes place, or a compensating use tax if the item is delivered outside the state.

Once you purchase an item you must pick it up or arrange transportation at your expense. If you do not pick it up by a specified deadline, auction houses customarily have a warehouse where they deposit items until you take them and pay storage charges.

You have to know all these conditions of sale before you begin bidding because it is embarrassing to run afoul of the way the auction house does business. Actually, the catalogs tell you everything you need to know, provided you read all the type, large and small, and simply get used to auctions and bidding. There is nothing more formidable about buying at auction than in buying from a department store or a dealer. It is just a different way and many collectors consider it a more exciting way to buy anything.

Getting the Most from an Auction Sale

1. Get the catalog of the auction in which a desired collectible will appear. What is the price it is expected to achieve? Does this seem in line with other recent prices already achieved? If it is unusually high, is there a plausible reason (scarcity, quality of specimen, unusual provenance) for the difference or is it just fond hope on the part of the seller and the auctioneer who is his agent?

From the auctioneer's viewpoint, it is better to estimate expected sales prices conservatively; it makes for better postsale publicity to announce that such and such a piece "exceeded presale estimates of x amount of dollars by 30 percent" than to report that the piece went for "less than presale estimates." In the latter case the actual prices may have been quite strong, even at record levels, but nonetheless *below* exuberant presale estimates. Reporters in various media sometimes have a bias for emphasizing failure rather than success. You, as a collector with increasing expertise, will have to be able to read between the lines.

2. View the items yourself once you have studied the presale catalog or list of items that will be up for auction. Unlike museums, auction houses expect you to touch and examine closely the pieces you might want to buy.

If the items are extremely fragile or valuable (rare books or manuscripts) or easily stolen (precious jewelry) the house may have them in a locked display case. But you can examine even these items in the presence of a staff member who usually is able to answer questions you might have about the imprisoned treasure. Naturally the auction house, in such circumstances, also has armed guards on the premises. The more you visit an auction house the less you will cause suspicion or questioning. And, of course, if you are recognized as a frequent and knowledgeable buyer, the more you will be encouraged to examine items without challenge or close surveillance.

Behavior at an Auction

In the catalog you may be told how bidding proceeds and whether bids by mail and/or telephone are accepted. The auctioneer will probably tell the audience how bidding will proceed if anything exceptional is expected. All you have to do, really, is read your catalog thoroughly and get to the auction in plenty of time to observe the bidding before any item comes up that interests you. In so doing, you will get the feel of the manner and rhythm of the sale and you may recognize certain dealers and competitors and note where they are sitting, what paddle numbers they have and so forth. This will give you an orientation and forearm you for the competitive bidding on objects you want.

Every bit of advice on bidding at an auction will include a sentence to the effect that you should *make up your mind before an auction* how high you will go for an individual item. *Then stick to that limit.* It does not matter what reason you give yourself for the limit; simply make the limit and do not exceed it. In that way you will not overbid in the excitement. Of course, you can make a mental note to buy regardless of the price, and in that case you simply hang in with the bidding until you have won. You will witness the experts dropping out at a certain level and you may then have only a single competitor bidding against you, and he probably wants the item as much as you do. The price you can afford, then, is the amount of money it is worth to you to (1) get the piece as a part of your collection, and (2) win the pleasure of beating out a rival. There really is no rational limit on that amount of dollars. This may be the reason certain pieces make records that similar pieces never achieve again in the wake of a spectacular sale. The prudent collector usually avoids such emotional bidding, except in unusual circumstances when a single item will complete a collection and add to it a greater value than the individual piece is worth on its own. Any other motive amounts to pride of possession or beating a rival; it is not going to bring you a profit in dollars.

Ways of Entering a Bid

Collectors who frequently attend an auction sometimes develop discreet bidding signals with the auctioneer in order not to advertise they are anxious to get a particular piece. Sometimes they are aware that rival collectors or dealers are in the room; at other times they want to maintain an anonymity for a variety of reasons.

For the most part, a brief holding up of your hand or paddle (if paddles are used) will indicate you are willing to raise the bid by whatever unit, $10, $50, $100, or $1,000, the auctioneer is handling at the time. Your verification comes with his announcement of your higher offer or a nod in your direction. The auctioneer will then usually maintain eye contact with you or a rival as the bidding proceeds. Sometimes, in a crowded audience, the auctioneer will use spotters, members of the staff, who relay bids to the auctioneer's podium. If that is the case, focus your bid on the spotter who covers your area. If you have developed special signals, let him know what you are up to; despite the trade-wide joke about the collector who blew his nose to signify he was willing to go higher, most auctioneers discourage such esoteric or eccentric bidding; it simply confuses the proceedings. If you must be secretive, develop a signal beforehand with the house and make it simply a natural movement such as a small nod of the head, a discreet wave of your catalog or raising your index finger. For the most part, auctions are auctions, business transactions where rivals will drop out when and only when bidding has reached a price beyond which they cannot justify going. There is no need to be coy; in a large auction even a fairly obvious bid will pass unnoticed by everyone except the auctioneer and his spotters. *But do stick to your predetermined limit in bidding.* Collectors, particularly the most enthusiastic kind, are most apt to blunder in their overbidding.

Mail and Telephone Bids

Once collectors have established their credit and identity with auction houses, they often, for the sake of convenience and/or anonymity, make bids by mail or telephone. Many catalogs carry a "bid sheet" that can be used to make a bid—the top price you will pay—on a specific item. You will not win that item if bidding goes higher but you will surely get it—at a lower price—if bidding does not make the limit you have set. In other words, the auctioneer will try to get the item for you at a lower price and always under the limit you have set.

If you are a regular bidder this way, you probably will establish an account with the auction house. This will facilitate the movement of goods to you; when you are a relative stranger, the auction house may hold the goods you bought until you have honored its invoice with a check that has cleared.

A written bid can be placed in person the day of your visit to the exhibition preceding the show. This will prevent two trips; auction houses often clear the walls of items a day or so before the auction takes place. The items customarily are lined up backstage or viewed via photographic slides so that they are presented to the audience in a predetermined order, almost always by chronological lot number. By the time of the sale, in the busy houses, other items are being hung in the exhibition galleries. Most galleries, if you want to check out an item at the last minute before an auction begins, will let you behind the scenes and will help you try to find and inspect the item. You will get this kind of service more readily if the house recognizes you as a collector and identified buyer and if you do not abuse this privilege.

Of course, you can mail in or telephone in your bid anytime before the sale and you can monitor the sale via telephone if you have prearranged these communications. Particularly in a sale of art, several collectors may prearrange communication with the house the day of the auction. A staff member may be near the podium relaying bids to the auctioneer as the auction proceeds. During one of the most dramatic sales of American paintings, the sale of Frederick Church's *Icebergs* (which sold for $2.5 million), the winning bid was completed by telephone. At the time, it was the highest amount of money ever paid for a painting by an American painter.

Dealer Bids on Your Behalf

If you deal primarily with a dealer/expert and you hear of an item coming up for auction, you may employ him to obtain it for you. He will apply his expertise to evaluate the piece and its condition and determine the price it will likely achieve, and then discuss with you the highest bid he should make. Most dealers will give you this service for a 10 percent commission on the gross price of the piece.

Carting the Prize Away

As purchaser of a piece, you are responsible for picking it up and taking it away. If you are going to a country auction of furniture, take a station wagon. If you are going to an auction in the city, prearrange delivery with a trucker recommended by the auction house. You will probably get a good price as well as competent handling of possibly fragile material. Beware of taking just any trucking service. You may receive your prize in pieces, scratched or, in the case of multiple items, with some items missing. Be systematic about checking bills of lading to see what the trucker picked up at the auction house and what he delivered to you. Take whatever insurance is recommended by the auction house and do not settle your account with the auction house until you are satisfied you got what you bought. In the case of discrepancies, notify the auction house immediately so that adjustment can be made, omitted pieces possibly found and the like. You usually have three days after the auction to pick up items and a reasonable length of time after that to report discrepancies and to make requests for adjustment (three days after receipt of collectible stamps, for example). By and large, at smaller regional auctions and at country auctions especially, you are expected to take small items with you and pay for them before you go. At most country auctions, in fact, you buy on a cash and carry basis. Thus you have to be more shrewd in your purchases at these auctions. On the other hand, you are not likely to put up very much money for an individual item at a country auction; the really valuable pieces have a way of going to speciality auctions where they are most likely to get the best exposures.

Sources of Collectibles—Shows

Wherever collectors gather—at educational seminars given by dealers and auction houses, at conventions of dealers, at annual get-togethers for collectors—you can be sure to meet someone with something to sell, barter or trade. Because these conventions and gatherings attract such a large audience in some collectible categories, such as coins, stamps and books, museums put on special shows, auction houses schedule special auctions and dealers have a kind of gala open house. This occurs more and more frequently in New York City, Los Angeles and Chicago, but particularly in New York where the collectibles "complex" certainly has its worldwide capital. New York also has the hotel facilities, entertainment facilities and full panoply of dealers in hundreds of different collectibles. Thus collectors can take a theme holiday, often a business tax-deductible trip, for pursuing their hobby-business.

You will, of course, through experience, have to weed out the shows you find worthwhile attending and those that are not for you. But, on the whole, this type of meeting attracts the most vital elements of any market, those who have the supply and those who want to buy. As at any convention or meeting, you are there to get to know key people and to learn without necessarily committing

"Nobility, celebrities, you name it—all the biggies. Kid, I've got a collection of owners you wouldn't believe!"

yourself to any purchase at all. And you have the advantage of getting transportation and hotel rates at a group discount, depending on the number of people the show will attract and how effective the show's management is in getting breaks for attendees. You can find out about local, regional and national gatherings by getting the newsletter or magazine that covers your collectible.

Shows vary in quality and the level of dealers who come to display their wares. In general, a show sponsored by a leading charity (which gets part of the admission charge and sometimes a percentage of items sold) is worth attending and you can assume that dealers have been screened before they are invited to exhibit. Other, strictly commercial, shows may be less selective and you will have to check out a dealer's reputation on your own if you intend to do serious business.

Regardless of whether you buy or not, a show is a good place to get acquainted with dealers, ask questions, examine good examples of your collectibles and rub elbows with a number of fellow collectors.

Sources of Collectibles— Flea Markets and Attic Sales

The fair or bazaar, flea market, garage sale, attic sale, rummage sale, thrift shop, or tag sale recycles more collectible items in the

United States each year than all the auction houses and dealers put together.

In general it is safe to say, though, that these informal fun affairs deal in secondhand goods of all kinds that are probably not more than a century old and frequently only a few decades old. They cannot be said to deal in antiques and seldom offer very significant or big-ticket collectibles. But you can find modestly priced coins, stamps, old books, records, printed material of all kinds, glassware, ceramics, folk art, clothes, old tools and many kinds of useful items. Household machinery that is not longer produced may have some use still, but is interesting partly for its sentimental value and for collectors who snap up what others consider ready for a rummage sale. These sales are a good way for neighbors to convert to cash whatever they have that they do not want to keep any longer.

So it is worth spending some time at these sales; you can usually find something to eat there as well, and if the day is pleasant, the whole event can prove a rewarding excursion.

At such sales, you are on your own about authenticity and pricing. They are open ground for pickpockets who know these are largely cash-and-carry events with no guards. Vendors, in fact, risk pilferage; if you have serious thoughts about selling some of your collectibles at such sales, think twice about offering anything of value. It is safer to have a dealer handle it for you.

Such sales encourage very heterogeneous pricing and both the possibility of a bargain and of a trap. There is a tendency to overprice anything with a manufacturer's mark that is well known in furniture and porcelain, as well as any very popular items such as record albums of pop stars, baseball cards and Art Deco and art moderne pieces. The manufacturer's mark proves the authenticity and the fame; then the mystique accounts for the bold prices.

At the same time, if you know what you are looking for, you can often recognize pieces of authentic art pottery that slip in and that you can buy for a few dollars because no one has bothered to research their origins.

Go to such a sale with notes on exactly what you are looking for, a Xerox copy of identifying marks, possibly a price guide of your collectible and the means for carting away the treasures you find.

Sources of Collectibles— Fellow Collectors

Much of your fun in collecting may be in trading or swapping information, stories and specimens with fellow collectors once you have the hang of pricing and identifying quality in your field.

You will find great pleasure in swapping items; a friend obtains a wanted object and so do you. You need not require that each item bartered in this way has an immediate place in your collection. Sometimes you will accept several items useful for later trading in order to keep one long-sought-after piece. Dealers experience this same acceptance of marginal material when they buy an estate or a major collection. The sale, from the standpoint of an executor, is neater if marginal items are included with the major and most valuable core of the collection. Dealers and collectors know the reasons for this. If the seller were to handle each minor item separately, the process might go on for years, produce mediocre results and even wind up with leftovers that cannot be sold or given away.

When you are trading thusly with fellow collectors, remember that you may get some pleasure (and other profit) from the sheer excitement or process of the trade. You may be high on your acquisition as you make it but realize later that the "high" was personal pleasure and your collection is no better off for the transaction. In fact, you may hope it is no worse! Collectors sometimes offer questionable items in trade for the sake of trading; you may have to accept some of the nonsense simply to get at one or two particularly valuable items. In some cases, it may be wiser to have a dealer handle the swap for you with the understanding that he will get some of the lesser objects as his commission. That clears all chances and leaves the unwanted pieces in the hands of the man most likely to sell them.

These marginal acquisitions, by the way, may benefit another collector who specializes in them and who may negotiate a bargain piece for relieving a dealer or a collector of odd items not normally handled or collected but nonetheless accumulated over the years of accommodating sellers and friends. For example, an avid collector of paperweights may have in his collection peripheral bits of glassware and perhaps antique marbles that fascinated someone because of their relationship to the paperweight. But the peripheral glass or marbles were largely miscellaneous; they may represent good quality of their kind but were not the main attraction for paperweight collector A. Collector B, however, may find he can obtain them for a good price simply because collector A wants to upgrade and tidy his collection. Surely some of these peripheral items will generate cash and buying power that can be applied to the central collection.

Not the least benefit or profit to you as a collector is the fact that the IRS now considers these exchanges in kind as nontaxable. (However, you may want to have your accountant's current advice on this matter before you pursue it on a large scale.) Thus you can prune and improve your collection and its value without incurring immediate additional tax liability.

4

Protecting and Insuring Your Collectibles

Consider the bad news about theft, first. Only about 5 percent of all stolen antiques and collectibles *are ever recovered.* As you have gathered by now, the markets for collectibles are many and varied: swapping, bartering, buying on one coast and selling on another, fly-by-night dealers, street fairs, all are means for acquiring and disposing the goods, whether they be honestly or dishonestly offered and represented.

So the burden of protection against theft is on you, not on your landlord or the police, neither of whom may know a collectible from a kitchen utensil. Unfortunately, the more educated and thriving thieves do; they have been known to ransack a house and take selectively the most valuable collectibles that have a good market. It is the same principle that makes it so hard for business offices to retain the IBM Selectric, self-correcting typewriters they buy. They are a wanted commodity. Stamps, coins and jewelry, all things valuable and relatively small, are high on a thief's most-wanted list. Of the burglars who are arrested, about half turn out to be teenagers, some of whom have taken the trouble to learn (or to be taught by master thieves with the skill of Dickens' arch-thief, Fagin) what to take and what to leave behind.

It was not always so. Collectors thought, with good reason, that their collectibles were safe in a locked display cabinet in a house that usually had someone inside, the owner or a servant, but might sometimes be empty. They had no special concern for their safety.

The safety of collectibles fell victim to the progress of communication technology and their popularity as tangible capital. Some highly profitable collectibles have, in some instances, value as currency and uses as money. This is especially so with silver and gold coins and with stamps—particularly those that have intrinsic and numismatic or philatelic value but are not so rare and valuable that any buyer would be suspicious of their provenance and authenticity of ownership. This means that good, run-of-the-mill collectibles that are not easily identified one from another among hundreds more of the same are especially vulnerable.

Electronic Protection

Fortunately, the same technology that spreads the news so quickly about collectibles, which is popular among thieves at the moment—TV pictures of stolen objects in the nightly news report—also can be used as protection in the form of monitoring cameras. There are on the market now all manner of electronic gadgets that can trip up entering burglars. Roughly, they are of the type that makes a noise and lets the neighborhood know that an intruder has entered the premises. This is a sensitivity type of installation that handy collectors can install themselves with either a ray or a receptor disguised as an electric plug or wires placed beneath a doorsill or doormat. The difficulty with these sensitivity alarms is that you can set them off if you enter when they are "on." Or your cat or dog can play burglar and create havoc when, in fact, they are simply going from one room to another in search of something to eat. If this happens too often—false alarms that raise an awful racket—you are likely to hear about it from your neighbors.

These local alarms, both for fire and for theft, are effective to the extent that they warn of a fire or intruder. But at the sound of the alarm some person has to call the fire or police department to take effective action. In the case of thieves, the noise alone will frighten away quite a few amateurs but the pro, recognizing the nature of the system, will simply know it as an early warning and regard it as an exit cue.

The professional thief, who unfortunately may simply be the nimble first echelon of a highly organized crime syndicate, will have previously calculated the remaining minutes for finishing the caper and getting off the premises. It will depend on the value of your collection and your vulnerability to theft whether you install a more professional alarm system. There are two more foolproof types and both require professional installation. One is a system that sends an alarm into a central station. It is usually wired to that station, a commercial alarm company, through a leased telephone line. In a matter of seconds after a disturbance, the central office will have notified the police or fire department and may send an inspector itself to check out the threat to your security. Other electronic systems notify the fire or police departments directly and immediately.

Often the mere sight of a security system, such as the familiar metal foil strips that outline a window, are enough to deter many potential burglars from entering obviously protected premises. Decals announcing that "these premises are protected by a Foil Thief Protection System" accomplish a similar purpose.

It is very hard to choose which system is the best protection for you. The person to ask about this is your insurance agent. Do not buy electronic gadgetry off the street from someone you do not know or from someone who advertises in the local newspaper and then uses high-pressure sales tactics in person and by telephone.

Yes, you do need someone to come to the premises and make a survey of your needs. But arrange to invite a representative from a reputable company recommended by your insurance agent or by a fellow collector who knows from experience that the product and/or service is good. Another source of reference is your local police or fire department, either of which is aware of results obtained by various protection systems. You will want to get to know both departments, anyway, if you have a system installed that requires their prompt response.

How to Buy Insurance at the Lowest Feasible Rates

Working with the police and fire departments and with your insurance agent, you will find that you can obtain the protection you need and that your insurance premium may be lower than expected. Here is why. The chances of loss are much less with an effective protection system installed. For this reason it is important to bring your insurance agent into the decision on what protection system you use. It is his business to know how to minimize loss.

You may be surprised to learn that your comprehensive homeowners' policy (or tenant homeowners' policy, if you rent your home or apartment) automatically covers your personal property as a fixed sum, one sum for the dwelling and another for your personal possessions. Because antiques, art objects and most other collectibles are considered personal property, they are covered. The usual policy protects against fire, theft, smoke, vandalism, explosions, sleet, ice, hail, windstorm, weight of snow felling trees, falling airplanes, water from frozen pipes and collapse of the building. Some of the situations in which you will not be protected include normal wear and tear or loss in value caused by rust, rot, mold or corrosion. Book bindings, for example, can simply dry out and dust away, or fall apart. Your comprehensive policy will not reimburse you for that.

The major drawback in using a comprehensive homeowners' policy for protection of fine arts or special collections such as stamps or coins is the sharp difference in intrinsic value between your collectibles and other, more ordinary, personal articles such as clothing, household furniture, kitchenware and tools. It will be hard to prove that a drawerful of coins is worth the thousands of dollars you claim; or that a stamp collection that is now a sodden, damp, soggy mass of cinders and charred album pages contained stamps conservatively estimated as worth $75,000.

For these special collections you need "scheduled insurance" that identifies the individual items and includes individual appraisals of worth. Here again, you will be wise to work closely with your insurance agent and take his advice about getting the kind of supplementary insurance that will protect your special collection. You will find that the agent will work out with you a communication system so that you will periodically notify the insurance company as to which items you have sold and which ones were added and their appraisals.

"I was over chatting with the weathervanes for a while. A nice bunch, but—well—a bit two-dimensional."

Operation Identification

You have probably heard about this new deterrent to thievery: a police sponsored system for etching indelible numbers on all manner of solid objects with an electric etching tool, or a stylus that scratches the number on fragile ceramics that might shatter from the vibrations of a power tool. Paper documents can be identified by indelible numbers in ink. Then your premises are marked (usually with a sticker or decalcomania) as recorded with Operation Identification. The rationale behind the system is an easier recovery of stolen goods because they positively can be identified and registered as yours. A thief or his disposal outlet, or "fence," cannot get rid of them so easily. Given a choice, a thief prefers to steal unmarked goods rather than traceable ones. The same principle operates as with marked money paid in ransom—the marked object can be used as evidence against the person trafficking in crime.

Records to Keep

Although it is difficult to keep records on every piece of your collection, it is really the only way to prove anything in the case of loss and/or if you are challenged by the IRS on any losses or gains you report for tax purposes. Records also make it easier for your appraiser and insurance agent, and for you when you talk to a dealer about selling your collection. In the last analysis, you have to manage your collection like a business if you want to get the most financial profit from it. Not many people have the interest or the will, the sheer energy, to do this. They prefer a lackadaisical approach—the fun of picking up a piece here and there, possibly selling it later and telling endless tales about acquisitions at low amounts twenty years ago selling for great multiples at present. While these tales may be true in their rough figures, they omit telling what has happened to the dollar over a period of twenty years. To be honest, you must consider that the dollar in 1980 bought only about half of the goods and services it bought in 1960, so a collectible would have to be sold for at least two times what you bought it for in order for you to break even on the venture. That is talking in dollars terms, only; you may have enjoyed incalculable pleasure simply in looking at your stamps, coins or Oriental vases. All well and good. That is a valid profit, too, as long as you are aware of both kinds of profit: the personal pleasure and the financial gain.

If you do have a strong motive for financial profits and do not like to keep records, you will have to employ a part-time "curator" of your collection or choose a collectible that does not require thousands of units to become a whole. Limit yourself to a collectible with high value per unit, such as gold or silver coins, oil paintings or Oriental ceramics. You can concentrate your protective worrying, insurance and record keeping on relatively few items that nonetheless add up to considerable value. This is also a factor in displaying your collectibles and/or storing them (spaces on shelves, case, drawers, closets or storage warehouse) and the cost in providing and maintaining each of these.

In Chapter 5 which covers selling and taxes, you will find a simple record form that you can arrange to have duplicated in a variation that suits your needs. It can serve as a single-unit record for appraisals, insurance, and buying and selling.

The Bank Vault or Safe Deposit Box, or Storage Warehouse

Certain types of collectibles such as rare coins, stamps and jewelry might be best kept in a safe deposit box when you are not using or working with them. If this is the type of collecting you prefer, and you do not want to handle your collection frequently, this is probably the best type of protection you can have as they increase in value. Of course, there is some expense involved, depending on the size of high-security storage you need. If you collect paintings, you may want to keep some of them in a storage warehouse where you will want to consider insuring them against theft and damage in handling, in storage and to and from storage.

Most collectors prefer to have their treasures around them but some, because of the risk and space required, will simply have to put some items out of circulation for a while. Still other collectors, attracted by potential profits they can realize on their surplus items, will sell and pare their collection, thus limiting expenses for protection and storage at the same time.

5

Selling Your Collectibles
at a Profit

It is more than likely that you will get maximum financial profit from your collection if you manage it like a business. First of all, you choose the collectible that seems to have a future, that will attract people, just as you would choose merchandise for a store. Then you develop a sense of timing, when to buy and when to sell what items. You will also want to develop a sense of display so that fellow collectors and budding collectors will see the decorative value or simply the scope and fascination of your collection.

As has been mentioned before, you will want to keep records, so that you know what you own, how it is protected, what you have been offered, what comparable pieces have brought at recent auctions.

You will probably want to keep file folders on various topics pertaining to your collection—articles that appear in the press; new ways of preventing theft and fire; reminiscences of fellow collectors that often record in print the location of noteworthy collections; and finally, auction records of prices achieved and price annotated catalogs of auctions you may have attended. Whether you realize it or not, as a seasoned collector you have become part scholar, part businessperson. You can add to the printed knowledge on your subject if you choose to publish your research findings or prepare a monograph covering territory not yet researched by fellow collectors. This may be in the form of a scholarly article or something more popular for a magazine, even a literary essay.

In short, you will get the most profit by preparing to market your collectibles at a profit and doing this enthusiastically, within the context of your collectors' association and fellow collectors. They will think of your collection as yours, the John Doe Collection of Paperweights, for example, and if you have communicated your fondness for your orderly and significant collection, they will automatically give it the benefit of something whole and distinctive, as compared to a vague assembly of individual pieces with little shape or meaning as a collection. The latter type of collection is the frequent achievement of a beginner and amateur. If the individual items are well chosen, they may have considerable value, but not as much as they will as part of well-managed collection that belongs to you, a collector of stature and prominence. No matter what your profession or trade, you may very well become best known in your family, locally, and nationally as a collector, a benefactor of your local museum and author of significant works on what once was a "little hobby" for you. It is a wonderful accomplishment, both tangible and intangible, that you can pass on to others, including your heirs.

Where To Sell Your Collection

Although you might consider selling or trading individual pieces to fellow collectors, the best place to sell most items is the same source where you bought them, be that a dealer, an auction or a show (through a dealer there).

If your collectible was picked up willy-nilly over many years from many sources, go to the most reputable dealer or auction house that specializes in your collectible.

If you are now the proud owner of a significant collection, a dealer or auction house will be glad to sell all or part of it for you. If they sell a part successfully now, they will naturally look forward to selling the rest of it one day, for you have valuable items to offer. You have put together something that is more significant and valuable than the mere sum of its parts.

You will be pleasantly surprised at how the pieces have gained in value over the years! When you sell, be sure to keep track of the paperwork that reported the sale, the commissions and whatever expenses you had in preparing the object or objects for sale. Also remember that you can deduct repairs you may have made over the years when you calculate the gain on the piece.

Your Tax Situation on Your Gains

Because purchases and sales of collectibles are not reported to the IRS via your Social Security number, even though they are traded and handled and rightly regarded today as an investment medium, you are on your own about reporting major gains you make. It would be a good idea to talk over these matters with your accountant so that he outlines a procedure that will benefit you as much as it can, depending on your personal financial situation. You may find that it would be to your advantage to give a core collection of your best pieces to a museum, so that others can share in viewing and learning about your beloved objects and what you have done with them to make them a joy for future generations.

Keeping Track of Your Collection

The "Collector's Tracking Sheet" which follows is suggested as a handy way to keep track of the significant items, or groups of items, in your collection. It is useful when you have your collection appraised or insured and when you calculate the gains you have made. Have a sheet like this typed up and then run off as many Xerox copies as you need.

COLLECTOR'S TRACKING SHEET

*Code Number	Identifying Mark	Artist/ Craftsman/ Manufacturer	Date of Purchase	Where Purchased	Price	Appraised (Date/ Amount)	Date of Sale	Where Sold	Gain

* Many collectors develop a personal numbering system so that each object has a code. Sometimes this is simply a number inked to paper or scratched into other material in an inconspicuous place, based on chronological date of acquisition. Other collectors supplement this numbering system with 3 × 5 cards that carry the number and all of the above information, plus bits of history that form the provenance of the article. All of these systems help keep a large collection in order and build up its worth, and also protect it. This numbering system, for example, can tie into an Operation Identification registry with your local police department.

A Jar That Brought Its Owner 1000 Times the Value He Expected   *A man brought this wine jar into a Phillips regional salesroom, hoping to get about $400 for it. It was authenticated as a 16th-century Ming wine jar. Phillips sent it for sale to its London auction rooms, where it would have the full advantage of the international interest in fine Chinese ceramics. A Japanese collector bought it for $440,000 (£220,000). (Photo: courtesy of Phillips.)*

Black Memorabilia Often Feature Stereotyped Characters *This collection included a pair of china salt and pepper shakers (one a maid, the other a chef), a Staffordshire figure of Uncle Tom and Little Eva, a cloth doll of the Cream of Wheat Man, a pair of salt and pepper shakers as seated mammies, an ashtray and match holder formed as a porter carrying suitcases, and the cast-iron bust of a boy that may have served as a sprinkler head. The highest price paid at a Christie's auction of these memorabilia was $100 for the Uncle Tom and Little Eva. Production of these items began at the turn of the century; they were popular until the 1960s, when a strong sense of black dignity and achievement discouraged manufacture of these comic and servant stereotypes. They are now collected and often displayed as part of black history lectures and demonstrations. (Photo: courtesy of Christie's.)*

Clay Teapot Turns to Gold   *Probably the most expensive teapot of European porcelain is this small one in red stoneware created by the draftsman Bottger, who worked for Meissen in the early 18th century. Bottger was also an alchemist who spent many years trying to find a way to turn base metal into gold. Two centuries after his death, his artifact may have done it for him. It brought $60,000 (£30,000) at a recent auction. (Photo: courtesy of Phillips.)*

Model Butcher Shop with Unusual History   *This framed three-dimensional model of a Victorian butcher shop, complete with colorful joints of meat, staff, utensils and a fat cat, was sold recently at a Phillips Collectors' Centre sale in London for about $1,440 (£720). It was offered by a pub that had had it on display for years. An owner of the pub, years ago, had accepted it as payment for drinking debts. (Photo: courtesy of Phillips.)*

Famous Model, Famous Sculptor, Famous Style   *Several collectible features combined to gain a high price—$8,000—for this Art Nouveau gilt bronze figural lamp. It was cast by Raoul Larché in about 1900; the model was the dancer, Loie Fuller, holding swirling drapery above her head. (Photo: courtesy of Christie's.)*

Rummage Sale Donation of $1 Buys Rare Mirror Case   *The donor of $1 to a church rummage sale took this fragment of ivory home and kept it in his bureau drawer for more than twenty years. Recently, because an auction house had sold his mother's old wedding dress "rather well for me," he decided to inquire about the piece of ivory. This circlet, about 4" in diameter, was identified as a French 14th-century mirror case, beautifully carved and still in excellent condition. It sold for $72,000 (£36,000). (The mother's wedding dress had sold for $40!) (Photo: courtesy of Phillips.)*

Pieces of Aged Wood with Unusual Potential   *These pieces of seasoned maple brought more than $1,000 (£500) at a Phillips auction in London. The maple proved to be ideal wood for violin backs. It had been estimated to go at one-fourth or one-fifth of the amount it actually brought; a violin craftsman apparently needed this fine wood badly. (Photo: courtesy of Phillips.)*

Wormy Wood Chunks Identified as Valuable Carving *Three wormy chunks of wood carving were brought to Phillips in London for possible sale by the owner. When they first broke into three fragments he had thrown them away, had second thoughts, and retrieved them from the garbage can. He was glad he did. A Phillips specialist identified the carvings as a rare Flemish work from about the year 1500. They portray St. Hubert, patron saint of hunters. A previous owner (a wood preservation firm) had been using the piece as an example of "what woodworm can do to your home." At the Phillips sale the three pieces were sold to a dealer—and expert in this kind of antiquity—for $21,000 (£10,500). (Photo: courtesy of Phillips.)*

6

Popular and Profitable Collectibles

ANIMATED FILM CELS

Cels are names for the material, celluloid, from which most of the early animated cartoon transparencies were made. The material, now of varying chemical compositions, often Mylar, enables translucent coloring of designs that can be moved against a painted background that shows through so that slight changes in the photographed posture of figures in successive cells suggest motion when projected.

The genius of the animated cartoon probably reached its height as an art in the five full-length film features produced by Walt Disney Productions: *Dumbo, Bambi, Fantasia, Pinocchio,* and the supremely realized and unforgettable *Snow White and the Seven Dwarfs.*

Other popular cartoon characters were Betty Boop, created by Walter Fleischer, Walter Lantz' Woody Woodpecker, and Paul Terry's Terrytoons.

In historical fact, the animated cartoon, as an experimental form, came to life long before actual movies. The first film with a story line probably dated from about 1900 when an anonymous artist in the Edison motion-picture company produced *The Enchanted Drawing.* It projected an artist sketching a sad-faced tramp on a drawing pad. As the artist draws a "light" from the cigar in the tramp's mouth, the whole drawing magically comes to life and the tramp puffs up a storm of smoke to the playful surprise of the artist.

About 1909, Winsor McCay, who created the comic strip *Little Nemo,* projected an animated film of his character that won wide and frequent showings. McCay took his films on tour and acted as an emcee at each showing.

J. R. Bray's studio arranged to have films go out on their own. His *Colonel Heeza Liar* series began in 1913 and helped to train such animators—later famous—as Walter Lantz, Paul Terry, Max Fleischer and Carl Hurd.

During the 1900's a number of cartoon characters were animated, including Mutt and Jeff, Krazy Kat, the Katzenjammer Kids, and Maggie and Jiggs from *Bringing Up Father.* Then came the Disney creations, Mickey and Minnie Mouse, Donald Duck and Pluto. Studios such as Warner Brothers brought out *Looney Tunes* and *Merrie Melodies,* and created such familiar characters as Porky Pig, Daffy Duck, Bugs Bunny and Roadrunner. MGM created Tom and Jerry. And United Productions of America created the near-sighted Mister Magoo.

In the early days, the cels, backgrounds and storyboards were not particularly valued or even filed away. Sometimes an animator took them home when the film had been shot; some were given away to studio visitors.

As a popular collectible, the animation cel dates from the 1930's when a California art dealer, Guthrie Sayre Courvoisier, made a deal with Walt Disney Productions. He foresaw a market for the cels in museums, school art departments and interior decoration, and as collectibles. "Without half trying," he reported, he sold 65 cels of a group of animals and Snow White looking through a window for prices ranging from $5 to $50. Today, those same cels bring ten times or more their original price.

Where To Find Animation Cels— The Market

Cels are a relatively new and specialized collectible. You will not find them, usually, at flea markets, attic sales and the like. They are usually sold at shops that handle prints, drawings and inexpensive oils. Now and then they come up at collectors' carousels at the major auction houses but they have yet to build a large market and wide following. If they particularly appeal to you as something decorative to have in the house, they are a good buy at current prices. You can use them as decoration as well as collect them and wait for wider demand to raise the price. In this situation, the supply from the animation studios and the *reproductions* on Mylar and other contemporary film material of *originals* can keep the market well supplied and the prices down. Be sure you know the difference between reproductions run off as duplicates of the original and the originals themselves. Walt Disney Productions authen-

ticates and identifies both and has made a small subsidiary industry of reproducing scenes of its most famous characters; they are
usually done as "limited editions."

Museums Notable for Their Collections of Cels
  Baltimore Museum of Art, Baltimore, MD 21218
  Museum of Modern Art, New York, NY 10019

Clubs and Organizations
  ASIFA, International Animated Film Society, 1680 North Vine,
    Hollywood, CA 90028

Books Worthwhile for Collectors
  Cabarga, Leslie, *The Fleischer Story*, Crown Publishers, New
    York, 1976
  Finch, Christopher, *The Art of Walt Disney*, Harry N. Abrams,
    New York, 1973
  Madsen, Roy, *Animated Film Concepts, Methods, Uses*, Inter-
    land Publishing, 1969
  Maltin, Leonard, *Disney Films*, Crown Publishers, New York,
    1972

ARROWHEADS

Most "arrowheads" never flew through the air, powered by an Indian bow. Rather they are properly identified as spear points; they were affixed to shafts thrown or hurled by Indians. The bow appeared in the New World only about 500 A.D.

Spear points generally are larger than arrowheads and longer, too. The true arrowhead tends to be triangular and small.

Points were chipped from many materials from about 10,000 B.C. when flint was the principal material used. Later, quartz and quartzite became popular and in the Plains and Western regions agate and obsidian were frequently used.

Different regions of the United States produced different shapes of points and they usually were made of the hardest materials found in the region—quartz, flint and quartzite in the East and agate and obsidian in the Plains and Western regions.

The size of the points diminished with craft and evolution. During the Paleo-Indian period before 8000 B.C., hunters sought bison and mammoth; points were three inches or more in length; they had to be long to penetrate the thick, hairy hide of these large animals. Archaic points, dating from 8,000 B.C. to about 1,000 B.C., are usually notched or stemmed at the base, which made for easier fastening to a shaft. The hunter who used them went after smaller game and also fished and used berries and grasses as part of his diet.

During the Middle period, 1,000 B.C. to about 1,200 A.D., people had begun to settle in villages. They developed more distinctive local styles and designs in points. A final "late" period stretched from 1,200 to 1,600 or 1,700 B.C. and points became very small, often barely an inch long and hard to tell sometimes for real arrowheads. Other chipped artifacts, found with points and arrowheads, were knives, daggers and scrapers for cleaning animal hides. Other variants were drills, perforators, gravers and hammer-stones—a tool-making tool.

But points are the most sought after by collectors and, in the United States alone, more than 400 distinct types are recognized by archeologists. They can be identified by region, material, shape and the distinctive pattern in which they are flaked.

Where To Find Arrowheads—The Market

Points and arrowheads are essentially archeological finds and are still found in abundance throughout the United States on natural sites of use. If Indians once lived in the region you now occupy, you can still find arrowheads in fields newly plowed and washed by rain, and along the edges of lakes and rivers. In parts of the West and Northwest, collectors find points by prospecting for them: sifting the soil of sites known to have been occupied by Indians. Of course, other people do this, too—or their ancestors have done it— and previously collected arrowheads and points will come out in flea markets and in attic sales from time to time in towns and villages where Indians once dwelled. Often museums will have sales of excess items. Arrowheads, as such, seldom bring high prices and they make a good beginner collectible. Heads, points and fragments can be purchased for a few dollars. But much of the fun is in prospecting for them in the open.

Museums with Notable Collections of Arrowheads

If you are in arrowhead and point country, check first of all your local municipal, county or state museums. They will usually have the best collection of regional artifacts you can find. Here are some prominent museums with worthwhile collections:

Field Museum of Natural History, Chicago, IL 60605
Museum of the American Indian, New York, 10032
National Museum of Natural History, Smithsonian Institution, Washington, DC 20560

Clubs and Organizations
Central States Archaeological Societies, Inc., 6118 Scott Street, Davenport, IA 52806
Eastern States Archaeological Federation, RD #2, Box 166, Dover, DE 19901
Ohio Archaeological Society, 35 West Riverglen Drive, Columbus, OH 43085
Oregon Archaeological Society, P.O. Box 13293, Portland, OR 97213

Books Worthwhile for Collectors
Bell, Robert E, and Perino, Gregory, *Guide to the Identification of Certain American Indian Projectible Points*, Special Bulletins Nos. 1–4, Oklahoma Anthropoligical Society, 1958–1971
Ceram, O. W., *The First American*, Harcourt Brace Jovanovich, New York, 1971

Miles, Charles, *Indian and Eskimo Artifacts of North America*, Henry Regnery Company, Chicago, 1963

Vanburen, G. E., *Arrowheads and Projectile Points*, Arrowhead Publishing Company, 1974

ART POTTERY

Art pottery, if one must define it, was decorative rather than useful, although most of its shapes could be used as vases or bowls. The imaginative, even fanciful, variations of these creations are often so fragile that most owners prefer to put them on a safe shelf or sill and admire but not use them.

The history of the art pottery movement in the United States stems from the Englishman William Morris' concept of individual crafts and arts done at home. The Philadelphia Centennial Exposition of 1876 brought from abroad some brilliant examples of European art pottery. Almost overnight U.S. collectors began gathering and making art pottery. And the craze continued until shortly after World War II. In fact, a case can be made that it has only entered a new phase of individual potters (somewhat more commercial than the former talented amateurs), who can be found at every arts and crafts fair with often dazzling arrays of their pots.

The movement in the United States was part of an early women's movement; many of the early and most important potter-

ies were founded and sponsored by women as an outlet for feminine creative energies.

Rookwood Pottery, for example, was founded by Marian Longworth Nichols Storer, a wealthy woman from Cincinnati who gathered together, in 1880, a work force of craftswomen. Most of her early workers had experience in the Victorian lady's hobby of china painting—applying a design to blank plates and porcelain pieces and having them fired to set the colors and glaze. Rookwood's pattern of success led to the success of many hundreds of other potteries coast to coast in the United States—wherever clay for pots was available. The craft began informally with designs improvised, sometimes daring for their time and sometimes "flops" but rather exuberant flops nonetheless. As commercial success took hold, the potteries became larger, had to become more businesslike to face competitors who got away with close imitations of the most popular designs.

The Miller, Owens and Roseville potteries, also located near the Zanesville, Ohio, clay fields, all had varieties of Rookwood Standard, a brown-glazed ware—background colors of brown, yellow and green covered by a hard, clear, pale yellow glaze.

The collector of art pottery, to profit from this hobby or mania, should probably specialize in one pottery or potter and collect typical examples of the product in as perfect a condition as possible.

Other potters whose signed works can bring prices of thousands of dollars at auction are Hugh C. Robertson, who had a factory in Dedham, Massachusetts; George E. Ohr, of Biloxi, Mississippi, who featured unusually eccentric shapes and very thin walls,· causing a high price if you can find a specimen in perfect condition; and Theophilus A. Brouwer of East Hampton, New York, who fire-painted his products and created most interesting runs of colors.

William E. Grueby of Revere, Massachusetts, rediscovered and developed the art of mat glazing, which left the tile or bowl with a dull or nonshiny finish.

An itinerant British potter, Frederick H. Read, wandered through the United States from one commercial pottery to another and developed brilliant new designs and glazes that the factories continued and/or modified as Read moved on to yet another employment. There were also Artus Van Briggle and Louis Comfort Tiffany, who turned to the French Art Nouveau style for inspiration.

Three women offered a final flair to the art pottery movement. One was Adelaid Alsop Robinson of Syracuse, New York. Another was Mary Chase Perry of the Pewabic Pottery of Detroit, and the third was Mrs. James J. Storrow of Boston. All of these women

Early Unpopularity of a Rookwood Glaze Caused Scarcity—and High Prices Today *From left to right, these Rookwood vases with iris glaze were popular when first produced in the 1890s. A good quantity is available to collectors today. Even more rare is a sea green glaze or an aerial blue glaze, which were unsuccessful among the public when they were first produced. These glazes were quickly discontinued; their scarcity makes them considerably more valuable today than the iris glaze. Prices vary according to shape, glaze, condition, and possibly an artist who signed the decoration. A vase might run today from several hundred to several thousand dollars. (Photo: courtesy of Gem Antiques.)*

created a distinctive flow of pottery forms from their patronage of a group of potters.

Where To Find Art Pottery—The Market

The various factories and groups of "cottage" workers came and went; some were more successful than others. The more successful, such as Roseville and Weller, standardized their wares and produced quantities of items for collection. As such, they are still modestly priced and are a good place for the beginner to start. Other art pottery of quality and small production, such as a Rookwood vase, can bring $7,000 to $8,000 and one art pottery vase not long ago brought a record of $32,000 at Christie's.

Collectors have been awakened to the high values of art pottery from the artists mentioned above, as well as Necomb, Teco, Fulper, Weller, Buffalo and Dedham ware; the prices achieved at major auction houses are a good measure of current values. Backwoods dealers, even floating flea market merchants, are apt to know the going values, too. To find bargains, your best bets are garage sales and rummage sales where the sponsors and pricers may not recognize one of the name potters.

Museums Notable for Their Collections of Art Pottery
   Chicago Historical Society, Chicago, IL 60614
   Cincinnati Art Museum, Cincinnati, OH 45202
   Everson Museum of Art, Syracuse, NY 13202
   Freer Gallery of Art, Washington, DC 20560
   Metropolitan Museum of Art, New York, NY 10028
   Museum of Fine Arts, Boston, MA 02115
   National Museum of History and Technology, Smithsonian Institution, Washington, DC 20560
   Newark Museum, Newark, NJ 07010
   Zanesville Art Center, Zanesville, OH 43701

Books Worthwhile for Collectors
   Arnest, Barbara M., ed., *Van Briggle Pottery: The Early Years*, Fine Art Center, Colorado Springs, Colo., 1975
   Blasberg, Robert W., *George E. Ohr and His Biloxi Art Pottery*, J. W. Carpenter, 1973
   Clark, Robert J., ed., *The Arts and Crafts Movement in America*, Princeton University Art Museum, 1972
   Evans, Paul, *Art Pottery of the United States*, Charles Scribner's Sons, New York, 1974

Hawes, Lloyd E., *The Dedham Pottery and the Earlier Robert-son's Chelsea Potteries*, Dedham Historical Society, 1968

Henzke, Lucile, *American Art Pottery*, Thomas Nelson, Camden, N.J., 1970

Huxford, Sharon and Bob, *The Collector's Encyclopedia of Rose-ville Pottery*, Crown Publishers, New York, 1974

Kovel, Ralph and Terry, *Kovel's Collector's Guide to American Art Pottery*, Crown Publishers, New York, 1974

Pack, Herbert, *The Book of Rookwood Pottery*, Bonanza Books, 1963

Purviance, Louise and Even, and Schneider, Norris, *Roseville Art Pottery in Color*, Wallace-Homestead, 1976

——— and ———, *Weller Art Pottery in Color*, Wallace-Home-stead, 1971

AUTOGRAPHS

Nothing is so personal a collectible as an autograph, the intimate touch of a famous person. But you have to be careful in what form you collect these personal remnants, whose you collect, and what order or rationale is the basis for your collection.

Autographs were routinely collected during earlier periods by many families in the U.S. and elsewhere who had a visitor's book in the parlor. Sometimes this amounted to an autograph book—the kind schoolchildren use for collecting written mementos of friendships, verses or signatures or simply as a record of visits, travels and friendly people they meet and want to remember with their addresses. It is therefore entirely natural that this activity should expand into passionate and profitable collecting.

In the United States this amounts to collecting signatures of the famous: sports heroes, politicians, presidents, literary people, Nobel prize winners, movie stars or some other fairly homogeneous group—opera singers, for example, where there is a good chance of finding an abundance of signatures and possible access to the person.

Autographs are considered more valuable by collectors if they are part of a basic document—a personal letter, a business transaction, a work of art, even a publicity photograph in the case of movie stars. Of course, the content of the letter or document can influence the value of the signature. Lincoln's letter to Mrs. Bixby, consoling her on the death of her sons, or Lincoln's terse "Let him have a pardon" on the back of a letter requesting mercy for a young drummer boy who fell asleep on watch during the Civil War are the kinds of signatures that, if they can be bought at all, command much higher prices than a social invitation or a reply to a business request.

Collections have greater value, too, if they have a theme and can be considered as a whole. An autograph of each of the signers of the Declaration of Independence is still feasible as a collection today, even though a "John Hancock" (from Massachusetts) is scarce and you may have to pay $35,000 to $50,000 for a "Button Gwinnett" (from Georgia).

Or you may want to collect dated signatures of every U.S. president, *dated while he was in office.* You would have a hard time finding such a signature for James A. Garfield (he had been only six months in office when he was shot July 2, 1881, he died

September 19 of the same year). And think of the difficulty with President William Henry Harrison, who was inaugurated March 4, 1841, caught cold at the inaugural ceremony and died a month later of pneumonia!

Autographs, aside from the fame of the writer, can be classified in degrees of descending value as follows (with the most valuable items on top). Physical condition of the item also counts, of course, and the subject of the writing can also affect values. (As an example, some of Lincoln's letters are more valuable than others, simply for what they say.)

1. Manuscript of literary or historical value in the hand of a celebrity and signed by the author.
2. Letter in the hand of the person and also signed.
3. Document, such as a receipt or check, signed by the celebrity.
4. Items in another's hand (the "other" person may have historical significance, too) signed by the celebrity.
5. Typewritten material, such as a manuscript, letter or legal document, corrected by the person and signed. If the author did his own typing, so much the better.
6. Clipped signature of a celebrity.

Naturally some of the most valuable handwritten material has long since been collected and cannot be recollected by others unless an entire collection goes to market and is broken up.

Where To Find Autographs—The Market

Clipped signatures, properly authenticated by dealers or auction houses, are perhaps the most accessible and can be purchased for a few dollars each. You may buy them in a "mounted format" from dealers with a photo of the author/celebrity, his/her clipped signature and perhaps some informative historical material to go wtih the handwriting and the photographic image. Clipped signatures of even such famous people as John F. Kennedy can still be purchased for less than $100. In Kennedy's case you will want to be sure he actually signed. While he was in the White House his staff made increasing use of a signature machine that automatically signed his name to countless routine letters he sent out each day. Attics, of course, produce amazing bundles of letters, often of ancestors who knew and corresponded with celebrities. But these letters are usually sold to dealer experts rather than offered at flea markets or attic sales.

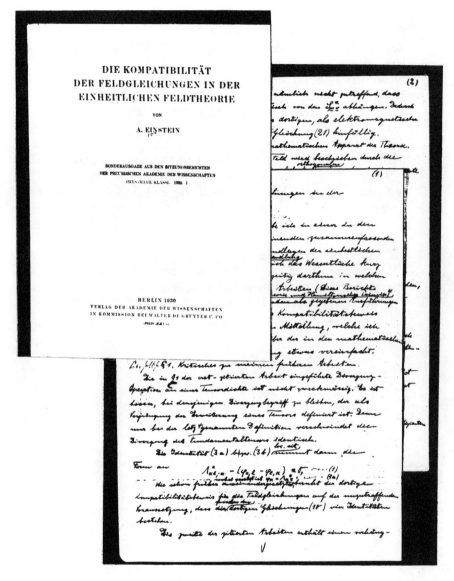

Safecracker Discovers "Lost" Einstein Manuscript   *This is a first-draft autographed manuscript, corrected and signed, written in ink in German by Albert Einstein. This draft of "The Compatibility of the Field Equation in the Unified Field Theory" remained for years in a huge iron safe in the basement of the Brooklyn Jewish Center. The contents of the safe were unknown and the combination had been lost. A safecracker was promised the safe if he could open it. He did, and found a box filled with papers including the Einstein draft. The manuscript was subsequently sold via telephone at a Phillips auction to a California physicist, who got it for $31,000. (Photo: courtesy of Phillips.)*

Museums with Notable Collections of Autographs
  Bancroft Library, Berkeley, CA 94720
  Bentley Historical Library, Ann Arbor, MI 48109
  Huntington Library, San Marino, CA 91108
  New York Public Library, New York, 10018
  Newberry Library, Chicago, IL 60610
  The Pierpont Morgan Library, New York, 10016

Clubs and Organizations
  Manuscript Society, 429 North Baisy Avenue, Pasadena, CA 91107
  Universal Autograph Collectors Club, P.O. Box 102, Midwood, Brooklyn, NY 11230

Books Worthwhile for Collectors
  Hamilton, Charles, *Collecting Autographs and Manuscripts*, University of Oklahoma Press, Norman, Okla., 1970
  Patterson, Jerry E., *Autographs: A Collectors' Guide*, Crown Publishers, New York, 1973

BASEBALL CARDS

Sports heroes as pictures on durable cardboard, easily filed in a shoe box or in display albums—what more durable and popular U.S. collectible can you imagine, especially for boys and men bitten by the baseball bug?

It may be that the 1930's, 40's and 50's will prove to be the peak years for baseball card production even though cards still come off the presses today by the millions and help promote the sale of hot dogs, bubble gum, beverages, conceivably any of the staple and fun foods to which the American mouth is addicted and for which the mouth will ask if given an incentive to prefer it over the competition.

The cards were born as gimmicks in the 1880's when Goodman & Company, a tobacco manufacturer, devised them as a way to sell more cigarettes. Other cigarette manufacturers got into the act and the card craze flourished.

When the American Tobacco Company, at the turn of the century, was created out of many smaller firms, competition fell off and so did the production of baseball cards. Antitrust action and the breakup of American Tobacco and other similar tobacco trusts revived competition and ushered in a second period of popularity for baseball cards. More than 200 cigarette brand names were advertised by cards, which usually showed the heads and shoulders of major league stars as well as regional stars for those who remained loyal to local teams. A few nontobacco companies such as Cracker Jack and Tip-Top bread brought out their own version of cards. The period 1916–1932 produced poor quality cards, partly because German printing inks, cut off during the war period, were supposed to account for the higher quality of printing during the prewar period. The fourth period began about 1933 and extended to 1941. It provided collectors' cards as they are still printed today. This phase brought the bubble gum manufacturers into the game, where they remain dominant even today. Among the gum companies who gave away cards during that period were the Goudey Gum Company and the De Long Gum Company, both of Boston.

Immediately after World War II, a fifth period began when such gum companies as Leaf Confectionery, Bowman, Frank H. Fleer Corp. and Topps Chewing Gum, Inc., took over the field. Topps continues to produce and use the cards today. Clubs of collectors began forming in the 1960's and were never more active than they are today.

Where To Find Baseball Cards— The Market

You can find cards offered at most local flea markets and garage sales. Many families threw them away (to their regret) when the young collectors outgrew their hobby. So some attics will provide these contemporary treasures, others will not. Baseball cards are probably best obtained at national conventions or local meetings of collectors. There you can barter to your heart's content, cast out your duplicates, fill gaps in your collection and trade up for cards in better condition. The most popular cards show up more frequently now at auctions.

Prices of cards vary with quality and scarcity. Unlike stamps, cards with oddities or misprints generally do not bring higher prices than unflawed cards. The cards from the first period are the most prized; one Honus Wagner card printed for American Tobacco Company in 1910 is considered to be worth more than $5,000. The card was part of a set of 561 but only 19 are known to survive today. Wagner sued the company because he did not smoke and the company discontinued printing his image. If you happen to find a T-206 (as the card is known among collectors of Wagner) you have really found a treasure.

Other prized cards are the Eddie Plank of the same series. The plate broke during printing and only 25 known cards survive. The Mickey Mantle card fans got with a nickel pack of gum in 1952 sold at a Philadelphia auction in September 1980 for $3,100. Cards of contemporary players tend to rise in value with the player's game or perhaps when a player is due for election to the Baseball Hall of Fame.

Museums Notable for Their Collections of Baseball Cards
  Metropolitan Museum of Art, Burdick Collection, New York, NY 10028
  National Baseball Hall of Fame and Museum, Cooperstown, NY 13326

Clubs and Organizations
  See the newsletters listed below for possible groups in your locality.

Magazines and Newsletters
  Baseball Advertiser, The Card Memorabilia Association, Amawalk, NY 10501

Sports Collector's Digest, John Stommen, Milan, MI 48160
The Trader Speaks, Dan Dishley, Lake Ronkonkoma, NY 11779

Books Worthwhile for Collectors
 Burdick, R., Jr., ed., *The American Card Catalog,* Nostalgia
    Press, 1967
 Clark, Steve, *The Complete Book of Baseball Cards,* Grosset &
    Dunlap, New York, 1976
 Douglas, John, *Sports Memorabilia,* Wallace-Homestead, 1976
 Sugar, Bert Randolph, *Classic Baseball Cards,* Dover Publica-
    tions, New York, 1977
 ————, *The Sports Collectors Bible,* Wallace-Homestead, 1975

BEER CANS

Collecting beer cans only recently emerged as a hobby and quickly became a popular but well-recognized craze. They were not made in quantity until 1935, first by Krueger's Finest (U.S.) Beer; they only came into widespread use by brewers after World War II. Collectors discovered them in the late 1960's. At that time isolated collectors got together, encouraged by a news story about one collector and his extensive collection. The wildcat nature of this collectible quickly matured until the present when whole collections of beer cans may appear at specialty auctions.

Certain technical breakthroughs were necessary to make possible today's seamless, extruded aluminum can with the ringed tab on top. Earlier, more primitive cans came with a cone top and a cap that resembled that of a glass beer bottle. Naturally there was experimentation with size and one company, for a time, offered an economy *gallon* can but that container soon lost out to the more convenient six-pack carton.

Oddly enough, although colored glass beer bottles and their labels have been collected for decades, they are not at present anywhere near as popular (or as expensive) as the can version with its extensive capacity for color and good lithography on metal.

After early use of rolled steel—the old-fashioned tin can—manufacturers and brewers switched to a seamless, nonrust aluminum. A few went through an intermediate stage, a can with a cone top and cap. But all variants faded in the 1960's with today's durable, stackable, unit container that just asks to be lifted from grocery and liquor store shelves and makes an ideal, durable, relatively small collectible with many display possibilities. Unlike many other collectibles, the *interim stages* that preceded the current beer can are also collected for historical value. In many instances, the unsuccessful innovations, because they proved unpopular, are now more valuable because of their scarcity. Primo Beer of Hawaii, for example, introduced its entry among the new aluminum cans in the late 1950's with a *paper* label that did not last long. As a result, it is extremely rare and valuable today. When pull tabs were introduced in 1962 they were popular with the public and gave collectors another variant. In 1965 a more convenient ring replaced the pioneering tab and the ring continues to this day.

Among collectors there is always the question of what to do with the beer inside a discovered can. Most collectors let it out by making a triangular hole with a hand can opener, or in the case of a rimless can, a bartender's opener that safely punches a hole without requiring leverage on an edge. Other collectors carefully use ice picks. Regardless of the method of making the hole, it is made *in the bottom* of the can where it will not show when the can stands upon a display shelf. This preserves intact the characteristic and possibly unique top design—an important concern of collectors—as well as the physical condition of the can.

Through March 1, 1950, the U.S. government required that the message "Internal Revenue Tax Paid" be stamped on every can. The presence or lack of such a legend is a sure way to date a U.S. can before or after March 1950.

You may collect beer cans by size or by regional breweries. Of the approximately 800 breweries making beer in 1935 when beer cans first appeared, there were less than 150 makers remaining by 1975, only 40 years later. Thus many collectors specialize in cans from *regional* or *local* breweries or *foreign* breweries, if they choose. Because of the popularity of beer drinking throughout the world and the economies of packing and transporting made possible by the light-weight aluminim can, there is still a large supply of most cans available—somewhere—although their physical condition may vary greatly. The trend toward recycling them will also cut into the collectible supply in future years.

Where To Find Beer Cans—The Market

Collectors of cans are great swappers. Your well-preserved old can found in a dump in California may prove highly swappable for two or more contemporary regional cans in Boston. Rare regional cans, particularly when the brewery and brand no longer exist, can sometimes cost several hundred dollars but can be bartered for with duplicates you may have reserved for that purpose. You will find an active trading traffic in cans at meetings of the Beer Can Collectors of America and via its newsletter.

Cans have not made it to the top auction houses (nor to museums) but eventually stellar *collections* of cans probably will. Cans are available most inexpensively through dump and roadside ditch scavenging. They often are found in rooms of buildings that were used as beer warehouses or taverns. And you may find them in new buildings, in the rafters or mortared into dead spaces by beer-drinking workmen. Picnic area trash baskets are other good places, particularly where the picnic areas attract out-of-town motorists who may have "imported" an unusual regional can. The

Beer Can Collectors of America has issued a uniform code for describing can condition and type as well as type of beer and in that respect resembles the standardization of description used by stamp collectors.

Clubs and Organizations
   Beer Can Collectors of America, 747 Merus Court, Fenton, MO 63026
   World Wide Beer Can Collectors, P.O. Box 1852, Independence, MO 64055

Books Worthwhile for Collectors
   Beer Can Collectors of America, The, *The Beer Can: A Complete Guide to Beer Can Collecting*, Greatlakes Living Press, 1976
   ———, *Guide to United States Beer Cans*, Greatlakes Living Press, 1975
   Cady, Lew, *Beer Can Collecting*, Tempo Books, 1976
   Dolphin, Richard R., *Collecting Beer Cans: A World Guide*, Bounty Books, 1977
   Martells, Jack, *The Beer Can Collector's Bible*, Ballantine Books, New York, 1976
   ———, *The Cone Top Collector's Bible*, Greatlakes Living Press, 1976
   Russell, Darrold, *Foreign Beer Cans*, Wallace-Homestead, 1977

BELLEEK PORCELAIN

Belleek porcelain collectors have an Irish potter, McBirney & Co., of Belleek, Ireland, to thank for their collectible. In that town of northern Ireland, McBirney began making this attractive porcelain ware in 1863. The pottery, now called Belleek Pottery, Ltd., continues to this day to produce its fragile, translucent, cream or pearl-glowing ware. Typical Irish Belleek may be woven ceramic baskets or marine shapes such as shells, or local Irish plants, including the shamrock. From the start, Belleek was made to be collected and a mark of the manufacturer can usually be found at the bottom of every piece.

This mark is important because collectors often specialize in the products of their favorite manufacturer. The original Belleek combined the qualities of a British pottery known as Parian ware that had a marble-like tone and a creamy glaze developed by the French.

An American Belleek was created in 1833 by Ott and Brewer of Trenton, New Jersey, thanks to the artisans pirated from the original Irish manufacturers. Among many collectors of Belleek, the products of Ott and Brewer are the most sought after; they manage to get the highest prices at auction.

Other well-known American Belleek factories were also in the vicinity of Trenton. They were Morris and Willmore, Willets Manufacturing Company, and Rittenhouse, Evans and Company whose Belleek often bore the name of American Art China Co.

Another manufacturer, the Ceramic Art Company, formed in 1889 by employees of Ott and Brewer, is known today as Lenox Inc. It produced a Belleek porcelain from 1889 to 1924.

In Ohio there were several potters who specialized in Belleek. Between 1891 and 1896 The Knowles, Taylor & Knowles Co. of East Liverpool, Ohio, turned out "Lotus Ware," which was really a Belleek supervised by a potter imported from the original factory in Ireland. In the late twenties, just before the Great Depression began, two other Ohio potters, The Coxon Belleek Company and the Morgan Belleek China Co. began to manufacture production. Later, in the 1940's and 1950's, other companies that started to make Belleek were the Bellmark Pottery Company, Perlee, Inc. and the American Beleek Company [sic].

Because Belleek was made primarily for collectors, the various potters put their marks at the bottom of most pieces. Some of the manufacturers produced blanks for decorating by silversmiths or by lady painters, some of whom did unusually professional decorations and perhaps added their initials to the potter's mark. Belleek from both commercial and amateur decorators also attracts collectors but the value of the pieces from the "amateurs" will depend on their demonstrated talent. Belleek decorated by staff artists Hans Nosek or George or William Morely of Lenox is collected avidly and some of the plates the Morelys decorated with game birds, fish or fruit and flowers have brought over $150 each at recent auctions.

Where To Find Belleek—The Market

You will find the Irish as well as American Belleek at leading auction houses. As a form of art pottery, it had its peak days at the turn of the century but has enjoyed a revival as a collectible today; the Irish pottery is still produced for collectors. Because of the great number of pieces that were produced over many years, there are many items still available for collectors today. But there are fewer in top condition every year because it is a fragile porcelain; its web and basket tour de force designs seemed to ask for chipping and breaking. You can find it coming out of attics and at flea markets but real bargains are scarce. Everyone seems to recognize Belleek as a popular and valuable collectible; it is not a "come-lately" stranger to collectors. You *may* run across sellers who have on display Belleek look-alikes, or creamy-glazed ware in familiar shapes. But real Belleek *usually* has a confirming mark on the bottom. It is actively traded at auctions and thus the price guides for ceramics will pretty well settle the going value. In less formal circumstances, such as attic sales, you might run across a piece or two. Younger generations of a family may not know what they are selling when they offer remnants from Grandma's estate. Perhaps you can spot a good piece before a dealer does!

Museums with Notable Collections of Belleek
  Museum of Ceramics, East Liverpool, OH 43920
  New Jersey State Museum, Trenton, NJ 07625

Clubs and Organizations
  Belleek Society International, P.O. Box 2661, Houston, TX 77001

Books Worthwhile for Collectors
Barber, Edwin Atlee, *The Pottery and Porcelain of the U.S. and Marks of American Potters*, Feingold and Lewis, 1976
Hughes, G. Bernard, *Victorian Pottery and Porcelain*, Macmillan, 1959
Shinn, Charles and Dorrie, *Victorian Parian China*, Barrie & Jankins, London, 1971

BENNINGTON POTTERY

The name of these special ceramic creations come from Bennington, Vermont, where potteries flourished during the last century. Captain John Norton established the earliest pottery in 1793. It turned out useful, sturdy kitchenware and tableware fashioned from a local brick clay. Later it used a clay imported from New York via the Hudson River and then carted to Bennington. The pottery prospered for more than a century and left a good quantity of surviving examples for collectors.

But, oddly enough, it was another potter in the same town whose pottery operated for less than two decades, Christopher Webber Fenton, who produced a more decorated, finer pottery that collectors prize most highly and that commands ever-rising prices.

Fenton married into the Norton family and in 1847 started his own studio in part of the Norton buildings. Later Fenton's Works left for its own, separate facilities in Bennington and became known as Lyman, Fenton and Co., and finally as United States Pottery Company, Bennington, Vermont. It closed in 1858.

Fenton experimented with glazes and hired an English designer, Daniel Greatback, who created bottles and pitchers in Toby Jug patterns and also animal forms, including a famous hound-handled pitcher.

Today collectors seek the rare, early Fenton ceramics with a mottled brown and glazed finish. This pottery resembled the wares of the Rockingham Potteries of England. Though imitated by many potteries throughout the United States, Fenton invented a variation of Rockingham with a glowing brown finish known as "dark luster ware" and another spattered variation that combined the yellow of the basic clay to give a tortoiseshell effect.

In 1849 Fenton created and patented another glazing effect called Flint Enamel. He added metallic oxides to a still-wet clear glaze. As they melted when fired they streaked and ran together at random. Thus no two objects of the same shape had quite the same colored effect.

Fenton also fell in love with a porcelain made from kaolin. He fired it to produce the effect of Parian (white) marble, very similar to English Parian ware, and he used this material for classical shapes, such as urns and ewers, and for small figurines.

Where To Find Bennington Pottery— The Market

You can find Bennington ware at auction houses specializing in art pottery and, of course, you should always be on the lookout for that odd piece that may come out of an attic and appear at a garage or rummage sale.

Today, prices of Fenton's best pieces can range from $25 to $175.

Museums Notable for Their Collections of Bennington Ware
Bennington Museum, Bennington, VT 05201
Brooklyn Museum, Brookly, NY 11238
Greenfield Village and Henry Ford Museum, Dearborn, MI 48124
New York Historical Society, 170 Central Part West, New York, NY 10024

Books Worthwhile for Collectors
Barret, Richard Carter, *Bennington Pottery and Porcelain*, Crown Publishers, New York, 1958
Ketchum, William C., Jr., *The Pottery and Porcelain Collector's Handbook: a Guide to Early American Ceramics from Maine to California*, Funk & Wagnalls, New York, 1971

BIBLES

Collecting editions of the Bible can prove a highly expensive adventure if you want to compete for the 48 known copies of the Bible printed by Gutenberg. At auction, a copy is likely to bring $2 million or more. Copies of this first book printed by Johann Gutenberg at Mainz, Germany, in 1455, are now mostly in the hands of wealthy collectors or in library museums.

Or you can actually collect in leaf form an authentic but incomplete Gutenberg Bible that was cut up into individual pages in 1921 by an enterprising bookseller. Individual leaves, depending on condition, occasionally come up at auction and can bring as much as $4,000, if they contain a well-known passage.

The Bible has always been the most published book in the world. There are many millions of copies available in every conceivable language, elegance or plainness of binding, quality of type, beauty of translation, country of origin and condition.

A collector deciding to collect Bibles usually specializes in one kind or another if only to prevent a storage and insurance problem of too many books in the wrong atmospheric conditions. Like any book, Bibles, especially the oldest and those with the finest bindings, can depreciate in value rapidly if their physical condition deteriorates. You always have a shelving, storage and climate problem with old books.

Still, rare books, and particularly Bibles with all their emotional and religious appeal, are known to appreciate in value as consistently and rapidly as any collectible. But if you collect them, you had better bone up on storing and preserving books.

The beginning Bible collector, with modest funds, had best start with a 19-century U.S. Bible. There have been more than 2,500 editions of the Bible printed in the United States over the past two centuries and they form a generous supply (like U.S. stamps and coins) to meet demand. Thus their price is relatively low.

Nineteenth-century Bibles were printed in the United States in the most remote places, in small towns by obscure printers who wanted for one reason or another to fulfill a local need. Perhaps the leader of a small local religious denomination or sect wanted its own binding, translation or commentary on the Bible. These volumes can, because of the curiosity given them, be quite valuable and still turn up at local auctions and fairs.

As you become familiar with U.S. Bibles, you should read *The English Bible in America*, prepared by Margaret Hills (see books below) to prepare yourself for small discoveries. Also bone up with *Rare Bibles* by Edwin A. F. Rumball-Petre.

Some Bibles belonged to famous Americans and may contain their signature somewhere and hence have added value. Some Bibles have illustrations by famous artists. After 1870, a great quantity of family Bibles included now celebrated illustrations by Gustave Doré.

Where To Find Bibles—The Market

You can find Bibles turning up at almost any kind of sale, but the best copies appear at auctions specializing in books. Also, if you collect Bibles or any kind of book, you should get acquainted with the bookseller in your vicinity who handles older books.

Museums and Libaries Notable for Their Collections of Bibles
   American Bible Society, New York, NY 10023
   Bridwell Library, Southern Methodist University, Dallas, TX 75275
   Henry E. Huntington Library, New York, NY 10018
   Northern Bible Society Bible Museum, Duluth, MN 55802
   Pierpont Morgan Library, New York, NY 10016

Clubs and Organizations
   International Bible Collectors Society, P.O. Box 2485, EL Cajon, CA 92021

Books Worthwhile for Collectors
   Herbert, A. S., ed., *Historical Catalogue of Printed Editions of the English Bible 1525–1961*, American Bible Society, New York, 1968
   Hills, Margaret T., ed., *The English Bible in America: A Bibliography of the Bible and the New Testament Published in America 1777–1957*, American Bible Society and the New York Public Library, New York, 1961
   Rumball-Petre, Edwin A. F., *Rare Bibles*, Philip C. Duschenes, 1954

BOOKS

The contemporary book collector has the pleasure of associating with venerable and distinguished company. J. Pierpont Morgan, to name one famous collector, eventually gave civilization his Pierpont Morgan Library at 29 East 36th Street in Manhattan.

You can spend a lot of money to collect a single book, such as $2 million for a Gutenberg Bible in good condition. Not so long ago a 15th-century manuscript anthology of English verse, including 15 previously unknown Middle English poems, sold at Sotheby's in London for $280,000. Most book prices are under $100, with rarer first editions of United States authors going for a few thousand at the most. Thus the market is open for beginning collectors who are willing to study its opportunities and choose a specialty.

As George Lowry of Swann Galleries, Inc., a book auction specialist in New York City, says, "Do not buy books primarily as a speculation or investment. Collect books for intellectual stimulation and personal pleasure. This should be enough reward, though there is virtually no downside risk in value for the informed collector. A good book is legal tender anywhere in the world."

All highly civilized cultures have produced manuscripts, scrolls and finally bound books and with them, just a step behind, has been the discriminating collector who usually combines the skills of a scholar with the aesthetic lust of a collector of historical fragments of beauty, art and the printed word.

Prices are still low in many book specialities; the average person can begin a worthwhile collection even today in the midst of inflation. Although books as a group have not made spectacular gains, they do manage to keep ahead of inflation in sheer dollar value; a few race spectacularly ahead of it.

By and large the book collecting field is one of the most professional and stable there is. There is enough knowledgeable competition among dealers to assure a going market price for any item. There are also many regular auctions and certain auction houses (such as Swann Galleries mentioned above) that specialize primarily in books and related material such as photographs and manuscripts.

You can best start your book collecting with a private dealer who can educate you in the field and act as scout for the books you have decided to collect. When you have defined your goals and made a good start, you can then round out your collection at auction or on your travels in the United States or abroad, which might take you to large cities that have booksellers specializing in collectible books.

To identify dealers and their specialties in the United States, you might want to ask for a free copy of the membership directory of the Antiquarian Book Sellers Association of America (see below). It lists dealers alphabetically, geographically and by subject matter. It includes a brief and useful section of guidelines for the sale or the appraisal of books. If you are in New York City, it will pay you to stop by at the ABA's permanent exhibition where more than 75 booksellers display samples of their specialities and where staff personnel can answer questions collectors may have. The association sponsors an annual fair in New York City and the leading auction houses usually plan to have special book auctions at that time.

When Is a First Edition Really a First?

In collecting books of modern authors where there are usually a quantity of copies printed, collectors seek first editions only. This peculiarity may not seem entirely logical; it isn't. But these manias of collectors, nonetheless, determine the market price for books as well as many other collectibles. First editions should be the first impression, i.e., the first run off the press. If there is a second impression of the same type, minus perhaps a few errors picked up from the first group of copies printed, it is the first segment that is considered the first edition. And that first edition should have its dust jacket (cover) in excellent condition, no tears or wear marks.

The copy should be as close as possible to "just off the press and from the bindery." Other copies have value but quite a bit less if they are a second impression, if their condition has deteriorated or if the book is without a dust jacket.

In the history of successive editions, as type is reset, etc., there is a tendency for errors to creep in. Thus you have the curious paradox of errors in the *first edition* valued because they are proof of the first edition *before* a proofreader caught certain mistakes and made a final correction. Then, in later editions, the text begins to deteriorate and the impressions made by type or the "worn" illustrations become less clear and sharp and the book depreciates rapidly in value, just like the family car.

There are certain categories of books published in the United States that attract collectors more than others. They are *Americana*, which can be either early or unusual ventures in producing books by American publishers. Americana can also mean books about the United States printed in the United States or in Europe.

Other highly attractive categories are books about *sports*, *medicine* and *science*, and *19th-century* classics (earlier books are either prohibitively expensive or have been bought up by wealthy collectors of the past who have their collections in the family still or have donated them to libraries and museums—in either case leaving slim and unaffordable pickings for the beginning collector). Still another attractive and affordable category is private press books. Some of these are the Kelmscott Press, the Limited Editions Club (still publishing on a subscription basis), the Ashehendene, Vale and Daniel presses in England and the Mosher and Merry-mount presses in the United States. Virginia Wolfe fans will treasure Hogarth Press books—and pay dearly to collect them. These press books, to be worth their maximum, must be in virtually untouched condition with dust jackets intact.

This rule applies, too, to *modern American authors*, except in cases where dust jackets did not exist. They come into widespread use after the turn of the century.

A special kind of first edition of modern American authors is the *limited first edition*. Most of these are printed from the same plates as the ordinary trade edition but they may be designed, and produced, really, like a fine press edition on better paper, with better binding and nearly always with a slip case rather than a dust jacket. They are invariably numbered and signed by the author with a standard statement telling the number of copies in the limited edition and identifying each copy by the number in that special series.

Where To Find Collectible Books—
The Market

Books for a long time have been a mature collectible and will turn up at all sources from attic sales and flea markets to specialized dealers, as noted before, and at the most prestigious auction houses. Prices can be astronomical for a Gutenberg Bible or a fragment of one, but most 19th-century books can be had for a few hundred dollars. Limited first editions can be valuable; for example Hemingway's *A Farewell to Arms*, which sold for about $10 when it was published in 1929, brought more than $500 in 1979. Prices are highly dependent on the popularity of modern authors, the condition of the book and whether it has its dust jacket and/or slip case.

Museums and Libraries Notable for Their Collections of Books
　　Henry E. Huntington Library, San Marino, CA 91108
　　Newberry Library, Chicago, IL 60610
　　New York Public Library, New York, NY 10016
　　Pierpont Morgan Library, New York, NY 10016

Clubs and Organizations
　　Antiquarian Book Sellers Association of America, 50 Rockefeller Plaza, New York, NY 10020
　　Grolier Club, 47 East 60 Street, New York, NY 10021

Magazines and Newsletters
　　AB Bookman's Weekly, AB Bookman Publications, Inc., Clifton, NJ 07015
　　The American Book Collector, Arlington Heights, IL 60005
　　American Book-Prices Current, Columbia University Press, New York, NY 10027

Books Worthwhile for Collectors
　　Bennett, Whitman, *A Practical Guide to American Book Collecting (1663–1940)*, Bennett Book Studios, Inc., 1941
　　Carter, John, *The ABC for Book Collectors*, 5th ed., Alfred A. Knopf, New York
　　Haller, Margaret, *The Book Collector's Fact Book*, Arco Publishing Co., New York
　　Johnson, Merle De Vore, *American First Editions*, Mark Press, 1965

————, *High Spots of American Literature*, Jenkins Publishing Co., Austin, Tex., 1969

Lepper, Gary M., *A Bibliographical Introduction to Modern American Authors*, Serendipity Press, 1975

Randall, David and John T. Winterich, *Primer of Book Collecting*, Crown Publishers, New York, 1966

Ransom, Will, *Private Presses and Their Books*, AMS Press, 1976

Tannen, Jack, *How to Identify and Collect American First Editions*, Arco Publishing Co., New York, 1976

Thomey, Alice, ed., *World Bibliography of Bibliographies 1964–1974*, Rowman, 1977

BOTANICAL PRINTS

Biologists, doctors, botanists, even plain dirt gardening enthusiasts may often combine their professions or hobbies with collecting something in the area of their enthusiasm. Such is the case with botanical prints. They are artist's renderings of plants that are then reproduced by engraving, by lithography and, today, by silk screening processes. Thus they are essentially prints, not original art, even though hand colored and related to an original work of art.

The earliest compilations of botanical drawings go back to Greek and Roman manuscripts; these drawings were models of both accuracy and simplicity. They were drawn from close, actual observation.

Unfortunately for scientists, for almost ten centuries thereafter these classical models were simply copied and recopied, usually by a scribe who looked at an older print rather than at the natural object. Thus stylizations, distortions and inaccuracies crept into the picture of the specimen.

During the Renaissance such famous artists as Leonardo da Vinci and Albrecht Durer went again to nature for details and their renderings set a new level of quality for botanical prints. Few collectors, however, can afford the prints of these artists. Yet they were the pace-setters for lesser artists who, for many centuries thereafter, created prints that are still affordable today. During the Renaissance the prints were useful primarily in professional and scientific work—medicine, botany, horticulture and similar pursuits where accurate identification was a prelude to scientific and medical use.

It was during the collector-crazy 19th century that the artistic value of a botanical print came into its own after ages of scientific use. Today, of course, as with Audubon's prints of birds and animals, botanical prints have soared in popularity and value both as sophisticated household decorations and as worthwhile collectibles.

Some famous editions, in book format, though sometimes dismantled and sold separately as prints, are Nicolas Robert's *Recueil des Plantes*, first published in 1701, a book of engravings; and Robert John Thornton's *The Temple of Flora*, published in the late 18th century by an English doctor and featuring hand-colored illustrations of plants, executed by various artists and engravers.

Probably the most famous single botanical publication of the 18th century was the *Species Plantarum*, published in 1753 by Carolus Linnaeus. His system for classifying plants was immediately adopted for many works published both before and after his, which went into many editions as the popularity of such books grew.

Among famous illustrators are George Dionysium Ehret, a German who furnished nearly 500 illustrations for the early volumes of an 80-book set, *Phytanthoza Idonographia—An Illustrated Record of Flowering Plants*, which began publication in 1937. Later in France, a group of botanical artists flourished and the best known was Pierre-Joseph Redouté. Other artists are Ferdinand and Francis Bauer, Pancrace Bessa and William Baxter. Today, examples of their work are usually found as individual illustrations, removed from a book, and they can sell for more than $100. Prints from lesser-known artists can be purchased, even today, for much less and the supply is large. The older the print, the more likely that the artist has left his signature or device in some way. A magnifying glass can help identify the name.

Where To Find Prints—The Market

Prints come up for sale in many places—attic sales, thrift shops, galleries or print shops that specialize in them and the finest auction salons. The best advice that can be given the beginning collector is to read up on the subject, keep in touch with other collectors of botanical prints and at first, buy through a reputable dealer until your own knowledge and confidence can discover bargains at out-of-the way sales.

Special Care Required

Prints require special care lest they deteriorate physically. Separate each print from the next with nonacid tissues such as museum barrier paper or glassine tissue, which you can obtain at an art supply store. Never handle the print in such a way as to make it bend, and never touch the face of the print itself lest it absorb oil and dirt from your finger. Foxing, a brown stain caused by mold, flourishes in an environment where the temperature is fairly high (above 75°) and where it is humid. Avoid, too, exposure to sunlight or even steady artificial light.

Museums

You can find a good selection of botanical prints for viewing at the Hunt Institute for Botanical Documentation, located in Pittsburgh, PA 15213, or at the National Agricultural Library in Beltsville, MD 20205.

Magazines and Newsletters

Periodicals for botanical print collectors include the *GNSI Newsletter*, published by the Guild for Natural Science Illustrators, Washington DC 20044.

Books Worthwhile for Collectors

Blunt, Wilfred, *The Art of Botanical Illustration*, Collins, 1967

Bush-Brown, Louise, *Men With Green Pens: Lives of the Great Writers on Plants in Early Times*, Dorrance & Company, 1964

Sigrosser, Carl, and Gaehde, Christa M., *A Guide to the Collecting and Care of Original Prints*, Crown Publishers, New York, 1965

BOTTLES

Antique bottles have attracted the fastest growing swarm of collectors in the country during the past few years. There is an especially avid species that discovers and hoards "dug" bottles. The places to find these are in vintage dumps, old foundations, seashores, ancient picnic places and where privies once stood.

The purist bottle collector regards machine-made bottles beyond collectibility, except for Avon, Jim Beam, J. W. Dant, Luxardo and a few other brand-name bottles still available on retail shelves today. Avon limits the production of its imaginative shapes simply to please its collectors. But most serious bottle collectors consider such fads as amusing—to be tolerated rather than indulged.

The mainstream of U.S. antique bottle collectors goes in for specimens hand-molded or blown between 1810 and about 1910. There was not much of a glass industry in the United States before 1810. After 1910 or so the machines took over. However, during a flourishing century, glass makers had a field day with bottles, particularly those for containing liquor and patent medicines.

As with most collectibles, you had better get into collecting with a specialty in mind. One of the most popular specialties is flask- or calabash-shaped bottles. Liquor dealers of the 19th century would buy the bright glass containers and fill them from barrels and demijohns. In addition to historical and pictorial flasks, you can also collect medicine, poison, ink, bitters, soda, food, beer, wine, perfume, pepper sauce, candy and fire-grenade bottles, as well as such esoterica as "witch balls," target bottles (predating clay pigeons) and glass floats.

The same bottles may exist in several color variants, have whimsical shapes or carry quaint embossed advertising slogans. Mexican Mustang Liniment bottles, for example, usually had all their "N"s printed backwards.

Color variants will affect the price of bottles. Dark green amber or brown amber are the natural color of glass and are the most common and least expensive, if other features are equal. Cobalt blue tends to be the most expensive because of its rarity and the cost of the dye. Other relatively rare colors are yellow, puce and purple. Clear antique glass probably had manganese added to bleach out the natural amber color. And antique glass thus bleached tends to turn a lovely, much-prized amethyst when left exposed to the sun for a number of years.

A strange thing happens to glass that has been soaked in the brine of the sea. It acquires a fluorescence. In a damp soil, depending on the mineral content, a bottle may gain fluorescence or simply get frosted, or "sick." Sometimes this frosting or fluorescence seems to enhance the beauty of the bottle, but it usually makes it less valuable than one of the same kind that has retained its original color and clarity. Sick or diseased bottles are sometimes "oiled"—rinsed with oil inside to temporarily restore a high degree of clarity. But the alert collector will detect traces of oiling and rejects the bottle.

Where To Find Bottles—The Market

"Bottle collectors have always had to watch for two deceptions," says Stirling Watlington, a veteran bottle collector already on his way to a second collection after selling his first at a profit. "The one is "oiled" bottles; the other is straight scratch lines on the bottom—to make bottles appear worn by age—when normal wear causes scratches in all directions." Over the years, Mr. Watlington has bought approximately 1,100 bottles, mostly from out-of-town dealers. He mentions that the old-line dealers now dead or retired—such as the "giants" George McKearin and Abraham & May—priced their bottles on the basis of cost plus a comfortable profit margin. Many dealers today also add a bargaining margin, a practice more and more common with dealers in most collectibles. Thus you will always want to offer less than the asked price: the dealer will quickly tell you if his prices are fixed.

Bottles can sometimes crop up in flea markets and street fairs, but you had better know your bottles well before you attempt to discover bargains in these places. One good fair is the White Plains Antique Show in the spring and fall at the County Center, White Plains, New York. Also the Skinner Auction Galleries in Bolton, Massachusetts, conducts regular auctions featuring antique bottles.

Museums Notable for Their Collections of Bottles
  Bennington Museum, Bennington, VT 05201
  Corning Glass Museum, Corning, NY 14830
  Henry Ford Museum, Dearborn, MI 48121
  Museum of Art, Toledo, OH 43697
  New York Historical Society, 170 Central Park West, New York, NY 10024
  Bottles Unlimited, 75 East 78th Street, New York, NY, 10021 carries a representative selection of antique bottles and is a kind of minimuseum in itself.

Clubs and Organizations
  Genesee Valley Bottle Collector Association, P.O. Box 7528, West Ridge Station, Rochester, NY 14615
  Iowa Antique Botleers, 1506 Albia Road, Ottumwa, IA 52501
  Memphis Bottle Collectors Club, 232 Tilton Road, Memphis, TN 38111
  The Pennsylvania Bottle Collectors Association, 743 Woodberry Road, York, PA 17403
  San Jose Antique Bottle Collectors Society, P.O. Box 5432, San Jose, CA 95150
  Western Slope Bottle Club, Box 354, Palisade, CO 81526

Magazines and Newsletters
  Antique Bottle World, 5003 West Berwyn, Chicago, IL 60630
  Bottle News, Collector's Media, Inc., Kermit, TX 79745
  Old Bottle Magazine, Maverick Publications, Bend, OR 97701

Books Worthwhile for Collectors

McKearin, George S. and Helen, *American Glass*, revised ed., Crown Publishers, New York, 1948

McKearin, Helen, and Kenneth M. Wilson, *American Bottles and Flasks and Their Ancestry*, Crown Publishers, New York, 1978

Ketchum, William C., Jr., *A Treasury of American Bottles*, Bobbs-Merrill Co., Indianapolis, 1975

Munsey, Cecil, *The Illustrated Guide to Collecting Bottles*, Hawthorn Books, New York, 1970

BUTTONS

"Button, button, who's got a button for my charming string?" This could have been the cry of a young lady in the 1860's when the female youth of the United States made "charm strings" of buttons contributed by friends, and according to one custom, accepted a final button from her husband-to-be.

The earliest buttons on clothing were probably few and ornamental; clothes were kept together with ties and/or pins. The earlier buttons, from up to about the 18th century, turn up in museums, for the most part, either as independent objects or as a part of antique clothes. They are not really profitable to collect because most are not artistically distinguished and the supply is not sufficient to make them a popular collectible. They are worth accumulating only as historical specimens or, sometimes, as jewelry.

Collectors, today, concentrate on buttons from the 18th, 19th and 20th centuries and those made in France, England, the U.S. and Japan. Most prized are elaborate buttons, often of precious or semiprecious metals and/or stones and sometimes of richly embroidered fabric.

During the 18th century the most decorative buttons were created in sets for *men's* clothing. Paintings or carvings or ivory scenes of the countryside, pictures of famous battles or landmarks, all under a glass covering, were used in the men's fashion trade. Occasionally a set of buttons showed variations on a theme rather than four, six or a dozen duplicates. A twelve-button set showing horses and riders in different equestrian poses recently was sold for $2,500. Some collectors try for one good button from any set, others feel challenged to collect toward a full set that exhibits all the variations on a theme.

Another collectible category of button is the metal button made for men's clothing in the 18th and early 19th centuries. There were flat with shanks, and rather large in size—some up to 1.5 inches. In general the thicker the shank the older a specimen button. Metal buttons of this type in good condition have brought as much as $20 in recent auctions. Sometimes these buttons bore monograms of their owners, personalized designs or commemorative emblems, and these features add a historical plus to their basic value.

What collectors call "the golden age" of buttons flourished during the 19th century. The best of these are finished in gilt: brass with a thin film of gold. Gilt buttons had their heyday during the first half of the 19th century. Some of these gilt buttons bear their makers' names in the rear. This is known as "back marking." The father of Charles and Nelson Goodyear made gilt buttons but when his sons perfected their rubbers process, he converted to making hard red rubber buttons backmarked with his name, A. Goodyear, and a date such as "1851" when he was in the midst of making his rubber novelties.

Another kind of collectible 19th century button was made of silver or brass for uniforms of clubs and military regiments, the livery of servants or the blazers of a sporting group. All bore appropriate designs.

Scenic buttons from the second half of the 19th century form the largest of contemporary collecting categories. An adaptation of a Currier & Ives print, "Skating in Central Park," is such an example. One of these, which sold for about $8 in the 1940's, now sells at auction for $190 or more.

Shell buttons from the same approximate period, some bearing designs, some pierced, some engraved, are now much valued by collectors. During this later part of the 19th century, Japanese potters adopted techniques for making Satsume ware, with its crackled ivory-colored glaze, to button making, and these ceramic buttons form another category.

Collectors consider 1900 to be the birthday of the "modern" button. Since then buttons have been made of every typical 20th-century material, many of them plastic, and they come in every contemporary shape.

Some buttons, especially those made of fabric, are perishable and need special care. There is also the challenge to keep your buttons in order. The best of a quality collector's buttons are often hung on a wall in wood frames; the remainder of the collection is stored in the collector's "organizer." If you follow such habit, you won't have to paw through an entire collection to look for the specimen you thought sure you had but cannot find at the moment.

Where To Find Buttons—The Market

Many people have button collections and have never taken proper care of them, have not even sorted them out. They like the tumble and quantity rather than individual quality. If you are a quality collector, it is often worth picking through a bowl of buttons at a street fair, a flea market or attic and garage sales. If you know what you are looking for, you can still discover a treasure. Prices could run less than a dollar. Collections of buttons and prized individual buttons do appear at auctions and can easily go for thousands of dollars depending on the quality and completeness of a set. Individual buttons have sold for hundreds of dollars each.

Museums Notable for Their Collections of Buttons
  Just Buttons Museum, Southington, CT 06489
  Viviane Beck Ertell Button Museum, Flemington, NJ 08822

Clubs and Organizations
  National Button Society, P.O. Box 39, Eastwood, KY 40018 (request from it information on state societies)

Magazines and Newletters
  Just Buttons, Sally C. Luscomb, ed., 45 Berlin Avenue, Southington, CT 06489
  National Button Bulletin, National Button Society, P.O. Box 39, Eastwood, KY 40017

Books Worthwhile for Collectors
  Chamberlin, Erwina, and Minerva Miner, *Button Heritage*, Faulkner Printing Co., 1976
  Ertell, Viviane Beck, *The Colorful World of Buttons*, Pyne Press, 1973
  Luscomb, Sally C., *The Collector's Encyclopedia of Buttons*, Bonanza Books, 1976
  Nicholls, Florence Zacharie Ellis, *Button Hand Book*, Art Craft of Ithaca, 1943

CAMERAS

Cameras that can reproduce images more or less permanently date from the pioneering photography of Matthew Brady and Louis Daguerre in France, circa 1835. The camera box or camera obscure was used more than 400 years before that to make sketches from images viewed and projected on a screen or flat surface at one end of the apparatus.

What has changed from the rather simple box and screen has been the material for preserving the image and the materials and convenience items attached to the box for taking pictures in all weather, light and focusing conditions. Huge camera with plates are still used in portrait studios; mini-cameras have been ingeniously concealed in all manner of ordinary objects such as cigarette cases, cane handles, tie clasps and the like for the purposes of spying.

A well-made, rare example of an early camera such as the Skaife Pistolgraph manufactured around 1860 brought about $6,000 at auction in 1977.

Cameras from the first quarter of the 20th century are often found in attics in good condition and can be bought advantageously at country auctions and flea markets. But an early vintage Leica is likely to be found only at the major dealers and auction houses for $20,000 or more. A typical folding camera might go for $15 to $125. A Kodak Bantam Special circa 1930 that has a metal case in the Art Deco style and is in good condition could be worth over $1,000 today. On the other hand, a twin-lens Rolleiflex, even the first model of 1929, can still be found for a few hundred dollars. The difference lies in the quantity produced; many more of the Rolleiflexes were manufactured.

To spot a bargain among fairly ordinary cameras requires a certain skill and a knowledge of camera technology. You can separate highly collectible cameras into two categories: (1) those that pioneered new features, and (2) those that were limited editions, that were manufactured only in small numbers yet had unusual features.

The original daguerreotype (invented by Louis Jacques Mandé Daguerre) was manufactured for only a short while; it produced only a single picture on a coated metal plate that had to be held at the proper angle to the light in order for the image to be seen most clearly.

In Vienna in 1841 Peter Wilhelm Friedrich Voigtlander imitated the sliding box of Daguerre. So popular was the Voigtlander model that in 1938 and again in 1956 the company sold working reproductions of its 1841 daguerreotype camera for as little as $150. These curious collectors' items were worth more than $2,000 in the late 1970's.

In England, Henry Fox Talbert made a very small box that introduced the negative-positive technique with paper as the medium. He did not get very far until the glass plate method took over because of its greater clarity of image. The first glass plates, used by Matthew Brady for his Civil War album and by William Henry Jackson for scenery of the West, incorporated the wet-plate process. This continued to be popular from 1851 to about 1881 when dry plates took over. The camera boxes were essentially the same but a camera stained with chemicals dripped from a wet plate

A Camera That Took Lincoln's Portrait   *In the first major New York auction of photographic equipment in more than ten years, this camera sold for $5,000 at Christie's in October 1980. It was owned by Mathew Brady, the pioneering photographer, and is believed to be the one Brady used to photograph Lincoln. (Photo: courtesy of Christie's)*

is more valuable today, other things being equal, then the same camera used (apparently) only with dry plates.

Eastman's innovation—roll film—opened photography to the masses. The first Kodaks were sold with a roll of film. You pointed the camera, pressed a button, shot your roll and then sent—after the 100 or so frames were shot—the camera, roll of film still inside, to the factory for developing and printing. Such pioneer Kodaks, selling for $25 in 1888, could easily bring $2,000 to $3,000 today.

Focusing technology made particularly fast strides after World War II. The old Rolleiflex used two lenses geared together. You adjusted one to see your image and the second, geared to the first, was synchronized to take a sharp image based on the distance from the object. The single lens reflex (SLR) system, so familiar in 35-millimeter cameras, revolutionized the popular camera market. The SLR, essentially, uses a mirror system that reflects the image onto a ground glass for focusing but the mirror swivels out of the way during the actual picture-taking.

Where To Find Cameras—The Market

As you can see, cameras can fetch a wide range of prices at dealers and at auctions. It is a much sought after collectible with considerable price appreciation potential. For it is a mechanism, it has a certain style, and in many models there are quantities available to collectors. But there are also limits to the quantity of each model and certain ones can easily bring several thousand dollars today. Others can bring a few hundred if in good condition. You will find cameras offered at the best auction houses. By observing values and acutely studying more comprehensive collections at museums, you will be able to spot values that come out of attics and turn up at flea markets and fairs. Start your collection with old family cameras you know about or discover in your attic. Condition and workability count with cameras. Part of the fun in collecting cameras is the taking of pictures with them to prove how they worked and the quality of their product.

Museums Notable for Their Collections of Cameras
  American Photography Museum, Inc., Baraboo, WI 53913
  International Museum of Photography, George Eastman House,
    Rochester, NY 14607
  Museum of History and Technology, Smithsonian Institution,
    Washington, DC 20560

Clubs and Organizations

Bay Area Photographic Association, P.O. Box 2366, Sunnyvale, CA 94087

Chicago Photographic Collectors Society, P.O. Box 374, Winnetka, IL 60093

Florida Photographic Historical Society, 9410 Live Oak Place, Fort Lauderdale, FL 33324

Leica Historical Society, 2036 Brightwater Boulevard, St. Petersburg, FL 33704

Midwest Photographic Historical Society, 19 Hazelnut Court, Florissant, MO 63033

Photographic Historical Society of New England, P.O. Box 403, Buzzard Bay, MA 02532

Photographic Historical Society of New York, P.O. Box 767, Cooper Station, New York, NY 10003

Western Photographic Collectors Association, P.O. Box 90607, Whittier, CA 90607

Magazines and Newsletters

Modern Photography, ABC Leisure Magazines, New York, NY 10022

Northlight, Photographic Historical Society of America, Simsbury, CT 06070

Photographica, Photographic Historical Society of New York, Inc., New York, NY 10019

Popular Photography, Ziff-Davis Publishing Company, New York, NY 10016

Books Worthwhile for Collectors

Auer, Michel, *The Illustrated History of the Camera from 1839 to the Present*, New York Graphic Society Ltd., Greenwich, Conn., 1975

Gilbert, George, *Collecting Photographica: The Images and Equipment of the First Hundred Years of Photography*, Hawthorn Books, New York, 1976

Lothrop, Eaton, *A Century of Cameras from the Collections of the International Museum of Photography at George Eastman House*, Morgan & Morgan, Hastings-on-Hudson, N.Y., 1973

Permutt, Cyril, *Collecting Old Cameras*, Da Capo Press, New York, 1976

CANES

King Tut used canes as a symbol of his authority. The walking stick—simply a stout limb of a tree cut to suit the walker—probably has been used and marked or shaped as long as man has walked upright.

One has only to see the bundle of walking sticks or canes beside the hiker's favorite entrance at any resort hotel to discover the woods and lengths popular for canes at any one time.

But the cane, or walking stick, has developed a thousand uses beyond walking support, beyond a way to alleviate the pressure upon an arthritic joint.

Canes, made by many an anonymous craftsman, have been fashioned cleverly to become concealed guns, cameras, cigarette and cigar holders, whiskey flasks, magicians' tables, umbrellas, collapsible seats, whips, undertakers' tools to give coffin lids a final closing twist, probes for merchants testing the bottom of a barrel or produce, holders of poison, valuables, or cosmetics or holders for concealing such weapons as daggers and stilettos.

A whole collector's category is made up of gadget canes with subcategories including weapon canes. If your cane actually contains a working gun, you, as a collector, may be subject to the Federal Gun Control Act.

Another category of cane collectors devotes its enthusiasm to materials such as wood, ivory, plastic, bamboo and metals, with almost an infinite variety of decoration, inlay and upholstering.

Canes generally bear no maker's mark. The skill of carving sometimes can be traced to a famous craftsman but, by and large, canes are anonymous and are not collected by makers but by types and approximate vintage. You can date a cane roughly by its handle. Through the early 19th century canes had handles in the shape of a knob of a size suitable for sturdy gripping. About 1840, makers fashioned handles at right angles to the shaft; they often had an eyelet for a carrying loop, cord or tassel. About 1865, the right angle became the familiar crook of today that enables the bearer of the cane or umbrella to carry it along on his arm, thereby freeing hands and wrists entirely.

The value of a cane varies with its workmanship, scarcity and age. Primitive canes, if found at all, qualify as primitive art and may have considerable value.

On the other hand, a gadget cane or weapon cane may have

value depending on the ingenious workmanship of the mechanism concealed by the cane and not at all dependent on its use as an aid in walking. A camera cane, concealing a camera, for example, could easily bring several thousand dollars because of its value as an unusual camera rather than its function as a cane.

Where To Find Canes—The Market

Canes, of course, turn up at every conceivable outlet for collectibles—attic or garage sales, flea markets, fairs, rummage sales and, of course, primitive art auctions and collectors' sales at the most prestigious auction houses. The most publicized sales will generally bring out the experts, who will bid items up to about their going value. Your best strategy is to develop a theme for your collection, know about your speciality thoroughly and then spot bargains where sellers, and perhaps other collectors, may not be as knowledgeable or astute in bargaining.

Museums Notable for Their Collections of Canes
  Division of Extractive Industries/Political History, Smithsonian
    Institution, Washington, DC 20560
  Essex Institute, Salem, MA 01970
  Independence National Historical Park, Philadelphia, PA 19106
  Remington Arms Company, Ilion, NY 13357
  Valley Forge Historical Society, Valley Forge, PA 19481

Books Worthwhile for Collectors
  Boothroyd, Albert E., *Fascinating Walking Sticks*, Salix Books,
    1970
  Stein, Kurt, *Canes and Walking Sticks*, Liberty Cap Books, 1974
  Von Boehn, Max, *Ornaments: Lace, Fans, Gloves, Walking
    Sticks, Parasols, Jewelry and Trinkets*, Benjamin Blom, Inc.,
    1970

CARNIVAL GLASS

This collectible is the poor man's Art Nouveau or Art Deco glass. It was frankly a vulgarized imitation of such fine art glass as Tiffany, Favrille or Corder's Aurene. It features a rapidly fadable iridescence and natural, flowing shapes in half-hearted homage to its models. But it was pressed by the thousands from molds without much care as to whether the glass came out perfectly or irregularly or boasted bubbles, or whether the seams or the parts showed or not. Thus if you find an exceptionally finished and pretty piece of Carnival glass, you have something unusual.

Carnival glass generally comes from one of four companies that produced 90 percent of all this kind of glass. They were the Millersburg Glass Company of Millersburg, Ohio (1909–1919); the Northwood Glass Company (1902–1923) of Wheeling, West Virginia; the Fenton Art Glass Company of Williamstown, West Virginia (circa 1900) and the Imperial Glass Company of Bellaire, Ohio (circa 1900). This special glass had its heyday from about 1907 through 1925 and then declined to the point where huge overstockings of these wares were sold or remaindered to carnivals and fairs as prizes or favors awarded to customers at various games of skill or chance, or as attendance incentives. Hence the name "Carnival glass."

There was such an outpouring of this glass that collectors must specialize or drown in the variety. You should limit your scope by manufacturer, pattern, individual shapes (tumblers, for example) or iridescent color.

The uses of the ware paralleled those of any set of dishware but the odd or unusually colored pieces, as usual, have greater value than the standard items for a place setting. There is even a category of "whimsies" such as vases or bowls in the shape of a lady's hat or a hatpin holder.

Because of the huge supply of the glass, it still goes for modest prices: a few dollars for standard pieces such as tumblers. But an odd, elaborate piece such as a punchbowl with twelve cups might go at auction today for as much as $1,000, although it cost but $5 for the whole set in the first decade of this century.

Where To Find Carnival Glass—
The Market

You can best begin collecting Carnival glass by choosing a segment of the production, such as a pattern or a shape, then scouting them out at garage and attic sales and flea markets. Try to find pieces that have retained their iridescence and were crafted with some finesse. You will have to watch out for new, contemporary versions of this glass, generally brighter and better crafted than the old. It is attractive and is sometimes made from the old molds but it does not bring as high a price among collectors. The quality and modest pricing of Carnival glass encourages overbuying of specimens, particularly when you uncover a group of pieces in good color and fine condition. You can later swap off or sell duplicate pieces or barter them to bring into your collection an item or two it lacks.

Museums Notable for Their Collections of Carnival Glass
   Fenton Art Glass Company, Williamstown, WV 26187

Clubs and Organizations
   American Carnival Glass Association, 1555 Blossom Park, Lakewood, OH 44107
   Heart of America Carnival Glass Association, 3048 Tamarak Drive, Manhattan, KS 66502
   International Carnival Glass Association, Lee Markley, R.R. 1, Mentone, IN 56439

Magazines and Newsletters
   Carnival Glass News and Views, c/o Joe Olson, 606 East 66th Street, Kansas City, MO 64131

Books Worthwhile for Collectors
   Cosentino, Geraldine, and Stewart, Regina, *Carnival Glass, A Guide For the Beginning Collector*, Golden Press, New York, 1976
   Edwards, Bill, *Millersburg, the Queen of Carnival Glass*, Collector Books, 1976
   Hand, Sherman, *Colors in Carnival Glass*, Books 1–4, Wallace-Homestead, 1967–1974

CAROUSEL ANIMALS

Remember the marvelous horses prancing on a carousel. Who can forget the thrills of riding these flashing, colorful beasts during childhood? Realistic manes, a certain wildness of eye and gnashing teeth or panting tongues give to the spectator the impression of horses drinking the wind as they race about on their circular track.

Partly because of this nostalgia—intact classic carousels still operating can be counted on one's fingers—the individual horses, other animals and incidental ornaments such as heraldic shields, garlands of fruits and flowers, and mythical as well as ordinary cats, deer, dogs, giraffes, camels and lions have been collected assiduously as prime examples of the woodcarver's art brought to bright heights by imaginative enameling, gilding and silvering.

The major builders of carousels in the United States were Carl Gustav Dentzel of Philadelphia and the Philadelphia Toboggan Company, which have a restrained "Philadelphia" style, Charles Looff of New York, Marcus Charles Illions of New York and Solomon Stein of New York, the last of whom featured the flamboyant "Coney Island" style of animal. Simpler and perhaps more charming were the "Country Fair" animals created by the Herschell-Spillman Company of North Tonawanda, New York, and the C. W. Parker Company of Abilene, Kansas. These makers influenced one another yet each retained certain stylistic characteristics readily apparent to the knowing observer. Among the artisans working for Dentzel (who himself specialized in horses, lions, tigers and giraffes) was Salvatore Cenigliaro (specialist in rabbits, cats and geese). Also with Dentzel were John Zalar and Frank Caretta.

The remaining collectible animals, mostly horses, can be grouped according to the three styles noted above. Collectors try for as many different examples as possible. Though the carousel originated in Europe, its art and carving came to its highest styles in the United States from the 1880's to about 1930 when the Depression shut down so many permanent as well as traveling fairs, circuses and amusement parks. You can recognize European horses because they are more elaborately decorated on the left side of the animal; European carousels turned clockwise. Carousels in the United States turned counterclockwise and decorators favored the right side.

On the oldest American carousels, too, there were generally three rows of horses or animals. Those in the outer row were the largest and the horses sometimes had three feet on the platform;

they were stationary. Inner-row animals were generally smaller. Also, after 1900 jumpers were added. If they had back hooves on the platform and forefeet in the air, they were called "prancers"; if they were suspended from the pole with all four hooves off the platform, they were known as "jumpers" and were perhaps the most thrilling to ride.

Where To Find Carousel Animals— The Market

Naturally it is rare to find any of these old figures with their original coats of paint intact. If you discover one, you have a real treasure, worth considerably more than its battered and chipped brethren. Restoration of shabby colors, if done well, enhances the value of an animal for collectors. You *may* find an occasional horse at a flea market or at an attic sale or in the barns of people who lived near old-time (now defunct) amusement parks, but the best now turn up when a collector buys from another collector or from a dealer. They may cost, depending on the carver, from $1,000 to $3,000.

Where You Can See Classic Carousel Horses Still in Action
  Playland at Rye, Rye, NY (Charles Carmel)
  State Fair Park, Dallas, TX (Carl Gustav Dentzel)
  Knott's Berry Farm, Buena Park, CA (Carl Gustav Dentzel)
  Greenfield Village, Dearborn, MI (Herschell-Spillman)
  Circus World, Orlando, FL (Marcus Charles Illions)
  Seaport Village, San Diego, CA (Charles Looff)
  Crescent Park, Riverside, RI (Charles Looff)
  Jantzen Beach, Portland, OR (C. W. Parker)
  Elitch's Gardens, Denver, CO (Philadelphia Toboggan Company)
  Central Park, New York, NY (Stein and Goldstein)
  Cedar Point, Sandusky, OH (Muller)

Museums Notable for Their Collections of Carousel Horses
  Heritage Museum, Sandwich, MA 02563
  Shelburne Museum, Shelburne, VT 05482
  Smithsonian Institution, WA, DC 20560

Magazines and Newsletters
  Carousel Art, Swenson's Graphic Arts Studios, Garden Grove, CA 92642

Books Worthwhile for Collectors
  Fried, Frederick, *A Pictorial History of the Carousel*, A. S. Barnes & Co., Cranbury, N.J., 1964

CASH REGISTERS

Perhaps one day 1980's versatile electronic input terminals on retail counters will become collectible. But whatever they have in efficiency they lack in charm, beauty and value, except as useful components of the marketing process.

Their predecessor, the cash register, appeared on the retail scene in the late 19th century. It was invented for the business purpose of keeping the flow of goods in a verifiable balance with the flow of cash. As models became more sophisticated they became a distinct aid in bookkeeping and inventory control.

James Ritty, a saloonkeeper in Dayton, Ohio, actually invented the machine and generated instant hate for it from clerks who felt that their honesty was being monitored. The early registers were of brass and bronze, solid because they held the day's cash receipts in safekeeping; they also tallied them in a number of ways, usually on a tape.

One of the saloonkeeper's customers was John Patterson, who bought two of Ritty's machines to stop cash leaks in a store Patterson ran. The cash register quickly put an end to the pilfering and Patterson bought into Ritty's business and changed its name to the National Cash Register Company.

Patterson was a dynamic, eccentric man, a pioneer in business, and his success with the cash register at once attracted competition, which he promptly knocked out with his superior manufacturing and management techniques. Between 1888 and 1895 there were 84 companies that made and/or sold cash registers. Only three others beside NCR survived for any length of time: the St. Louis, Ideal, and Michigan cash register companies, whose models can still be found occasionally by collectors. But NCR models are far and away the collector's darlings.

The most sought-after machines can be recognized by their appearance in decorated brass, bronze or wood marquetry and in part by means of NCR's neatly ordered serial numbers.

Each old machine has two sets of numbers on a metal plate, usually found on the front of the machine: (1) a model number and (2) a serial number. The machine with a serial number below 190,000 dates from the 19th century. 1900 to 1910 saw numbers rise to 800,000 and to 1,500,000 by 1916.

There is a way of identifying whether a machine is rebuilt or not. Serial numbers on rebuilt machines are preceded by an S for second hand, an R for rebuilt or an FR for factory rebuilt. These numbers are followed by a letter identifying when the work was done. If between A and P, the machine was rebuilt before 1916. Other numberings yield further information to the delight of avid collectors. If you know the NCR numbering system, you will know on sight a lot about the specimen you discover.

Where To Find Cash Registers— The Market

Machines turn up in antique stores, particularly in the country where long-established dry goods or other service stores may have one or more oldies still in use or for decoration. Or one that no longer works may be used in the storeroom. Do not be shy about asking any country shopkeeper you meet. Prices when new were modest—usually less than $50. But as collector's items, prices may run well above a thousand dollars. Cash registers also turn up at popular collectibles auctions, particularly when "Americana" collectibles are featured.

Books Worthwhile for Collectors
Allyn, Stanley Charles, *My Half Century with NCR*, McGraw-Hill Book Co., New York, 1967
Crowther, Samuel, *John H. Patterson, Pioneer in Industrial Welfare*, Doubleday Page and Co., 1923
Marcosson, Isaac F., *Wherever Men Trade: The Romance of the Cash Register*, Arno Press, New York, 1972

CHALKWARE

Not the least colorful and certainly not the most tasteful Victoriana that decorated middle class homes in the last half of the 19th century was chalkware. Call it plaster of Paris ware; by any other name it would remain as cheerfully colorful, breakable, chippable and tasteless.

It was first manufactured as a cheap imitation of porcelain and art pottery. You could buy pieces for a few nickels; many pieces could be had for less than 50 cents and most for less than a dollar.

But today it is collected as folk art and a single rare figure could bring over $1,000. Most of the popular designs were of animals and birds. Also there were fruits, buildings, candlesticks and some human figures. The usual figures were molded into two parts, head on body. But the head, sometimes, was suspended in the neck with a hook that encouraged a nodding when the figure was touched. When you find such a "nodder" you have found a piece of rare chalkware and it is likely to be quite valuable.

In making a piece of chalkware the craftsman used a mold greased with soap or a special oil. Into this he poured the plaster of Paris at the bottom, swished it around in the mold to form a thick sheet of successive coating and then allowed the excess plaster of Paris to run out. This method created a *hollow* figure. That is important to know because some of the old molds still exist and are used to create new versions of the old pieces that are a kind of fake if passed off as old pieces. Most of these modern versions are cast as *solid* figures. You might want to collect solid figures, old and new, but in general those that are new, even if bright and well made, are not as valuable as the old hollow version of the same subjects. Naturally the hollow figures were not exactly immortal; they broke easily.

Chalkware has added value if it is imaginatively painted. At first artisans used oils, then watercolors, usually in bright colors and with broadly painted lines to outline, almost as in a cartoon, a face or body features.

The figures and containers of chalkware have maintenance problems. Vase shapes cannot be used with water—they will "melt." Paint flakes off and the plaster of Paris cracks and breaks, but can be reglued and restored easily.

Because chalkware was a folk art, it usually cannot be traced to any specific artisan nor can it be easily dated. Thus dating is not important to collectors whereas color, distinction of figures and lively expressions are important and valuable. Also, the ingenious "nodding" feature of some animals and humans gives added value.

Where To Find Chalkware—The Market

Chalkware turns up mostly in the Midwest and in the East because it probably was created there at first by 18th- and 19th-century Italian immigrant craftsmen. They had learned their crafts in the long-established manufacture of plaster saints. Often the figures were sold by itinerant peddlers in the East. Many of the remaining chalkware "buildings" are churches or shrines useful for Christmas or religious decoration.

If you travel in Mexico you will see many examples of this art as it is still practiced. Mexican and other Latin American craftsmen may eventually produce chalkware rivaling the U.S. produced ware in popularity. And Latin American specimens are much less expensive. But as these trends strengthen, the most profitable pieces with the most immediate profit are those with a U.S. origin during the past two centuries. You can find the better and more expensive examples at antique shops, flea markets, country auctions and garage sales wherever that folk art comes out, but particularly in the East and Midwest where peddlers peppered the countryside with their wares. Prices can be modest but recently a finely featured cat in good condition was sold at a New York auction house for $950. There were good examples of chalkware in the Garbisch folk art collection that brought overall record prices at Sotheby's in the spring of 1980. Bargains, in relation to going prices, of course, can be uncovered by the eye that knows what it is looking for.

Museums Notable for Their Collections of Chalkware
  Brooklyn Museum, Brooklyn, NY 11238
  Greenfield Village and Henry Ford Museum, Dearborn, MI 48121
  Henry Francis du Pont Winterthur Museum, Winterthur, DE
    19735
  New York Historical Society, New York, NY 10024
  Philadelphia Museum of Art, Philadelphia, PA 19101
  Smithsonian Institution, Washington, DC 20560

Books Worthwhile for Collectors
  Adams, Ruth, *Pennsylvania Dutch Art*, World Publishing Co.,
    New York, 1950

Bishop, Robert, *American Folk Sculpture*, E. P. Dutton & Co., New York 1974

Comstock, Helen, ed., *The Concise Encyclopedia of American Antiques*, Hawthorn Books, New York, 1965

Lipman, Jean, and Winchester, Alice, *The Flowering of American Folk Art*, Viking Press, New York, 1974

CHESS SETS

They say that chess is the game of kings, but today you do not have to have a drop of royal blood in your veins in order to collect chess sets. But you may need quite a bit of money in your bank account to collect the more elaborate or vintage sets. They are available in all shapes, sizes and materials, and come from many centuries and cultures in which this ancient game has been played.

You need quantities of money—$2,000 to $5,000 or more—to buy sets designed by such famous artists as Alexander Calder, Max Ernst, Salvador Dali, Man Ray, Marcel Duchamp and the like or if you want sets decked out in precious mineral or metal, ivory, art glass, alabaster or fine porcelain. There are also more modest sets available in distinctively carved wood, cast metals, onyx and even plastic or glass. These are within the price reach of the average collector.

Chess as a game evolved as a pattern of medieval life and military action. Early sets portrayed two sides of famous battles. Another tradition of design has tried, over the centuries, to depersonalize each piece, to make it more general and abstract, so that no historical significance attaches to any particular piece.

The game probably developed in India about thirteen centuries ago and represented a king and the four branches of his army: foot soldiers, cavalry, elephant troops (castles) and charioteers (bishops). Persian versions are supposed to have added for the king's pleasure a wise man or queen.

The Arabs discovered chess when they conquered Persia in the 7th century but their rule against imaging actual people in their art accounts for their abstract design where the kings and queens have no faces. This artistic style developed into the Western version of the chess set.

The chessmen designed by J. Jaques and Norman Staunton, whose father was Howard Staunton, a 19th-century English chessmaster, are of ebony (the black) and boxwood (the white) and they have become standardized throughout the world for tournament play. They are the familiar abstract pieces with a slash or cut in the bishop's miter as probably the most distinguishing characteristic.

Nations varied the players. The American and British bishop became in French sets a fool or jester; in German sets a runner. In Russia the rook or castle became a boat. When you become a collector of chess sets you will realize that most sets are made for play but some highly collectible sets (often highly priced) are made for display. The latter are more decorative, are often larger in size and can cost several thousands dollars.

Where To Find Chess Sets—The Market

You will find collectible chess sets at dealers, art shops, gift shops, department stores and frequently the best auction houses. Be prepared to spend thousands of dollars for lavish sets of contemporary artists or sets associated with historic figures represented as players or sets that had distinguished owners. An original Staunton set, signed on the base of the king by J. Jaques, can bring hundreds of dollars even though it was mass produced at the Jaques factory in five sizes of ivory and six sizes of woods.

Museums Notable for Their Collections of Chess Sets
Metropolitan Museum of Art, New York NY 10028
Philadelphia Museum of Art, Philadelphia, PA 19101

Magazines and Newsletters
The Chess Newsletter, Rima Greenberg, ed., 320 West 86th Street, New York, NY 10024

Books Worthwhile for Collectors
Graham, F. Lanier, *Chess Sets*, Walier and Company, 1968
Mackett-Beeson, A. E. J., *Chessmen*, G. P. Putnam's Sons, New York, 1968
Wichmann, Hans and Siegfried, *Chess, the Story of Chesspieces from Antiquity to Modern Times*, Crown Publishers, New York, 1964
Wilkinson, C. K., and Jessie McNab Dennis, *Chess: East and West, Past and Present: A Selection from the Gustavus A. Pfeiffer Collection*, Metropolitan Museum of Art, New York, 1968

CHILDREN'S BOOKS

Not only are children's book classics collectibles, they are often sought for their illustrations as well. Some of the most famous illustrators collaborated with authors to produce such classics as *Alice's Adventures in Wonderland* (Lewis Carroll, author; John Tenniel, illustrator) and *The Wonderful Wizard of Oz* (L. Frank Baum, author; W. W. Denslow, illustrator). The original artist so realized the characters of each tale that subsequent versions of the story—theater, movie or other editions—tended to conform, lest a new version disappoint expectations and be rejected.

The impact certain books have on collector's childhood can alter the course of his or her tastes in later life. Perhaps the Tom Swift books attracted him to engineering; perhaps *The Wind in the Willows* led her to telling imaginative stories; maybe *Tom Sawyer* or *Treasure Island* led a boy to a life of exploration; the Hardy Boys and Nancy Drew certainly led generations of young men and women to adventure and delight.

Collecting children's books really began in earnest after World War II, although rare books have been collected seriously for centuries since the invention of printing.

The children's subsection of book collecting can reward the beginning book collector because children's books worth collecting are mostly products of the late 19th and 20th centuries; they are, by and large, in generous supply and the prices are low with no great emphasis and variance because of physical condition. Scribblings, tears and smudges from fingers of little readers have a certain charm and worth in this category of collectibles.

Before the 19th century, books for children were essentially educational—ABC's or books of manners. Some of these early books still survive, but not many; they served their purpose and perished in the process. John Newberry, an 18th-century publisher who specialized in children's books, lightened these lessons with verses and illustrations; today a prize for new children's books is named after him.

About 1850 Edward Lear began in London to babble his nonsense verses for children and Lewis Carroll (Charles Lutwidge Dodgson, a mathematician and teacher at Cambridge University) wrote the classics *Alice's Adventures in Wonderland* and *Through the Looking Glass.*

Some collectors may specialize in Carroll only, collecting as many editions of the two famous works as they can find. Another favorite is L. Frank Baum, whose first book, *The Wonderful Wizard of Oz* was published in 1900. Many copies are probably in existence but they remain hidden away in attics. A good copy can bring, therefore, as much as $750 today.

The Adventures of Tom Sawyer (1876) and *The Adventures of Huckleberry Finn* (1885) are perhaps the most popular among American collectors. A first edition of Finn can bring more than $500; of Sawyer, more than $2,000. Robert Louis Stevenson's *Kidnapped* (1886) in a first edition can bring today about $250 but his *Treasure Island* (1883) could bring close to $1,000.

Mass-produced adventure stories for young people, such as the Tom Swift, Hardy Boys or Nancy Drew series, have come out in floods since 1910, when the first five (now rare) Swifts—*Tom Swift and His Motor Cycle, His Motor Boat, His Air Ship, His Submarine Boat* and *His Electric Runabout*—all came out; first edition copies of these can still be found today at prices less than $25. They are worth collecting.

As for Nancy Drew, look for *The Secret of the Old Clock, The Hidden Staircase* and *The Bungalow Mystery* (all out in 1930). The first Hardy Books were *The Tower Treasure, The House on the Cliff* and *The Secret of the Old Mill.*

If you are inclined to favor illustrators, consider Kate Greenaway's *Almanacks* which, in their final editions in the late 1890's, introduced color photogravure. Special editions of standard favorites—*Tom Sawyer, Treasure Island, The Last of the Mohicans, Robinson Crusoe*—had for illustrators Howard Pyle, Norman Rockwell and N. C. Wyeth in this country. In England, John Tenniel illustrated the Alice books and E. H. Shepard helped make the characters in *Winnie the Pooh* memorable images, as did Kenneth Grahame for *The Wind in the Willows.* Arthur Rackham was another well-known illustrator of children's books.

Where To Find Children's Books—
The Market

In this field there is something for everyone; you may want to begin where your heart lies, with some of the titles that were your favorites when you were very young and the House at Pooh Corners was a favorite place to visit. Thus you are likely to find the beginning of a collection in your own books saved from childhood or perhaps passed on to younger relatives who now have no use for them. This is the story in many families; thus quantities of children's books show up at garage and attic sales, at charity fairs and at street fairs. The best books, usually those with valuable illustrations, come up for auction at the book specials now held by all the major auction houses.

Museums Notable for Their Collections of Children's Books
Free Library of Philadelphia, Philadelphia, PA 19103
Philip H. and A. S. W. Rosenbach Foundation, Philadelphia, PA 19103
Pierpont Morgan Library, New Nork NY 10016
Toronto Public Library, The Deborne Collection of Early Children's Books, Toronto 5, Canada
University of Minnesota, The Kerlan Collection, Minneapolis, MN 55455

Magazines and Newsletters
AB Bookman's Weekly, AB Bookman Publications, Inc., Clifton, NJ 07115
The Horn Book Magazine, The Horn Book, Inc., Boston MA 02116

Books Worthwhile for Collectors
Bader, Barbara, *American Picturebooks from Noah's Ark to the Beast Within*, Macmillan, 1976
Blanck, Jacob N., *Peter Parley to Penrod*, Mark Press, 1974
Maig, Cornelia, ed., *A Critical History of Children's Literature*, Macmillan, 1969
Quale, Eric, *The Collector's Book of Children's Books*, Clarkson N. Potter, New York, 1971

CHINESE EXPORT PORCELAIN

Chinese Export Porcelain, also known as Lowestoft, is not great art and is not of the quality of Chinese ceramics, such as the "dynasty ware" that has been the investors' delight of the past few years when their values have gone up more than 17 percent annually on average.

But Export Porcelain *does* participate in the general enthusiasm for Oriental ceramics; it simply starts from a lower value base. The quantities still available at reasonable prices make it a highly attractive collectible for pleasure and profit.

The finesse of Chinese procelain impressed early travelers from the West ever since about the 9th century A.D. when travelers to the East began to talk and write about it. Marco Polo, for example, exclaimed about the thin, white, translucent ceramics that far outshone the pottery then made in Europe. During the years of the Renaissance, however, European potters did not delay in finding the recipe for such highly desirable ware.

A large group of collectors today, however, prefer the Chinese original to the European imitations. The loyalty of collectors encouraged Chinese makers and East-West traders to create and handle pieces specifically for the export market during the 17th to the late 19th century. Political and economic disruptions in China and the ascendancy of European potters put an end to the Export Porcelain business and defined the later years of authenticity for collectors.

Of course, Chinese manufacturers continued to make porcelain for their domestic market but the style, shapes and colors that attracted Western taste were distinctively different and thus the knowledgeable collector can easily tell the Export Porcelain from the domestic. For one thing, Export Porcelain tends to be a bit heavier to withstand travel.

The highly organized Chinese made most of their porcelain in Ching-Te Chen, in the province of Kiangsi, near a famed and ancient source of clay, about 600 miles from the port of Canton. As the trade increased, more and more of the actual decoration of the pieces moved to Canton where designs could be customized to the order of Western merchants.

Oddly enough, the ingredients of fine porcelain in the vicinity of Ching-Te Chen were used earlier for finer ceramics; the royal potteries of the Ming emperors drew their clay from this same area.

Provenance Helps Bring Handsome Prices   *The very rare eaglet-decorated cider jug and cover was one of a pair bought by Mrs. Ward of Boston at the sale of George Washington's estate. (The Washingtons had many items of Chinese Export porcelain at Mount Vernon.) This piece remained in the possession of six different descendants of Mrs. Ward until recently, when it was sold at Christie's for $3,200. The large seal of the United States divides two blue enamel flower sprays, all between underglaze blue and gilt bands of the cell pattern. Its domed cover has a Buddhistic lion cub finial. (Photo: courtesy of Christie's.)*

Yet until the Chinese ports were opened to European trade in the 16th century, there were only a few private potteries operating in Ching-Te Chen. By the end of the 18th century there were more than 3,000 manufacturers in "Porcelain City." About a million people, almost the whole population, were involved in the pottery business and makers of Chinese Export Porcelain had evolved, centuries before the modern industrial production line, a manufacturing system in which *many* people contributed to each piece of porcelain their special skill—shaping a part, applying a single repeating element of design, etc.

Once the Export Porcelain began to flood European and American ports (at its peak more than a million pieces entered the United States each year), shapes and decorations, often with family coats of arms or mottoes, were made to order for wealthy families and then, finally, in vulgarized formats for the general, middle-income public that had a growing habit of imitating taste setters.

The most common pattern was classic Canton, a blue glaze on a white background usually featuring a bridge, a tea house and a weeping willow with a scalloped line inside the blue rim. Sometimes the serving pieces of a set had open work around their borders which, today, automatically makes them more valuable. Individual pieces at auction can go for well above $1,000.

A pattern called Nanking was slightly more elaborate with border variations and sometimes a gilt overlay. Both Nanking and Canton were often stowed in the bottom of a ship's hold to act as ballast and a cushion for finer imports, including tea and silk.

A higher quality of commercial procelain featured a rainbow of other colors, mostly in the red range. Such pieces were called Rose Medallion or rose palette and tended to include decoration with flowers and animals in a Westernized style. The Mandarin pattern used many of the same colors but emphasized a central scene of imperial court figures and furniture.

Still another pattern was called "Hundred Butterflies" because of the brilliant variety of those insects that decorated the center and borders. The quantity and availability of these patterns assure collectors of a continuing supply. New collectors can accumulate it, still, at fairly reasonable prices for ordinary pieces of a place setting. Service pieces, of course, can run into the thousands of dollars, depending on their rarity and condition.

Where To Find Chinese
Export Porcelain—The Market

Look for Chinese Export Porcelain in antique shops in the vicinity of U.S. and foreign ports known for their imports of Chinese porcelain during the 19th century. These would include New York, Philadelphia, London and Boston. In these environs, it is likely to appear at attic sales, fairs and bazaars, and the best pieces will appear at popular auctions. The British imitation is known as Lowestoft and you are likely to find a confusion about origin except where place of manufacture is indicated. Prices can run from a few hundred to a few thousand dollars for a piece, depending on supply and condition.

Museums Notable for Their Collections of Export Porcelain
  Art Institute of Chicago, Chicago, IL 60603
  Henry Francis du Pont Winterthur Museum, Winterthur, DE 19735
  Metropolitan Museum of Art, New York, 10028
  Museum of the American China Trade, Milton, MA 02186
  Museum of Fine Arts, Boston, MA 02115
  Peabody Museum of Salem, Salem, MA 01970
  Philadelphia Museum of Art, Philadelphia, PA 19101
  Western Reserve Historical Society, Cleveland, OH 44106

Books Worthwhile for Collectors
  Gordon, Elinor, *Chinese Export Porcelain: An Historical Survey*, Universe Books, New York, 1977
  ———, *Collecting Chinese Export Porcelain*, Universe Books, New York, 1977
  Howard, David S., *China for the West* (2 volumes) Sotheby's, 1978
  ———, *Chinese Armorial Porcelain*, Faber & Faber, 1974
  Hyde, J. A. Lloyd, *Oriental Lowestoft*, Ceramic Book Company, 1964
  Le Corbeiller, Clare, *China Trade Porcelain: Patterns of Exchange*, Metropolitan Museum of Art, New York, 1974
  Palmer, Arlene M., *A Winterthur Guide to Chinese Export Porcelain*, Crown Publishers, New York, 1976
  Phillips, John Goldsmith, *Chinese Trade Porcelain*, Harvard University Press, Cambridge, Mass., 1956

CIGAR BANDS AND LABELS

Europeans have smoked cigars since the 16th century when tobacco was introduced to fashionable society by such travelers, explorers and adventurers as Sir Walter Raleigh.

Yet cigars were not packaged with labels or banded until the middle of the 19th century, when gilt bands and colorful labels served as advertising and identification of various brands preferred by Victorian gentlemen and occasional Victorian gentlewomen.

It has been suggested that Cuban ladies introduced bands to prevent the tobacco from staining their fingers. Cuban ladies, of course, smoked cigars long before their sisters elsewhere. Another legend has it that English dandies encouraged the practice of banding to prevent the tobacco from dirtying their gloves.

Women began to collect these gaudy bits of printed paper and glued them to the bottoms of glass ashtrays or in scrapbooks and thus took them out of circulation. The hobby caught on and specialty printers *over*printed and sold bands directly to collectors as if they were postage stamps.

Printers sometimes created bands specially for give-away cigars that advertised something else such as Coca Cola. During the years 1927–1944, Coca Cola used bands extensively at company meetings, limited printings that make cigar bands advertising Coca Cola highly desirable; they can cost more than $100 each now, even if glued to the bottom of an ashtray!

A label from a presidential portrait series, available at $1.25 when first printed, may cost, if found at all, more than 100 times that amount today. When you collect bands, rarity increases value. Also, bands associated with famous people such as politicians, who had bands created for campaign advertising, or famous people who had bands created for their own private cigars (Rudyard Kipling, the English poet and author was one of these) with monograms or heraldic devices, because of their limited printing, if available to the collecting public at all are assured a special value.

Labels from cigar boxes ran to large sizes—4-inch squares, 7- × 4-inch rectangles—and they allowed the artist more room for self-expression. These are a subcategory of cigar band collections. Collectors usually do not collect the label, box and all; rather the label is soaked or steamed off the box and dried flat in a book of blotter paper and then pasted in a scrapbook.

Where To Find Cigar Labels—The Market

You can find labels in attics, at flea markets and in antique shops that specialize in paper ephemera. Major collections may come up at auctions of collectibles or at swap sessions between collectors at conventions. Since at the turn of the century there were about 350,000 brands—every village and whistle-stop in the United States had its cigar store with private brands and bands—you can sometimes discover local treasures when such stores go out of business, or their printers do. Printers who specialized in such labels and bands, if they will cooperate with you, may release quantities of overprinted labels kept for years in their storerooms. Naturally you will want to overbuy such discoveries! The trading between cigar band collectors is almost as avid as between stamp collectors. With such a discovery you may have cornered the market on one or two significant labels. This could help you to fill out your collection via swapping and bartering.

Museums Notable for Their Collections of Cigar Bands
  Metropolitan Museum of Art, The Burdick Collection, New York NY 10028
  Museum of the City of New York, New York, NY 10029
  National Tobacco-Textile Museum, Danville, VA 24541
  New York Public Library, The Arents Collection, New York, NY 10018

Clubs and Organizations
  International Seal, Label and Cigar Band Society, 8915 East Bellevue Street, Tucson, AZ 85715

Books Worthwhile for Collectors
  Back, J.B., *The Pleasures of Cigar Smoking*, Rutledge Books, New York, 1971
  Davidoff, Zino, *The Connoisseur's Book of the Cigar*, McGraw-Hill Book Co., New York, 1969
  Hyman, H. Tony, *Handbook of American Cigar Boxes*, Arent Art Museum, 235 Lake Street, Elmira, N Y , 1978

CLASSIC CARS

The sign before the sparkling town car at the rally of the Pierce Arrow Society announced a "1937 Pierce Arrow town car, body by Brunn, wheel base 147 inches, 10 in the world built at a cost of $7,500." Today it has appreciated in value ten times over.

The obstacle to collecting classic cars, even though they appreciate rapidly in value if restored and kept in good condition, is their size. Storage and maintenance problems immediately arise. But for the classic car buff and erstwhile mechanic, these marvelous remnants of the Age of the Classic Automobile (from the turn of the century to about World War II) are worth all the expense and effort. In the twilight of the automobile age, only a few mammoth car makers survive: Ford, General Motors, and far behind, Chrysler and American Motors.

Collectors who grew up or became collectors during the golden age know very well the family's pride and thrill when Dad brought home the new car, especially if it was somewhat grander and a better status symbol then the old.

Of course, you may have an attachment to a vintage Packard touring car your grandmother once used for driving you to the State Fair, but sentiment is not what makes a classic car valuable. Scarcity, working condition and appearance do! Or possibly a model exhibits some pioneering mechanical innovation such as the 1951 Chrysler Firepower V-8—the first mass produced car for the consumer market with a hemispherical combustion chamber that improved miles per gallon.

Where to Find Classic Cars—
The Market

If you have tens of thousands of dollars to put into fairly ordinary cars, you will want to limit the goals of your collection to a particular period or maker. The recent auction record of $400,000 for a single car was set in September 1979 by a 1938 Mercedes auctioned by Christie's to a customer in Monaco. Very unusual cars frequently exceed $250,000 at specialized auctions. You may find a restorable heap in a farmer's barn. Like old landmark houses, the scarcity of the essential model makes the expensive search for authentic parts and refinishing worth your while.

You will invest in cars more profitably if you select a particular period and try for the best appearing models designated as Classic Cars (by the Classic Car Club of America) or as Milestones (cars built before 1945).

Standard periods of specialization include the pre-World War I era, the period between the two World Wars and the post-World War II era. You can further limit your collection to one of the eight generally recognized subdivisions:

PRE-WORLD WAR I
Pioneers were built through 1905 with engines powered by steam, electricity or gasoline.
Brass and Gas cars were made from 1906 through 1912 with brass radiators and trim and acetylene-gas headlights.
Vintage cars were made from 1913 through 1919. Many had electric starters and headlights and enclosed bodies.

BETWEEN THE WARS
Production cars are assembly-line cars with unusual features or of a certain year's design.
Classics are Quality Cars chosen by the Classic Car Club of America.
Vintage Sports cars are cars with high performance characteristics chosen by the Vintage Sports Car Club of America.

POST-WORLD WAR II
Production cars are assembly-line cars with unusual features or of a certain year's design.
Milestones are cars chosen by the Milestone Car Society; they have outstanding design or engineering features.

Two of the most collectible cars available are Fords, the Model F and the Model T. Both offer significant engineering improvements over the brass and gas models of an earlier period. Model T's in good condition can bring $5,000. A Model A Ford Phaeton, of which 47,476 were made in the year 1928, might bring $3,500 today.

So choose your period and prepare to expand your garage space! As you must have imagined by now, you need a lot of money to collect classic cars. But then you can make a lot of money on that level, too.

Museums Notable for Their Collections of Classic Cars
Harrah's Automobile Collection, Reno, NV 89504

Long Island Automotive Museum, Southampton, NY 11968
Museum of Transportation, Brookline, MA 02146

Clubs and Organizations
Antique Automobile Club of America, 501 West Governor Road, Hershey, PA 17033
Classic Car Club of America, P.O. Box 443, Madison, NJ 07940
Horseless Carriage Club of America, 9031 East Florence Avenue, Downey, CA 90421
Milestone Car Society, P.O. Box 50850, Indianapolis, IN 46250
Veteran Motor Car Club of America, 15 Newton Street, Brookline, MA 02146

Magazines and Newspapers
Automobile Quarterly, Automobile Quarterly, Inc., Kutztown, PA 19530
Car Classics, Car Classics Publishing Co., Chateworth, CA 91311
Cars and Parts, George Slankard, Sesser, IL 62884
Classic Motorbooks Catalogue, Classic Motorbook, Osceola, WI 54020
Hemmings Motor News, Watering, Inc., Bennington, VT 05201
Old Cars, Chester L. Krause, Iola, WI 54945

Books Worthwhile for Collectors
The American Car since 1875, Automobile Quarterly, 1975
Georgano, G. N., ed., *The Complete Encyclopedia of Motorcars, 1885–Present*, E. P. Dutton & Co., New York, 1976
Nowak, Stanley, *Automobile Restoration Guide*, Crown Publishers, New York, 1974
Wheatley, Richard C., and Morgan, Brian, *Antique and Classic Cars, Their Maintenance and Operation*, Robert Bentley, Cambridge, Mass., 1976

CLOCKS

Collectors of clocks, it hardly needs saying, do not collect them to tell time in different ways. They collect them for their artistry, their unique movements, their cabinet work, sometimes for the achievement of the artist who painted the face of the clock.

Categories of clocks can vary widely; instruments to tell time have been around for centuries and before *that* there were sundials.

The mechanical clock, as far as collectors in the United States are concerned, reached a peak of popularity in the *present*; the current favorites were made in the 19th century by Connecticut craftsmen.

The earliest U.S. clocks come in two basic sizes: grandfather clocks that are 7 to 9 feet tall and are usually called "tall-case clocks," and grandmother clocks that are 3 to 5 feet tall. The handsome cases are of a size and shape to accommodate the weights that hang by cords. The weights cause the turning of the movement and are regulated by the long pendulum to assure timing.

The first tall-case clocks were crafted by hand and cost about $50. Some of the most famous makers were Peter Stretch of Philadelphia, William Glaggett of Newport, Rhode Island, and Simon and Aaron Willard of Boston. Any 19th-century tall-case clock today is worth many times its original price and clocks that still tell fairly accurate time (in other words—they work) bring the highest prices, often several thousand dollars.

In fact, even in the 18th century, tall-case clocks grew expensive enough to create consumer resistance to limit the supply the market would accept. Clock makers revised the technology of gears and pendulum and created shelf clocks. They abandoned expensive hand brass-finished "works" wherever they could and replaced them with cheaper wood parts.

Innovators at that time were Benjamin Cheng, Jr., of East Hartford, Connecticut, and Gideon Roberts of Bristol, Connecticut. Another Connecticut citizen, Eli Terry, in the latter part of the 18th century tried to mass-produce clocks made of standardized parts and used water power to drive his saws and lathes. In 1807 Terry received an order from a case maker for 4,000 works that he delivered three years later. One of Terry's apprentices in this project was Seth Thomas, probably the best known, now, of the Connecticut clock makers.

Both Terry and Thomas developed the shelf clock, which transformed the industry—they could be mass-produced and priced within a range a large number of consumers could afford, about $15 each. Today, at auction, such clocks could easily bring several hundred dollars.

Another clockmaker, Chauncy Jerome, reverted to works of brass which, when mass-produced, could be offered at less cost and could be advertised for their longer wear. These several innovations made a reliable clock available to the growing mass-family market. Shelf clocks often came in three typical variations in design, the banjo shape, the beehive and the pillar and scroll.

In the 1830's further innovation in manufacturing techniques led to the use of inexpensive springs to replace pendulums and weights. Long used in watches and often clocks, this expanded use of springs allowed miniaturization in household clocks, which again made possible mass production at popular prices. As a result, there is a generous supply of 19th-century U.S. manufactured clocks still working and in good condition.

Where To Find Clocks—The Market

There is a good number of collectors, too, and that makes for an interesting market with gradually increasing prices achieved by the rarest clocks in the best condition. Collectible clocks are now coming out of attics; they show up at flea markets and country auctions, and with fine cabinets they make American sales at the best auction houses—but be prepared to pay several thousand dollars for these prizes!

Famous Clock Makers
Prized to Collectors

Among the sought-after makers are the following, with the dates when they manufactured clocks:

Ansonia Clock Co.
Ansonia, Connecticut
(1859–1929)

William L. Gilbert Clock Co.
Winchester, Connecticut
(1871–1964)

E. Howard & Company
Roxbury, Massachusetts
(1840–1882)

E. Ingraham Company
Bristol, Connecticut
(1857–1967)

Joseph Ives
Bristol, Connecticut
(1810–1862)

Chauncey Jerome
Bristol, Connecticut
(1824–1855)

New Haven Clock Company
New Haven, Connecticut
(1853–1959)

Seth Thomas Clock Co.
Plymouth Hollow
Thomaston, Connecticut
(1853–present)

Sessions Clock Company
Forestville, Connecticut
(1903–1968)

Waterbury Clock Company
Waterbury, Connecticut
(1857–1944)

Eli Terry
Plymouth, Connecticut
(1807–1833)

E. N. Welch Manufacturing
    Co.
Forestville, Connecticut
(1864–1903)

Restoring Clocks

Clocks are a collectible worth restoring—both for the time-telling mechanisms and for the cabinets, which count as antiques and are often very valuable furniture. If you like to putter with restoring and refinishing cabinets and have a mechanical bent with broken gears, you will find it worthwhile in added value to buy ruined clocks and restore them to tip-top ticking order.

Museums Notable for Their Collections of Clocks
    American Clock and Watch Museum, Inc., Bristol, CT 06010
    Greenfield Village and Henry Ford Museum, Dearborn, MI 48121
    Museum of the National Association of Watch and Clock Collectors, Inc., Columbia, PA 17512
    National Museum of History and Technology, Smithsonian Institution, Washington, DC 20560
    Old Clock Museum, Pharr, TX 78577
    Old Sturbridge Village, Sturbridge, MA 01566
    The Time Museum, Rockford, IL 61125

Clock Collectors' Organizations
    Antiquarian Horological Society, New House High Street, Ticehurst, Wadhurst, Sussex, England TN5 7AL
    National Association of Watch and Clock Collectors, Inc., 514 Poplar Street, Box 33, Columbia, PA 17512

Books Worthwhile for Collectors
    Bailey, Chris, *Two Hundred Years of American Clocks and Watches*, Prentice-Hall, Englewood Cliffs, N.J., 1975

Battison, Edwin A., and Kane, Patricia E., *The American Clock, 1725–1865*, New York Graphic Society, Ltd., Greenwich, Conn., 1973

Britten, F. J. *Britten's Old Clocks and Watches and Their Makers*, E. P. Dutton and Co., New York, 1973

Distin, William H., and Bishop, Robert, *The American Clock*, E. P. Dutton & Co., New York, 1976

Palmer, Brooks, *A Treasury of American Clocks*, Macmillan Company, 1974

Tyler, E. J., *The Craft of the Clockmaker*, Crown Publishers, New York, 1974

A Clockmaker's Ingenuity *A talent for clockmaking has always included a dash of ingenuity as well as intricate engineering. Long before the age of electricity and electonics, there were illuminated clocks. The one above is a Davies Illuminated Alarm Clock made about 1880. As the alarm rings, a spring flies back, striking matches which then swing over to ignite an oil lamp. This clock is now part of the collection of the Watch and Clock Museum in Columbia, Pennsylvania. (Photo: courtesy of National Association of Watch and Clock Collectors Museum)*

CLOTHES/COSTUMES

In the recent past one would send "good" old clothes to a charity such as the Goodwill. Today, if the clothes are in wearable condition they may go to a resale shop—or perhaps, if by a "name designer," to a dealer in significant antique clothing. Sometimes, if part of a celebrated estate or the leavings of a society matron, the clothing may go directly to an auction house for sale. And it will bring good prices, even thousands of dollars per item for significant pieces of clothing in good condition, worn only once or twice by wealthy grande dames of society; such clothing is particularly valuable if worn by movie stars.

Although some collectors actually wear vintage dresses to high social or "period" occasions, most antique gowns are in too fragile a condition for risking such wear. Human perspiration, skin oils and ordinary friction all stain, rot and tear; precarious ancient seams easily split open with the stress of body motion.

Yet some collectors, when they buy at thrift shops and resale shops, value an old dress for its further wear as well as its distinction in design. They find it worthwhile to purchase even if the item can be worn for only a few occasions. Other collectors do everything they can to carefully repair old dresses, reweave some parts and restitch others with contemporary (but carefully matched) thread—in the same needle holes, if possible. That kind of collector profits most if gifted in needle skills that can repair, restore and clean. Such a collector often serves as a finder of historic gowns for museums and international collectors, thereby earning a second income discovering and repairing specimens as well as accumulating them.

Most collectors wind up in categories of clothing: evening gowns, undergarments or "whites," period items from the Victorian era, the 1920's, the 1930's, or men's or infants' wear. The most popular category is undoubtedly ball and evening gowns of certain eras. Of all clothing, they are the most highly styled and showy items. Hung on frames or manikins they make good displays. Still another subcategory of collectible gowns are the creations from the workshops of famous designers such as Worth, Poiret, Vionnet, Schiaparelli, Balmain, Dior, Mainbocher, Adrian, Balenciaga, Norell, Chanel and others.

When a collector has a truly valuable collection of vintage gowns, storage often becomes a challenge. Your most prized clothing should not be worn at all—particularly not by local amateur

Vintage Style Gown by Famed Stylist *This rose-pink silk pleated evening gown from the 1930s by Mariano Fortuny—a favorite with collectors because of his attractive pleats—sold recently at Christie's for $2,600. (Photo: courtesy of Christie's.)*

actors and actresses in period plays or, worse yet, by children playing dress-up with Granny's old gowns. Light fabrics do well on padded hangers; heavy, beaded fabrics should lie flat, wrapped in bleach-free white paper to separate the cloth from the wood or dark cardboard of containers. Use moth balls to inhibit attack by insects. Wool, of course, is most vulnerable to moths; heavy silk is likely to split on the folds with age.

Where To Buy Antique Clothes— The Market

Once you have studied your chosen category of clothing, you can find pieces through specialized dealers or featured at certain auctions. You can uncover possible bargains at all manner of local sales—estate, gargage and flea markets. Traders at such fairs know that antique (or merely old and used) clothes have their buyers if only for further use as wearable garments at modest prices. It will be up to you and your educated eye to spot the truly collectible garment from the mass of humdrum items.

Prices of antique clothing can range from below $100 to a recent high price of $3,200 for a shimmering Fortuny pleated silk evening gown (sold at Sotheby's). A Worth tea gown in silk grosgrain from the late 1870's with the Worth label intact recently went at auction for $300, which is the more usual price range for fine antique gowns.

Museums Notable for Their Collections of Clothes
    The Brooklyn Museum, Brooklyn, NY 11238
    Chicago Historical Society, Chicago, IL 60614
    Los Angeles County Museum of Art, Los Angeles, CA 90036
    The Metropolitan Museum of Art, Costume Institute, New York, NY 10028
    National Museum of History and Technology, Smithsonian Institution, Washington, DC 20560

Organization/Group for Collectors
    The Costume Society of America, c/o The Costume Institute, The Metropolitan Museum of Art, New York, NY 10028

Books Worthwhile for Collectors
    Arnold, Janet, *A Handbook of Costume*, Macmillan, London 1973
    Davenport, Millia, *Book of Costume*, Crown Publishers, 1972
    Kidwell, Claudia, and Christman, Margaret, *Suiting Everyone*, Smithsonian Institution Press, 1974

COINS

Coins, whether ancient, foreign or U.S., make excellent collectibles. They are durable, have an intrinsic value (because of their metallic content), a coinage value (based on the denomination they represent in a country's currency) and a numismatic value based on rarity, condition, history and beauty.

Coins have a certain convenience, too, in being compact and easily stashed away in, for example, a safe-deposit box if of unusual value (or if you want to safeguard them while on vacation). Also there is a very large group of collectors competing for a fixed number of coins.

For those who collect U.S. coins there is the added possibility of finding old coins in the attic—perhaps in the pocket of an old suit or purse—or even in one's hand as change. These are found treasures—a certain dime from the 1950's still could turn up as change and be worth $75.00 or more. Run-of-the-mill silver change (half dollars, quarters and dimes) with dates before 1965 are worth roughly four times face value simply because of their silver content. Wartime nickels coined in the United States during the years 1941–1945 are worth about five times their face value because they contain silver (substituted to conserve strategic nickel).

In fact, U.S. coins make a good choice for a beginning collector. This is because of their complex history, occasional errors and several mint markings, as well as their availability through dealers, auctions, fairs, attics and, to a limited extent (more limited by the year), current circulation. One or two of the guidebooks mentioned at the end of this section are indispensable, however. You simply have to know the history behind a coin to understand why it is worth little more than face value or many thousand times face value. A 1943 cent struck on old bronze blanks, instead of the wartime steel, is worth about $10,000 today. Only about a dozen of these coins went into circulation. (Beware of copper-plated steel cents.)

Collectors usually talk about coins in three categories: ancient (from about the 7th century B.C. to the fall of the Byzantine Empire in 1453 A.D., foreign (any coin not from the U.S. and minted after 1453 A.D.), and U.S.

Ancient Coins

For sheer beauty, coins minted by the Greek city-states have no rivals. Fortunately for collectors, the Greek city-states, the Roman

Empire and the Byzantine Empire showered silver, bronze and gold coins upon the world; ancient caches of them still turn up today. The coins of Lydia (mostly in museum collections now) had a design on one side only. According to legend, in the 6th century B.C. the Athenian tyrant Peisistratus authorized the first coins with designs on both faces—a profile of the goddess Athena on one side and her sacred bird, the owl, on the other.

Other Greek city-states followed the leader, with coins of patron gods and goddesses on one side and a city symbol on the reverse. Coins were predominantly in silver—drachmas about the size of a dime; tetradrachmas the size of a quarter. Nine very rare decadrachmas (about the size of a silver dollar) were recently put together by Nelson Hunt Barker, who bought the last one—for his "once in time" assembly of all nine—for $900,000. He had bought the other eight from another collector two years earlier. Some Greek coins rival Greek sculpture in their handsome relief and are priced accordingly when they come to market. To appreciate such artistic accomplishment the collector should visit a museum such as the American Numismatic Society in New York City, notable for its collection of ancient coints.

Foreign Coins

Although fascinating foreign coins have been produced for centuries since the fall of Rome and its Byzantine outposts, the collector today is best off concentrating on coins minted in the last 400 years. Most U.S. collectors, when they venture into foreign coins, choose Canada or Mexico as their target because both countries are accessible and have issued attractive coins for many years. Other favorites are French and British coins, or German states before the unification of Germany. Other collectors buy directly from the mints of third-world countries with the intention of buying brilliant uncirculated examples of every variation of a new country's vintage.

U.S. Coins

In 1652 the first coins were minted in the U.S. for use by citizens of England who lived in the American colonies. Bostonians, kept short of currency by the British Crown, took advantage of the period of the Commonwealth (when Oliver Cromwell ruled and the Crown temporarily lost its coinage monopoly). Thus the first crude coins were minted illegally; they were silver-clad wafers with NE for New England on one side and a Roman numeral designating value on the other. As the minting continued, always using the year 1652 regardless of the actual year of issue, the coins became smaller with a willow tree, an oak and, finally, a pine tree to make them distinctive. When the Crown was restored in 1660 it quickly shut down this colonial mint, but not before the mint had distributed many examples of its pine-tree coinage, some of which are still available to collectors at a cost of several hundred dollars per coin depending on condition.

Cut off from coining their own, the colonists faced the scarcity of English currency by using foreign currency widely—Dutch ducats, French ecus and Spanish dollars. These currencies had a value in silver or gold content approximately equal to their denomination and hence were readily accepted by merchants as legal tender. The Spanish dollar was so widely used, in fact, that it was legal tender into the 19th century, 60 years after the birth of the United States and the establishment of a U.S. mint. Because of its great acceptance, the U.S. founding fathers decided to base the new U.S. mintage on the dollar and the decimal system just being instituted by the French after their Revolution. The Mint Act of 1792 established a national currency.

Since then the coinage has pretty well followed the same pattern: ten cents to the dime, ten dimes to the dollar, with copper half-cents and cents, silver half-dimes, dimes, quarters, half-dollars and dollars and gold quarter-eagles ($2.50), half-eagles ($5), eagles ($10) and double-eagles ($20). Half-cents were discounted after 1857; silver half-dimes ended in 1873; and the nickel five-cent piece (manufactured of copper and nickel) first appeared in 1866. After 1933 the U.S. mints did not issue gold coins but have recently offered a medal containing an ounce of gold to compete with gold coins issued by foreign countries.

The designs were fairly uniform through the 19th and the early 20th centuries. Liberty, standing, sitting, or simply as a head, ruled one side of the coin and a wreath suggesting peace and the denomination appeared on the other. Beginning in 1909 portraits of past presidents began to appear in the place of Liberty with variants, too, on the reverse, such as the Lincoln Memorial on the cent and Monticello on the nickel. Of course, all of these motifs were redesigned from time to time and the fact that several mints throughout the country manufactured coins makes a fascinating situation for collectors. With the exception of the Philadelphia mint, all the others stamped their coins with an initial: D for Denver, S for San Francisco, O for New Orleans, C for Charlotte, North Carolina, CC for Carson City, Nevada, and D for a mint in Dahlonega, Georgia, that was active only between 1838 and 1861. Thus for each year, for each coin, you have varying amounts put into circulation by each mint.

Where To Find Coins—The Market

You can find U.S. coins anywhere collectors congregate. Coins are a mature collectible with well-organized groups of collectors, price guides, regular auctions and specialized dealers. The market represents trading of $3 to $4 billion worth of coins each year. The yellow pages of telephone directories usually list established coin dealers in a city.

A recent sale, in four parts, of the John Work Garrett collection netted the owner, Johns Hopkins University, many millions of dollars and a single coin, the Brasher doubloon (a gold piece handstruck in 1797) itself brought more than $800,000.

You can also find worthwhile examples at street fairs and flea markets. But at those sources, you had better have a firm grip on pricing; you will not be able to come back the next day and claim you could have bought the same coin, same year, same condition, at substantially less from a long-established dealer. Also, you have less protection from counterfeit currency, which has increased rapidly with the value of coins.

For the beginning collector, pennies and nickels are still affordable and there is a great quantity of all of these except the most rare items, which a collector can save for the last when the added value of a complete collection may justify the extra expense.

Museums Notable for Their Money Collections
  American Numismatic Society, New York, NY 10032
  Brooklyn Museum, Brooklyn, NY 11238
  Buffalo Museum of Science, Buffalo, NY 14211
  Federal Reserve Bank, Philadelphia, 19106
  Metropolitan Museum of Art, New York, NY 10028
  The American Numismatic Association, Colorado Springs, CO 80901
  National Bank of Detroit Money Museum, Detroit, 48207
  Newark Museum, Newark, 07104
  Smithsonian Institution, Museum of History and Technology, Washington, DC 20560

Clubs and Organizations
  American Numismatic Association, P.O. Box 2366, Colorado Springs, CO 80901

American Numismatic Society, 617 West 155th Street, New York, NY 10032

Canadian Numismatic Association, P.O. Box 226, Barrie, Ontario, Canada L4M 4T2

Magazines and Newsletters

Canadian Numismatic Journal, Canadian Numismatic Association, Barrie, Ontario, Canada L4M 4T2

Coin Prices, Krause Publications, Inc., Iola, WI 54945

Coin World, Amos Press, Inc., Sydney, OH 45365

COINage, Behn-Miller Publishers, Inc., Encino, CA 91316

Coins Magazine, Krause Publications, Inc., Iola, WI 54945

Hobbies, Lightner Publishing Co., Chicago, IL 60605

Numismatic Literature, American Numismatic Society, New York, NY 10032

Numismatic News, Krause Publications, Inc., Iola, WI 54945

The Numismatist, American Numismatic Association, Colorado Springs, CO 80901

World Coin News, Krause Publications, Inc., Iola, WI 54945

Books Worthwhile for Collectors

Bowers, Q. Davis, *Collecting Rare Coins for Profit,* Harper & Row, New York, 1975

Carson, R. A. G., *Coins: Ancient, Medieval and Modern,* Hutchinson & Company Ltd., 1962

Chamberlain, C. C., *The World of Coins,* Hodder & Stoughton Ltd., 1976

Clain-Stefanelli, Elvira and Vladimir, *The Beauty and Lore of Coins, Currency and Medals,* Riverwood Publishers Ltd., 1974

Coffin, Joseph, *The Complete Book of Coin Collection,* Coward, McCann & Geoghegan, New York, 1973

Doty, Richard G., *Coins of the World,* Bantam Books, New York, 1976

Grierson, Phillip, *Numismatics,* Oxford University Press, 1975

Krause, Chester L, and Mishler, Clifford, *Standard Catalog of World Coins,* Krause Publications, 1980

Yeoman, R.S., *A Guide Book of United States Coins,* Western Publishing Co., New York, 1980

————, *A Catalog of Modern World Coins,* Western Publishing Co., New York, 1978

Zimmerman, Walter J., *The Coin Collector's Fact Book,* Arco Publishing Co., New York, 1974

COMIC BOOKS

Comic books appeared in the 1930's in the United States and were a natural outgrowth of the popularity of the comic strip, which dates back to 1893 with the birth of the Yellow Kid in the *New York World*. The mother of the Yellow Kid was satire; the father was the deft pen of Richard Outcault, an illustrator/cartoonist for the *New York World*. Political and satirical cartoons, of course, have a much longer history.

Catoonists such as Outcault and Rudolf Dirks, father of the Katzenjammer Kids, gave continuity to characters and often, as in the case of Chester Gould with Dick Tracy, gave them the effect of a serial; the hero—Captain Easy, Terry of pirate fame or L'il Abner—faced challenges as perilous as those of Pauline! And you had to buy the next issue of the paper to find out what happened next.

Whether your favorite strip was Superman, Barnaby or Mickey Mouse, the pulp versions of the strip—the comic book—and in some cases the original art such as Al Capp's originals of Li'l Abner or cels from the movies made of Disney's characters, are highly collectible.

If you were of that once-in-a-culture's generation that doted on the comics in the print media, before TV, and before the onslaught of sleazy, weirdo and nearly pornographic strips appeared, you probably have great nostalgia for the medium as well as rewards if you collected it. The comics are assuredly not for everyone as collectibles, though they are assured of a firm position in U.S. cultural history (Classic Comics, for example, featured stories by the world's greatest authors) as something distinctly brash, lovable, romantic, educational, wry and, yes, comical and touching often at the very core of American humor. Whoever cannot laugh at the antics of Blondie and Dagwood (or could not laugh at Jiggs and Maggie of *Bringing up Father*) cannot bear to look in the mirror and admit the foibles of self.

Ironically enough, these put-down visions of ourselves now bring high prices at auctions and through bargaining among fans. A complete set of *Captain Marvel*, issued between 1939 and 1949, now goes at $5,000. It sold at newstand prices for 10 cents a copy. At newstand prices that would mean $12 for the full decade of issues. Not many collectibles have gone up in value 500 times during the 30 years.

But, of course, not all comic book series are as sought after as *Captain Marvel*. Needless to say, the lowly comic book has not yet made much of a mark in the swanky auction houses. But some of the cartoonists have. Originals by Al Capp for Li'l Abner sold at Sotheby's recently for $2,500 and Disney cels of Snow White or Mickey Mouse have gone as high as $1,500.

Where To Find Comic Books— The Market

You will get the greatest financial profit from comic books by collecting toward an entire series of books such as *Superman,* or collecting a character, such as Donald Duck, or in relatively rare cases, by collecting the original works of certain cartoonists such as Disney or Capp whose talent as artists and cartoonists have emerged on the market to the point where single originals have value. You will find these collectible items at art stores, and at occasional auctions of "American illustrators." Be sure what you are buying. Is it an original or a print in a very limited edition (as in the case of authenticated Disney cels)? Look for the artist's signature of authentication of some sort. Incidental strips or books found in your attic, however classic they may be (Maggie with her rolling pin has become American folklore; or, for example, the Al Capp strips on Sadie Hawkins Day), do not have much value by themselves. They might someday—do not discard them, use them for trading. But aim for a complete series. There is an active swap market in comic books at club meetings and at conventions. You can identify these gatherings by participating in fan clubs. In some cities you can find an old book shop or back-issue magazine shop that carries comic books as a specialty. The proprietor can fill you in about local resources and activities.

Museums Notable for Their Collections of Comic Books
  Cartoon Museum, Orlando, FL 32807
  Museum of Cartoon Art, Port Chester, 10573
  San Francisco Academy of Comic Art, San Francisco, CA 94116

Clubs and Organizations
  Classic Collectors Club, 1930 West Warwick Lane, Roselle, IL 60172

Books Worthwhile for Collectors
Blackbeard, Bill, and Williams, Martin, eds., *The Smithsonian Collection of Newspaper Comics,* The Smithsonian Institution Press, Washington, and Harry N. Abrams, New York, 1978

Horn, Maurice, ed., *The World Encyclopedia of Comics,* Chelsea House Publishers, New York, 1975

Lesser, Robert, *A Celebration of Comic Art and Memorabilia,* Hawthorn Books, New York, 1975

Overstreet, Robert M., *The Comic Book Price Guide, 1978–1979,* Crown Publishers, New York, 1978

Waugh, Coulton, *The Comics,* Luna Press, 1974

CURRIER & IVES PRINTS

Currier and Ives advertised themselves as publishers of cheap and popular pictures. They had a good thing going for them. Nathaniel Currier and James M. Ives soon became the largest lithographic company in the United States during the last part of the 19th century.

Both were horse-racing fanciers and not a few of their prints celebrated leading racers of the day. There are enough in volume and variety, in fact, to enable collectors today to specialize only in horse-racing prints.

Other categories and subjects were country views, comic situations, disasters, trains, panoramic vistas, hunting groups, yacht races, prize fighters, family groups and scenes showing American craftsmen at work. In sheer quantity the company turned out about 10 million prints on about 10,000 subjects.

There were other lithographers who produced similar works, such as Endicott & Company (good for steamboats), Henry R. Robinson, Nagel & Weingarten, and Major & Knapp, but they were not as popular among collectors then, nor are they now, as Currier & Ives.

The company flourished from about 1852 when Currier took his brother-in-law, Ives, as partner, until about 1907 when the children of the founders called it quits.

Pictures by well-known and lesser artists sold for from 20 cents to $6, depending on size and the fame of the artist. Today some of the rare prints, in good condition, can bring $8,000 to $10,000 at auction.

An offshoot of the print series was the trade card that retail and wholesale merchants bought in quantity as promotion giveaways. These were usually small "card" versions of the most popular prints and bore the name of the advertiser as well as identification with Currier & Ives. There are more than 100 known varieties of these. They often can be bought at bargain prices because they are a little-known variation of the main body of work.

The authentic Currier & Ives works were printed from a flat stone that ran through a press; the printer applied by hand damp paper sheets, one at a time. This left a black-and-white impression that artists then "filled in" with water color on a sort of assembly line for the small prints. For the larger prints, a single artist would do all colors as a batch of prints in his own studio and then return the finished product and pick up a newly printed group of black and whites.

The handmade nature of these "damp," shrinkable prints accounts for variants today in size and helps to identify old and authentic Currier & Ives prints in contrast to new reproductions made by the photo-offset process now. The popularity of the prints offered a motive for printers to print and sell reproductions. Unfortunately sometimes these are represented as originals and priced accordingly. The intended fakes usually give themselves away by their modern paper, while is generally whiter and brighter than the stock paper used by Currier & Ives in the last century.

Authentic modern reproductions are also run off in quantity in the form of calendars and decorative posters. Modern photo-offset methods apply all colors mechanically and can be identified by the dots (visible through a magnifying glass) that are characteristic of all photo-offset reproductions.

Where To Find Currier & Ives Prints— The Market

These prints are a staple collectible and have been for years. They thus come up for auction in the best houses for prices of hundreds, often thousands, of dollars, depending on their subject's rarity and the condition of the individual print. You can do better in price by knowing what you are looking for and then discovering examples at country auctions, local rummage sales and the like. It is best to settle on a subject of interest and then try for good examples of all the prints Currier & Ives did of your chosen subject.

Museums Notable for Their Collections of Currier & Ives Prints
  Boston Public Library, Boston, MA 02117
  Library of Congress, Washington, DC 20540
  Museum of the City of New York, Harry T. Peters Collection,
    New York, NY 10029
  Museum of Fine Arts, Boston, MA 02115
  New York Public Library, New York, 10018
  Philadelphia Museum of Art, Philadelphia, PA 19101

Clubs and Organizations
  American Historical Print Collectors Society, Inc., P. O. Box 962,
    Westbury, NY 11590

Magazines and Newsletters
Print Collector's Newsletter, New York, NY 10021

Books Worthwhile for Collectors
> Conningham, Frederic A., *Currier & Ives Prints: An Illustrated Checklist*, Crown Publishers, New York, 1970
>
> Conningham, Frederic A., *Currier & Ives, 19th Century Printmakers to the American People*, Heritage Plantation of Sandwich, 1973
>
> Digrosser, Carl, and Gaehde, Christa, *A Guide to the Collecting and Care of Original Prints*, Crown Publishers, New York, 1973

CUT GLASS

The U.S. Centennial Exposition of 1876 in Philadelphia generated interest in many collectibles, but probably one of its most lasting effects was the popularization of cut glass.

Forty-three U.S. glass companies exhibited at the Philadelphia fair; less than ten showed cut glass but it was this minority whose wares generated the fad that ran until about World War I. After that time manufacturing methods cheapened the artistry and killed the craze for giving cut glass for wedding and other assorted anniversaries.

Collectors today favor cut glass made in the United States but also accept the European counterparts that helped to generate the trend in the first place, but which do not have as avid fans in the countries of manufacture as they do in the United States.

The type of glass most attractive to collectors today is the "brilliant" style that sparkles grandly when deep cut, polished and suitably lighted.

Glass manufacturers deep cut a special "soft" glass containing red lead as a basic ingredient and then polished the cut on a wooden wheel with pumice or jeweler's rouge. After 1900 the makers sped up the process by dipping the piece in acid. As this practice spread, the quality and brilliance of the cut declined and so did the industry as it pushed shoddier pieces.

In the heyday of cut glass, makers produced versions of almost anything that had household use or could be used as decoration in the home. The spectacular 17-foot fountain of cut glass at the Philadelphia Centennial Exposition simply highlighted what cut glass artisans could accomplish when given the challenge.

Today the rarity of special pieces, such as lamps, clocks, loving cups, baskets, decanters and custom pieces for anniversaries or trophies bring the highest values.

The condition of the piece is more important than the motif. As with many glass pieces, chips, scratches and broken protuberances can be cut or ground off or reground to present the purchaser with a more perfect piece. Multipart pieces, such as decanter and stopper or decanter and glasses, can be mismatched—all parts are there to please the buyer but this assemblage does not please the serious collector with his eye on a good piece that can increase in value at the maximum rate.

Motifs in cut glass vary in popularity and price. Some are relatively rare. You will have to consult *American Brilliant Cut Glass* by Bill and Louise Boggess to bring yourself up to date on the availability and identification of the various motifs.

American companies that marked their glass were M. J. Averbeck of New York City; J. D. Bergen company of Meriden, Connecticut; T. B. Clark & Company of Honesdale, Pennsylvania; T. G. Hawkes & Company of Corning, New York; J. Hoare & Company of Corning, New York; the Libbey Glass Company of Toledo, Ohio; H. P. Sinclaire & Company of Corning, New York; and the Tuthill Cut Glass Company of Middletown, New York. One important and prolific company that *did not* generally mark its productions was C. Dorflinger & Sons of White Mills, Pennsylvania.

Collectors also seek 19th-century cut glass from such European manufacturers as Val Saint Lambert of Belgium; Harrachov and Riedel of Bohemia; Stevens & Williams, Thomas Webb & Sons of England; and Baccarat and Saint Louis of France. From Vienna came the glass of J. & L. Lobmeyr and a number of Irish firms produced cut glass now known as Waterford.

Some of the most visually attractive glass was in color (such as cranberry or amber) or with a clear base and a color overlay. The craftsman then cut through the color selectively to reveal the clear sparkling base.

In view of the wide variety of collectible cut glass, you should spend some time studying an authoritative book on makers and motifs and you should try to master the appearance of the different types by viewing them in museums with notable collections of cut glass.

Where To Find Cut Glass—The Market

Cut glass has been a highly popular collectible for more than 100 years. As such, and because of its intrinsic quality as an artifact, it regularly appears at the very best auction houses. Other sources are specialist dealers and, of course, its appearance from time to time at attic and garage sales, where a few pieces may be disposed of by a family whose ancestors bought it when new. Prices for odd pieces, such as a lamp, may run to several thousands of dollars. One lamp in the Plymouth motif, for example, originally sold for a respectable $300 when new in 1905. Now, according to one dealer, it could cost ten or twelve times that amount, with price levels rising annually.

Museums Notable for Their Collections of Cut Glass
  Chrysler Museum of Norfolk, Norfolk, VA 23510
  Corning Museum of Glass, Corning, NY 14830
  Historical Society of Western Pennsylvania, Pittsburgh, PA 15213
  Lightner Museum, St. Augustine, FL 32084
  Metropolitan Museum of Art, New York, NY 10028
  Philadelphia Museum of Art, Philadelphia, PA 19101
  Toledo Museum of Art, Toledo, OH 45697

Clubs and Organizations
  National Early American Glass Club, 55 Cliff Road, Wellesley Hills, MA 02181

Books Worthwhile for Collectors
  Boggess, Bill and Louise, *American Brilliant Cut Glass*, Crown Publishers, New York, 1977
  Daniel, Dorothy, *Cut and Engraved Glass, 1771–1905*, William Morrow & Co., New York, 1967
  Elville, E. M., *English and Irish Cut Glass*, Country Life Limited, 1953
  Evers, Jo, *The Standard Cut Glass Value Guide*, Collector Books, 1975
  Polak, Ada, *Glass, Its Tradition and Its Makers*, G. P. Putnam's Sons, New York, 1975
  Revi, Albert C., *American Cut and Engraved Glass*, Thomas Nelson, Camden, N.J., 1970
  Schroeder, Bill, *Collector's Illustrated Price Guide—Cut Glass*, Collectors Books, 1977
  Warren, Phelps, *Irish Glass*, Charles Scribner's Sons, New York, 1970
  Wales, Gustav, *Books of Glass*, Praeger Publishers, New York, 1971
  Wiener, Herbert, and Lipkowitz, Freda, *Rarities in American Cut Glass*, Collectors House of Books Publishing Co., 1975

DECOYS

The carving of decoys, principally ducks, geese and other waterfowl, is a distinctly American folk art. It was, in fact, originated by North American Indians, who were avid hunters and skilled at luring birds within range of their weapons.

Today decoys attract collectors more often than they do water- and shore fowl. But they are still made, mostly by anonymous carvers, although there are "name" craftsmen who sign or brand their products and bestow on them greater value among collectors.

Decoys, because of their Indian origin, have been used in the United States for centuries, but those made after the mid-19th century are the ones most prized by collectors. There is some correlation with quantity and necessity. During the latter half of the 19th century there was more extensive hunting of ducks and geese than there was in the years before or after. Today the best carvers of decoys are as likely to sell directly to collectors or to dealers as they are to hunters. There are two reasons for this: One is that the price of the specially carved and painted decoys is too high for hunters to actually use them. And the second is that duck and goose meat can be more successfully grown and marketed via specialized farms. There simply is not the mass taste for wild duck and goose, even though the species flourish up and down the major migratory flyways of North America. And commercial sport hunting has been severely regulated following the extinction of some species.

With the decline in volume of hunting, many creators of decoys turned to making more elaborate birds simply as ornaments and sculpture, some of remarkable realism and artistic presence.

This trend has supported the popularity of decoys made as late as the 1940's and 1950's and, in fact, some carvers still at work today have a ready market for their products. Such names as Charles "Shang" Weaver of Connecticut, Lem and Seve Ward of Maryland, Elmer Crowell of Cape Cod, Mark Whipple of Louisiana and Luigi Andreuceotti of California come to mind.

Problems enter the collection picture when it comes to positive indentification. Crowell, of the above artists, stamps his name on the base of his work. The others must be identified by characteristics of the painting, the "pose" of the bird. The Wards, for example, often carved ducks with heads turned to one side. Or it could be the manner of construction. The Wheeler decoys are hollow and carry weights as ballast so that they can swim at the right level.

Collectors usually specialize by maker, by bird or by species associated with the Mississippi, Atlantic, Pacific Coast and Central flyways (between the Rockies and the Mississippi) where most North American birds migrate. Or they may specialize by bird species, such as Canadian geese or mallards in as many styles and sizes as possible. They do not emphazise dates because decoys, particularly those that have actually been used in hunting, endured varying degrees of wear; they are difficult to date if you are not personally familiar with their history. Used decoys were often repaired, new parts added to old. Since collectors have taken up decoys, the practice of restoration has continued.

Decoys also can be categorized by basic types, the *floaters,* usually ducks and geese, and the *stick-ups,* mostly of shore birds and made full-sized and mounted on a stick to hold them upright in sand or marsh.

Where To Find Decoys—The Market

You can find decoys most easily in the areas where hunters used or may still use them. Factory-made decoys, popular before controls were placed on commercial hunting went into effect in 1920, were made by the Harvey A. Stevenson Company of Weedsport, New York. Stevenson decoys had the company name stenciled or burned into the bottom of its products. There were firms in Detroit,

Michigan: the Mason Decoy Factory and the Jasper N. Dodge Company. You can find remnants of their products throughout duck country but particularly close to home base.

Of course, decoys, because of their great popularity, show up regularly at flea markets, attic sales and even collectors' carousels of the major auction houses. Some beautiful decoys in excellent painted condition can easily bring $3,000 to $4,000, but most, rather banged-up specimens, bring less thatn $100 still and make a good beginner's collectible.

Collectors usually leave existing paint jobs alone. Hunters did not, of course, and some heavily used decoys may have been painted periodically, even every year, to help in their preservation and effectiveness as a lure. Sometimes the age of a decoy can be determined partly by its many coats of paint.

Condition and artistic beauty have a great influence on value. A good, identified specimen from one of the famous carvers is worth more, of course, than a tired specimen from the hand of an anonymous whittler.

The best way to get into the field is to train your eye by

Rare Dowitcher in Spring Plumage *This decoy was made by John Dilley of Quoque, Long Island. It weighs one ounce, is painted brown and tan with a red-tinged breast, and is generally in excellent condition. It was sold by William Doyle Galleries to a collector in Louisiana for $13,000—a record price for any U.S. decoy. (Photo: courtesy of William Doyle Galleries.)*

observing good and identifiable decoys in a museum and then give that developing eye some exercise by letting it run loose among dealers. Finally you will be able to search in the open market with a trained skill and to spot bargains that emerge from attics and pop up at flea markets. Prices at well-established auctions are usually what decoys can achieve at any particular time—there is a market for them active enough on that level to establish general prices. A record was set recently at $13,000 for a dowitcher, a rare shore bird, in exceptionally good condition. Most decoys at auction and elsewhere sell for a few hundred dollars.

Museums with Notable Collections of Decoys
  Cleveland Museum of Natural History, Cleveland, OH 44106
  Museum of American Folk Art, New York, NY 10019
  Shelburne Museum, Shelburne, VT 05482

Clubs and Organizations
  Long Island Decoy Collectors Association, 92 Helme Avenue, Miller Place, NY 11764
  Midwest Decoy Collectors Association, 1400 South 58th Street, Lincoln, NB 68506

Magazines and Newsletters
  Decoy Collector's Guide, edited by Harold D. Sorenson, 312 Franklin Street, Burlington, IA 52601
  Decoy World, edited by M. Clark Reed, Jr., 115 South Main Street, Trappe, MD 21613
  North American Decoys, edited by Bryan Cheever, P.O. Box 246, Spanish Fork, UT 84660

Books Worthwhile for Collectors
  Barber, Joe, *Wild Fowl Decoys,* Dover Publication, New York, 1954
  Bellrose, Frank, *Ducks, Geese and Swans of North America,* Stockpole Books, 1976
  Burk, Bruce, *Game Bird Carving,* Winchester Press, New York, 1972
  Earnest, Adele, *The Art of the Decoy: American Bird Carving,* Bramhall House, 1965
  Elman, Robert, *The Atlantic Flyway,* Winchester Press, New York, 1972
  Johnsgard, Paul A., *The Bird Decoy,* University of Nebraska Press, Lincoln, Nebr., 1976

Mackey, William J., Jr., *American Bird Decoys*, E. P. Dutton & Co., New York, 1965

Richardson, R. H., *Chesapeake Bay Decoys*, E. P. Dutton & Co. New York, 1965

Rue, Leonard Lee, III, *Game Birds of North America*, Harper & Row, New York, 1973

Starr, George Ross, Jr., *Decoys of the Atlantic Flyway*, Winchester Press, New York, 1974

Webster, David S., and Koho, William, *Decoys at Shelburne Museum*, Hobby House, 1961

DEPRESSION GLASS

You used to get what is called now Depression Glass free at the movies, one night a week—dish night at the local Bijou. If you were a movie fan and went regularly each week, you could acquire whole place settings; if you were only a sometime fan, you could complete your settings at the local five-and-ten for several cents a piece, or less than $2.00 for a place setting.

Like Fiesta Ware in ceramics, the cheerful colors and relatively simple, pleasing shapes plus the cheapness and usefulness of the object made them fun to buy and use and to collect today.

But today you talk about quite a few dollars *per piece* of Depression Glass in good condition. During the late 1970's almost any piece could be bought for less than $20. Yet today, special pieces in good condition could approach $1,000.

Actually some pieces of Depression Glass are still free—if you find them in your own attic or cellar where you or perhaps your parents packed them away when better times arrived and brought with them more expensive trends in home furnishing and decorating. Now they are out of place in use on the table but make a colorful display in collector's cabinets.

Look for bowls, pitchers, plates, measuring cups, teacups, saucers, sugar-and-creamers, salt and pepper shakers and domed butter dishes and gradually amass a set of sorts that you can then purify and upgrade to splendid specimens in the same color and in mint condition.

Depression Glass is not fine glass. The deep colors often obscure many flaws, bubbles and grit that come along with the piece. These pieces were machine-molded of cheap materials during the 1920's, 1930's and 1940's, but have become so popular today as collectibles that a few firms, not necessarily the original manufacturers, have revived the use of old molds or reproductions of them.

Companies originally manufacturing this glass were the Federal Glass Company of Columbus, Ohio; the Hazel Atlas Glass Company of Clarksville, West Virginia; the Hocking Glass Company of Lancaster, Ohio; the Indiana Glass Company of Dunkirk, Indiana; the Jeanette Glass Company of Jeanette, Pennsylvania; and the Macbeth-Evant Glass Company of Charleroi, Pennsylvania.

Some collectors try for whole sets in all colors (more than 25) from several manufacturers. Others stress complete sets of patterns, of which there are more than 95. Colors can be translucent, transparent or opaque, and there exist quantities of clear glass or "crystal."

Pattern, color, utility and rarity depending on pieces known to have been produced and apparently available affect current value.

Especially desirable patterns among collectors today are ultramarine Swirl, blue Royal Lace, amethyst Newport, Cherry Blossom, irridescent Iris, Florentine II, Mayfair, Cameo, Adam, Dogwood, Sarom and the very popular American Sweetheart pattern in several colors. To visualize these and others of the more than 80 remaining patterns, you need to refer to one of the profusely illustrated books listed at the end of this chapter.

Where To Find Depression Glass— The Market

Depression Glass makes a wonderful collectible because so many of the pieces are colorful, make a good display, are sturdy and can be bought still for a few dollars per piece. This is a growing market. Call it nostalgia for "hard times" or affection for a period when U.S. families were cruelly tested financially and made do with ingenious innovation. In this case, the glassware was practical, colorful and shapely at the same time.

This collectible also offers a challenge: You may discover some of the rare pieces or patterns that may bring premium prices. The market of Depression Glass is now one that is fully aware of itself. You are not likely to find bargains at the minor auctions where pieces crop up. It is a good collectible to buy indiscriminately because the prices are low and you can trade up to better pieces as you cull out duplicates or inferior specimens. That means sloughing them off or bartering them to less experienced collectors for either money or a rare piece you do not yet have.

The interest in Depression Glass is so lively these days that some commercial contemporary glass companies have brought out new pressings from the old molds or imitations of old patterns. These upstart pieces, of course, have their own utility but are worth considerably less as a collectible than the original series. You will have to school yourself in the difference by looking carefully at quantities of the real thing in well-known collections. The best Depression Glass has not yet made it with museums; you will have to seek out one of the many well-known collectors' clubs.

Clubs and Organizations

Central Jersey Depression Glass Club, 301 Maxson Avenue, Point Pleasant, NJ 08742

Del-Mar-Va Club, 7420 Westlake Terrace, Bethesda, MD 20034

Depression Glass Grabbers of Historic Charleston, Route 6, Box 529H, Summerville, SC 29483

Depression Glass of Northeast Florida, 1745 Flagler Avenue, Apt. 1, Jacksonville, FL 32297

Heart of America Glass Collectors, 721 Cambridge Drive, Lee's Summit, MO 64063

International Depression Glass Club, 2737 Wissemann Drive, Sacramento, CA 95826

Long Island Depression Glass Society Ltd., P.O. Box 119, West Sayville, NY 11796

Peach State Depression Glass Club, 4964 Bartow Street, Acworth, GA 30101

20-30-40 Society Chicagoland, 811 West Berkely Drive, Arlington Heights, IL 60004

Magazines and Newsletters

Depression Glass Daze, P.O. Box 57, Otisville, MI 48463

National Depression Glass Journal, P.O. Box 268, Billings, MO 65610

Books Worthwhile for Collectors

Florence, Gene, *The Collector's Encyclopedia of Depression Glass*, 3rd ed., Collector's Books, 1977

Klamkin, Marian, *The Collector's Guide to Depression Glass*, Hawthorn Books, New York, 1973

Weatherman, Hazel Marie, *Colored Glassware of the Depression Era*, 2 vols., Glassbooks, Inc., 1974–1978

DETECTIVE FICTION

Mysteries, crime stories, call the group what you will —collected stories of the great detectives can pay off so much better than the crimes depicted—and in honest money for the devoted collector. The detective story in the Western world was a child of the 19th century even though there is an earlier tradition that goes back centuries. Today, old and new examples of detective fiction are collected avidly but the older examples and the rarer editions bring higher prices. With the exception of occasional magazines that carried individual stories of collectibles authors (Edgar Allan Poe's first appearance was in a magazine), most detective fiction is in the form of books and behaves, as a collectible, like books.

The fictional detective becomes a more vivid character than most characters in other kinds of books. To the collector of detective fiction, the late Sherlock Holmes, with his cocaine habit, keen mind, violin playing, manias, wit and English class connections, was perhaps the most fascinating person in history. Hercule Poirot and Miss Marple, created by Dame Agatha Christie, the late queen of crime, have also entered that wonderful world where fiction becomes more real than fact. Not only do the characters spring alive from the words but movie after movie, seen again on television, give an image and an imaginative environment where these heroes and heroines excercise their wit and stalk their quarries as though unaware that millions dote on their every doing.

Mystery writers in the United States award their "Edgar" statuettes to contemporary craftsmen. The award is named after (and looks like, with moustache and all) Edgar Allan Poe, regarded as the father of the mode in detective story. Oddly enough, his M. Dupin, who appeared in the earliest stories, does not live today as does Sherlock Holmes, although it might truly be said that M. Dupin taught the great Holmes everything he knew about ratiocination and inductive reasoning. M. Dupin was introduced in 1845 when Poe published his short stories, *The Murder in the Rue Morgue* and *The Mystery of Marie Roget*, in magazine format.

Wilkie Collins introduced his sergeant Cuff in the *Moonstone* in 1868. A first edition of Poe's tales sells now for well over $10,000 and the *Moonstone* for over $5,000; early adventures of Sherlock Holmes wherever they appear command prices well over $10,000.

The general rules of book collecting apply to this spectacular specialty. For top value, books should be first editions, first impressions, in prime condition, with dust jacket (if there was one originally and there usually was, after the turn of the century, on books published in the United States).

Among the authors who have produced collectible detective fiction are Ellery Queen, John P. Marquand, Mickey Spillane, Erle Stanley Gardner, Dashiell Hammett, James M. Cain, John Dickson Carr, Raymond Chandler, Cornell Woolrich, Graham Greene, Josephine Tey, Agatha Christie, Dorothy Sayers, Rex Stout, John Creasay, Ross MacDonald, Margaret Miller, Ruth Rendell, Ngaio Marsh and P. D. James.

In most cases a first edition of an author's first venture into the field—the book in which he introduces a new sleuth—attracts the highest price of any of that author's works. Some of these, with dates of introduction are:

Author	Sleuth	Book Title	Year Introduced
S.S. Van Dyne	Philo Vance	*Benson Murder Case*	1926
John P. Marquand	Mr. Moto	*No Hero*	1935
Rex Stout	Nero Wolfe	*Fer-de-Lance*	1934
Erle Stanley Gardner	Perry Mason	*Case of the Velvet Claws*	1933
Ellery Queen	Ellery Queen	*Roman Hat Mystery*	1929
Earl Derr Biggers	Charlie Chan	*House Without a Key*	1925
Dorothy L. Sayers	Lord Peter Wimsey	*Whose Body?*	1925
Agatha Christie	Hercule Poirot	*Mysterious Affair at Styles*	1920
Dashiell Hammett	Sam Spade	*Maltese Falcon*	1930

Where to Find Detective Fiction—
The Market

This category of literature has been popular recreational reading since it was created for Western readers in the middle of the 19th century. Know your detective, author and significant dates and then prowl local sales, thrift shops, benefit sales, estate clearance sales, even the top book auctions. Your chances of still finding bargains are good at local sources, but are not good at specialized, rare-edition dealers and leading book auctions where the values are known and/or the supply has been picked over by collectors like yourself.

Where dealers have many miscellaneous books, you have a better chance. For some reason detective fiction, and for that matter "old books," are often lumped into boxes at local sales and clearances. You can buy an items box for a small flat fee. Much of what you get may be next to worthless, but now and then you can spot treasures worth collecting and other titles at least worth reading.

Many long-time readers of detective fiction are addicts as readers rather than collectors. Some *may* save the book for reading a second time. Most simply let the mysteries they have read pile up and may welcome an offer of purchase simply to clear out some shelves or a corner in the attic. They make a habit of reading a new mystery as soon as it comes out (first edition, first impression) but give little consideration to the value of the book as an eventual collectible. Ask any senior citizen who avidly reads mysteries whether he or she has saved earlier volumes and whether you might help clean up the attic.

Libraries with Notable Collections of Detective Fiction
Humanities Research Center, University of Texas, Austin, TX 78712
Lilly Library, Indiana University, Bloomington, IN 47401
Occidental College Library, Occidental College, Los Angeles, CA 90041

Books Worthwhile for Collectors
Barzun, Jacques, and Taylor, Wendell Hertig, *A Catalogue of Crime*, Harper & Row, New York, 1971
Penzler, Otto, ed., *The Great Detectives*, Little, Brown and Co., Boston, 1978
————, *The Private Lives of Private Eyes, Spies, Crimefighters, and Other Good Guys*, Grosset & Dunlap, New York, 1977
Steinbrunner, Chris, and Penzler, Otto, *Encyclopedia of Mystery and Detection*, McGraw-Hill Book Co., New York, 1976
Symons, Julian, *Mortal Consequences*, Schocken Books, New York, 1973
Winn, Dilys, *Murder Inc.*, Workman Publishing Co., New York, 1977

DOLLS

Perhaps you have a Shirley Temple "character" doll, perhaps a Madame Alexander doll with several changes of carefully sewn couturier frocks. Both make a good beginning for a collection of dolls. If you do not have a doll from your childhood but are attracted to dolls as a collectible, choose the elegant top of the doll population. You might become a collector, for instance, of pre-19th-century dolls, or Indian kachina dolls, or Raggedy Ann and Andy dolls. Then there is the Golden Age of dolls during the 19th century through the early 1900's. Also there are Kewpie dolls of the 1920's and 1930's, Barbie and Ken dolls from the 1950's; modifications are still coming off the line of persistent and creative manufactureres.

Jointed terra cotta dolls were playmates for children as long ago as the 6th century B.C. and it is probable that crudely shaped bits of wood, stone or molded clay served as dolls among the most primitive of people. For there is a primitive mystique about dolls as alter egos of the persons they resemble. They can act as avatars or substitute beings; they can be simple companions for a child who enjoys manipulating them and talking with them as a friend, or as a mother to a child. Dolls, after a certain age, varying with different cultures, seem to be the special province of girls or women. A boy can be interested in conventional dolls and teddy bears until about the age of 6 or 7; then he has to be weaned away or he will possibly collect and play with Buck Rogers and Lone Ranger effigies. John Noble, director of the Museum of the City of New York, is a noteworthy exception of that silly taboo. He is an authority and an avid collector of dolls. It is not surprising, therefore, that his museum has one of the world's better doll collections.

The majority of great doll collectors, nonetheless, are usually women such as the Coleman sisters, Evelyn, Jane, and Elizabeth Ann, of Washington, D.C., aided in their collection by their mother, Dorothy Coleman. Much doll literature has been produced by women; the Colemans are among these published authorities. Incidentally, most dolls are feminine in face and body though sexual characteristics, except in primitive images and in such contemporary realistic Barbie and Ken dolls (or even Gay Bob dolls), were suppressed and even the exceptions seem discrete compared with primitive sculpture.

Where To Find Dolls—The Market

In the Golden Age of doll-making, the 19th and early 20th centuries, there were a number of doll manufacturers who made their mark as artisans and whose dolls are considered highly collectible today. These dolls sometimes bring prices of $6,000 to $8,000 at auction and these prices could be exceeded in the near future if certain fine specimens should reach the market.

Golden Age dolls, from about 1880 to 1920, bring the highest values, particularly those from Germany and France. The U.S. product really never became significant until about the time of World War I. Today, of course, the popular Ken and Barbie dolls, plus celebrity dolls of movie stars such as Shirley Temple, are moving up quickly as collectibles.

Prominent firms that manufactured bisque dolls now considered highly collectible are the following, with their years of activity noted:

Bru Junior & Company, 1886–1939, Paris, France
Steiner Company, 1855–1903, Paris, France
House of Jumeau, 1843–1930, Paris, France
Société Française de Fabrication de Bébés et Jouets, 1899–1930, Paris
Kestner, 1804–1930, Waltershausen, Germany
Kammer & Reinhardt, 1886–1930 (doll bodies), Waltershausen, Germany
Simon & Halbig, 1870–1930 (doll heads), Koppelsdorf, Germany
Armand Marseille, 1865–1928, Koppelsdorf, Germany
Brothers Heubach, 1820–1930, Lichte, Germany

These manufacturers had a fairly sophisticated system for marking and dating their products. Fine specimens of such dolls can bring over $10,000 but many others, less fine and distinctive in dress or artistry of face, may sell for less than $100 at auctions, and even less if they appear at flea markets and fairs.

Once in a great while a doll will appear at a bazaar or rummage sale and the seller may not know the real value. It *you* do, you may find a bargain. At dealers who speacialize in dolls, such as Richard Withington, Inc., of Hillsboro, New Hampshire, the dolls will have price tags corresponding to current market values, for the doll market is a mature market with going prices well established. Of course, when you buy through reputable dealers and the major auction houses (who stand by their identifications) you can buy with greater confidence that your purchase is authentic as repre-

Petite Parisienne Sitting Pretty   *This doll—marked Daisy Paige, San Francisco—has a bisque head and shoulders. She was styled in a Parisienne manner. The doll has stationary blue eyes and a blonde wig; her head swivels and her joints can be moved. The trunk contains three dresses, hats, a pinafore, a blouse, undergarments, a fan, parasol, comb, brush, mirror and a picnic basket. She recently brought $3,000 at Christie's because she was in such fine condition and had such a carefully made wardrobe and accessories, also in fine condition. (Photo: courtesy of Christie's.)*

sented, that parts have not been substituted, clothes remade, and other alterations and restorations carried out that make the specimen less than authentic and possibly a clever fake. Museum visits and reading up on the category of doll you want to collect will develop your skill as a shrewd buyer and collector.

Museums Notable for Their Collections of Dolls
   Eliza Cruce Hall Doll Museum, Ardmore, OK 73401

Margaret Woodbury Strong Museum, Rochester, NY 14445
Mary Merritt's Doll Museum, Douglassville, PA 19518
Museum of the American Indian, New York, NY 10032
Museum of the City of New York, New York, NY 10029
Raggedy Ann Antique Doll and Toy Museum, Flemington, NY 08822
Santa Barbara Museum of Art, Santa Barbara, CA 93101
Smithsonian Institution, Washington DC 20560
Washington Doll's House and Toy Museum, Washington, DC 20015
Wenham Historical Association and Museum, Inc., Wenham, MA 01984
Yesteryears Museum, Sandwich, MA 02563

Magazines and Newsletters
The Doll Reader, Hobby House Press, Riverdale, MD 20840
Doll Talk, Kimport Dolls, Box 495, Independence, MO 64051

Books Worthwhile for Collectors
Angione, Genevieve, and Whorton, Judith, *All Dolls Are Collectible*, Crown Publishers, New York, 1977
Coleman, Dorothy, Elizabeth A., and Evelyn J., *Collector's Encyclopedia of Dolls*, Crown Publishers, New York, 1976
Colton, Harold S., *Hopi Kachina Dolls*, University of New Mexico Press, Albuquerque, N. Mex., 1977
Foulke, Jan, *2nd Blue Book of Dolls and Values*, Hobby House Press, Washington, DC, 1976
Revi, A. Christian, ed., *Pinning Wheel's Complete Book of Dolls*, Galahad Books, 1975

EGGS

The egg, "the perfect package," makes a perfect collectible. It has a pleasant shape, is relatively small and (if not a natural specimen but an imitation in stone, metal or plastic) has sturdiness and requires little care. Best of all, decorative eggs have a following, a market, are often very beautiful and make a good display.

If you collect eggs today you join a venerable tradition going back to at least the 7th century B.C. Burial sites from that date in Italy and Greece have revealed eggs of various kinds.

You may collect decorated (blown) Easter eggs, even the fabulous Easter eggs made by Peter Carl Faberge which are now mostly in museums or in the hands of wealthy collectors. Imperial Russian Easter eggs were created by Faberge between the years 1884 and 1916. Several of these precious eggs are in the Forbes collection, which can be seen on the premises of *Forbes Magazine* at 80 Fifth Avenue, New York City.

The price range of collectible eggs may start at pennies for darning eggs of wood and grow in cost for the delicately small ivory eggs for darning the fingers of gloves. Or they may fetch astronomical prices (such as the Faberge specimens) because they are of precious metals—gold and silver—studded with diamonds, rubies, sapphires and other precious stones.

Natural eggs, as a beginning collectible, are not really worthwhile in the United States because the collection of wild-bird eggs is restricted by federal regulations. And the rules apply to trading in natural eggs obtained outside the United States or obtained previous to the enactment of the regulation. The best place for disposing of natural eggs you may have inherited is a museum with a developed ornithological department. The curator will recognize the enhanced value of your eggs and will accept them or know a museum that will; thus you can take a legitimate tax deduction and relieve yourself of the worry over perishable collectibles that you cannot buy or sell legally.

Where To Find Eggs—The Market

Eggs of various materials pop up at all manner of fairs, flea markets, garage sales and auctions and with dealers. Some dealers have a special section for eggs, particularly stores that deal in mineral specimens. Ask such a dealer for his egg-shaped specimens. Faberge eggs and eggs of similar art value will, of course, appear at the most prestigious auction houses where their prices can easily exceed $40,000. Specimens of minerals in the shape of an egg may be purchased for as little as a dollar or two but when they are perfectly polished can bring $50 or more, depending on the value of the material from which the egg is made.

Museums Notable for Their Collections of Eggs
Egg Museum, Effort, PA 18330, and in Palm Beach, FL 33480 (winter quarters)
Forbes Magazine Collection, New York, NY 10011
Virginia Museum of Fine Arts, Richmond, VA 23221

Clubs and Organizations
Egg Art Guild, 1174 Glenwood Dale, Cape St. Claire, MD 21408

Magazines and Newsletters
Sunnyside Special, The Gold Egg, Inc., P.O. Box 59, Millersville, MD 21108

Books Worthwhile for Collectors
Disney, Rosemary, *The Splendid Art of Decorating Eggs*, Hearthside Press, Great Neck, N.Y., 1972
Newall, Venetia, *An Egg at Easter: A Folk Lore Study*, Indiana University Press, Bloomington, Ind., 1971

FANS

Among the elegant customs lost to contemporary Western civilization is the art of the fan. In certain cultures, the hand that wielded the fan ruled the country and the fan developed a gesture language of its own. It became a prop for the most elegant social occasions and a useful tool for coquetry as well as a mute way to express pleasure or displeasure; it was even a silent way to signal men to approach or hold back.

As social signals and as time-honored cooling devices, and because of their unusual beauty, fans have become a popular collectors' item with clubs, a newsletter and a bibliography all its own.

As part of a lady's attire, the fan had a certain usefulness to cool and soothe decorously. As such, it was used personally by women and via slaves or servants for men for centuries. Before air conditioning, who cannot remember an uncle or an aunt sitting on the front porch, sipping afternoon lemonade on a hot summer's day, fanning himself or herself with a bamboo or reed fan?

But collectors of fans seek more exotic items. Fan collecting was encouraged by a costume ball during the reign of the French king, Charles X, during the early part of the 19th century. The Duchess de Berry, in charge of the costumed quadrille, decided she needed period fans to go with the 18th-century costumes. She remembered a collection owned by a Parisian perfume manufacturer, Vanier by name, and arranged for fans from that collection to be worn at the ball. So taken were the court ladies by the languid elegance of those fans from an earlier century that they bought the collection piecemeal on the spot and began to order copies. Fan makers of the day entered a profitable era of faking fans from a century earlier, and many of these fans are in collectors' hands today.

Fans perhaps reached their highest degree of artistry in manufacture and their greatest integration into etiquette and social usage in the Orient. There are enough Japanese and Chinese fans extant for each catogory to provide a specialized field for any collector.

In fan manufacture there are essentially two types of fans—rigid and folding. Inexpensive forms, often with advertising printed on the leaf, are the familiar type—a round or oval cardboard attached to a stick for holding with much the shape and construction of a ping-pong paddle.

But for collectors of high–fashion fans, the folding form with individual wooden, ivory, mother-of-pearl, metal or plastic sticks to form a handle are the favorites. The stick is either glued onto or inserted into the "mount" or "leaf" of printed paper, cloth or vellum made from kidskin. This could be hand painted, lithographed, even gilded to offer an interesting or colorful scene as a lady moved her fan back and forth. It could—and usually did—become a conversation piece at social occasions.

Another type of high-fashion fan is known as *brisé,* from the French word meaning broken, split, cracked. It has no folding paper or fabric mount. Its sticks, plain or elaborately painted, spread out to form a semicircle and the ends of the sticks are held together with a colorful tape that limits their opening motion. As a result, the sticks overlap slightly and this forms the flat surface that moves the air gently. When you "fan" a hand of playing cards you are in effect creating a simple brisé fan (but with no tapes to limit its opening).

Not all popular 19th-century fans were fake reproductions of popular designs from centuries earlier. From Spain and China came authentic contemporary fans. In Spain the bullfight and its colors were popular for fan decoration and the sticks were likely to be of ivory or tortoiseshell. Ivory was also extensively used in Chinese fans.

Individual artists such as the Frenchman Pierre Jules Jolivet often signed these painted mounts and a house such as Martin or Duvellroy in Paris produced fans including Art Nouveau designs from the turn of the 20th century and Art Deco styles in the 1920's and 1930's. Duvellroy, among others, also manufactured ostrich feather fans with tortoiseshell sticks.

Where To Find Fans—The Market

Markets and auctions of fans have flourished in the United States. They are to be found as part of the rising craze for antique clothes, and also appear alone. In London, regular auctions are held and individual fans have brought recent prices of about $250 for an imported painted Chinese fan from about the year 1850.

Museums with Extensive Fan Collections
  Colonial Williamsburg, Williamsburg, VA 23185
  Museum of Fine Arts, Boston, MA 02115
  Shelburne Museum, Shelburne, VT 05482
  The Victoria and Albert Museum, London S.W. 7, England

Clubs
  East Bay Fan Guild, P.O. Box 1054, El Cerrito, CA 94530
  Fan Circle, 24 Asmuns Hill, Hampstead Gardens Suburb, London N.W. 11 6ET, England

Books Worthwhile for Collectors
  Armstrong, Nancy, *A Collector's History of Fans*, Clarkson N. Potter, New York, 1974
  de Vere Green, Bertha, *A Collector's Guide to Fans over the Ages*, Frederick Muller, New York, 1975
  Flory, M. A., *A Book About Fans*, Macmillan and Co., 1895
  Percival, MacIver, *The Fan Book*, Frederick A. Stokes Co., New York, 1921
  Rhead, George Woolliscroft, *History of the Fan*, K. Paul, Trench, Trubner & Co., Ltd., London, 1910

FIESTA WARE

If you have a Fiesta ware cup with handle intact and a matching saucer, treasure them as a rare collectible. They may be worth $15 though purchased at the five and dime in the 1930's for maybe only 25 cents.

The Homer Laughlin China Company of Newell, West Virginia, gave U.S. collectors a humble but highly popular collectible. Fiesta was an everyday dinnerware launched in the latter 1930's and produced as late as the early 1970's. Its revived popularity as a collectible may cause the company to bring out new versions, appropriately dated, of course, so as not to upset the supply of the "vintage" Fiesta pieces.

The line was introduced in 1936 in brilliant, cheerful colors and in a modernistic design at a time when Depression Glass and other depressingly cheap goods flooded the market. Fiesta ware was inexpensive, too, but was so bright and attractive that during the 1940's, 2,500 workers at the factory produced about 30 million pieces a year. They created a large supply—always chippable and breakable and therefore constantly diminishing in first-class specimens.

For beginning collectors, this is a dream situation. You can still get a representative set of every shape and color produced. And you are likely to find whole sets or substantial portions of whole sets at garage sales and flea markets, even in your own attic. From then on it is a matter of filling gaps and trading up the various items until you own fine specimens of every shape and size.

Few families that grew up in the 1930's and 1940's *do not* have memories of Wheaties spooned from an ivory Fiesta bowl or milk poured from a Fiesta pitcher with its cunningly shaped and mostly dripless spout with the oval lips.

And who does not remember the temporary tragedy when one of these bright beauties crashed to the kitchen floor while one cleared the table or washed the dishes?

Most Prized Pieces

Plates, saucers and bowls survive in abundance. In general pieces with handles or lids (often lost and/or chipped) are more scarce and thus more valuable. Colors that tend toward scarcity are gray, rose or chartreuse. This may vary by type and piece because equal quantities were not made in each color of each shape or piece. Fiesta red, so vibrant and attractive, was produced as a color in every shape (but not equal quantities for each shape) from the beginning in 1936 until 1973 when Homer Laughlin discontinued the line. During World War II and the years that followed with the development of the atom bomb, 1943–1959, however, red was discontinued to conserve uranium oxide, the mineral used to produce a red glaze. After 1959, the Fiesta red resumed production using "depleted" oxide, denuded of the atoms that made it useful to nuclear reactors. (At no time was this ingredient considered a health threat and it is not dangerous to collectors today.)

Colors can help distinguish the years of production. In 1936 the beginning colors were red, dark blue, yellow, light green and ivory. In 1937 came turquoise. In 1951 the light green, blue and ivory had been discontinued and the "Fiesta 50" took over: forest green, rose, chartreuse and gray. Medium green was added in 1959.

To distinguish real Fiesta ware from look-alikes (there are many of these), look for the concentric rings, six of them, on the rim of each plate or piece. Most pieces, plates and bowls, have a bull's-eye at the center when it is appropriate to the whole design. Almost all pieces made before 1969 carry the trademark of the manufacturer, HLC USA, in one form or another and the word "fiesta" in lower-case script.

Where To Find Fiesta Ware—The Market

You will find Fiesta ware in local garage sales and flea markets; perhaps a revival version will turn up in your dime store. It seldom appears at auction although whole sets of it may soon do so, particularly if they are in fine condition. Price inflation is phenomenal. Pieces that went for a fraction of a dollar when new might cost $5, $10, even $15 today. Fiesta ware has not yet made it to museums but undoubtedly someday it will, because it is a fine example of good design inexpensively produced in great quantity for the masses of people and purchased avidly by them.

Magazines and Newsletters
  Depression Glass Daze, edited by Nora Koch, P.O. Box 57, Otisville, MI 48463
  The Glaze, edited by Jo Cunningham, P.O. Box 4929 GS, Springfield MO 65804

Books Worthwhile for Collectors
  Huxford, Sharon and Bo, *The Collector's Encyclopedia of Fiesta, with Harlequin and Riviera,* Collector Books, 1976

FOLK ART

American folk art can be worth a fortune—the recent sale of the Garbisch Collection (the late Colonel Edgar William and Bernice Chrysler Garbisch) proved that point to the joy of all such collectors.

Despite the high prices on the best items, however, folk art is still a worthwhile collectible for beginners. The large supply is still out there—18th- and 19th-century examples coming out of attics and appearing at estate sales and being sold simply when collectors want to prune their holdings.

When the folk artist took paintbrush in hand, he or she produced "primitive" paintings that were not considered worth collecting at all until the early 20th century. Then Picasso began to adapt, deliberately, the primitive strength of African sculpture to his own style. And folk art came into its own as other contemporary artists followed his admiration.

A quality of the true primitive painter is untutored charm. A folk painter lacks perspective and easiness of the mastered line, anatomical proportions, and even an ability to paint a portrait that resembles the sitter (one painter specialized in portraits but painted almost all ladies' faces alike; this painter gave sitters different dresses and different postures and thus a certain individuality not seen in each face).

Folk art is often anonymous but a number of painters imitated the professionals by signing their names to the canvases once they had finished them. Such painters are Grandma Moses and early 19th-century painters such as a man and wife known as S. A. and R. W. Shute and Edward Hicks, whose *Peaceable Kingdom* variations now bring prices of thousands of dollars at auction.

Other forms of popular folk art include Spencerian (or calligraphic) script drawing by pen; mourning watercolors that serve to memorialize a famous person or a dear friend or relative; whittled and pottery figures; and many crafts and skills such as quilts, pottery and wooden utensils and figures, the handiwork of unsung artisans.

Frakturs form another classification of folk art. These were imitations of illuminated manuscripts based on a German typeface called Fraktur. They were done at first in this country by German immigrants to celebrate a family event such as birth, baptism and marriage. Today they are most often discovered in old German family bibles where they are usually interleaved with the family records for safekeeping.

Where to Find Folk Art—The Market

The most prized folk art now appears at the most prestigious auction sales. But if you know what you are looking for, you can make some actual discoveries of underpriced examples. If you have small pieces or photoreproductions of them, you can inquire in small towns where you might see something interesting in a local museum or public building, or even a venerable dry goods store. Knowledgeable locals will tell you where the home craftspeople were or are.

You can find folk art, too, at local fairs and at attic sales; simply ask where the pieces came from and get back to the source that way.

At recent auctions, a calligraphic lion was sold for $550, a Fraktur birth and christening certificate brought $500, a 19th-century naive portrait of a child of the Taylor family brought $26,000, a theorem (guided instructions) from an anonymous artist in New England brought $4,500, a watercolor of the Battle of New Orleans brought $6,750.

Museums Notable for Their Collections of Folk Art
   Abby Aldrich Rockefeller Folk Art Collection, Williamsburg, VA 23185
   Greenfield Village and Henry Ford Museum, Dearborn, MI 48121
   Museum of American Folk Art, New York, NY 10019
   Museum of International Folk Art, Santa Fe, NM 87501
   Old Sturbridge Village, Sturbridge, MA 01566
   Philadelphia Museum of Art, Philadelphia, PA 19101
   Shelburne Museum, Shelburne, VT 05482

Magazines and Newsletters
   The Clarion-America's Folk Art Magazine, Museum of American Folk Art, New York, NY 10019

Books Worthwhile for Collectors
   Ames, Kenneth L., *Beyond Necessity: Art in the Folk Tradition,* Winterthur Museum, 1977
   Bishop, Robert, *American Folk Sculpture,* E. P. Dutton & Co., New York, 1974
   Black, Mary and Lipman, Jean, *American Folk Painting,* Clarkson N. Potter, New York, 1966
   ————and————, *Folk Art in America: A Living Tradition,* The High Museum of Art, Atlanta, 1974

Hemphill, Herbert W., Jr., ed., *Folk Sculpture USA*, Brooklyn Museum, Brooklyn, 1976

——and Weissman, Julia, *Twentieth-century American Folk Art and Artists*, E. P. Dutton & Co., New York, 1974

Hornung, Clarence P., *Treasury of American Design*, 2 vols., Harry N. Abrams, New York, 1972

Lipman, Jean, *American Folk Art in Wood, Metal and Stone*, Dover Publications, New York, 1972

——, *American Primitive Painting*, Dover Publications, New York, 1969

——and Winchester, Alice, *The Flowering of American Folk Art; 1776–1876*, Viking Press, New York, 1974

Shelley, Donald A., *The Fraktur-Writings or Illuminated Manuscripts of the Pennsylvania Germans*, Pennsylvania German Folklore Society, 1961

FOUNTAIN PENS

Fountain pens are enjoying a renaissance as writing tools and as valuable collectibles.

Lewis Edson Waterman invented the modern fountain pen in the 1880's after he lost a customer for an insurance policy because the pen used for signing the contract flooded ink all over it; by the time a new policy had been written the customer had signed with a rival—or so the story goes! At any rate, Waterman found a way for a pen to carry its own supply of ink and to release it in a regular, controllable stream for writing. Waterman cut lengthwise fissures into the channel that carried ink from the container section of the pen to the nib. The fissures regulated the flow of ink by controlling the passage of air into the container to replace the ink.

The early mass-produced pens of Waterman are highly valued by collectors. Waterman soon had competitors and the most collectible of these are pens from the Parker Pen Company, the Conklin Pen Company and the W. A. Sheaffer Pen Company, all in the United States; the Mont Blanc Company of Germany; the Mable Todd & Dard Company of England; and the Wahl Company of the United States, a firm that got into the collectible pen business by first making mechanical pencils. Pencils of the mechanical kind are often collected with pens because they were sold as sets.

The various companies competed with one another to bring out refinements and attractive decorations. One of the most famous early pens was the Waterman #20, which sold in the early 1900's for an unusually high price of $10.25. Recent sales of this model in good condition have been for more than $450. The Parker Pen Company is perhaps best known for its Duofold Big Red, which has been recently selling at the $500 level. The German Mont Blanc Company made a specialty of using precious metals for its pens—gold, silver and platinum. These metals, naturally, increase the value of collectible pens. Most pen makers also participated in the Art Deco and other succeeding modernistic art movements; some manufacturers had elegant precious metal filigree around the usual hard rubber barrel. These pens can be purchased today for several hundred dollars depending on the quality of artistry and the condition.

Fountain pens *do not have to work* but they bring a premium among collectors if they *do* because many collectors enjoy using them and even perfect their penmanship and become addicted to a personalized color of ink as they progress in their hobby-investment.

Another category of fountain pens partakes in history—a pen used for an important occasion or owned by a famous person. For example, the pen King Edward VIII used to sign his abdication was recently sold in London for about $5,000. President Lyndon B. Johnson made a great gesture in giving to interested parties several pens he deliberately used in signing important legislative measures. Writers, too, have often cultivated idiosyncratic, even sensual relationships with their pens, pencils, even their typewriters. The love Virginia Woolf, for instance, had for her pens and her searches for the perfect model have been described in her biography by her nephew Quentin Bell and in her diary edited by Quentin's wife, Anne Olivier Bell.

Where To Find Fountain Pens— The Market

Collectible fountain pens can still be found in attics, particularly in drawers of old desks or tables, or perhaps among a collection of old letters or in purses and similar relics of the past. They will turn up at estate sales, flea markets, garage sales and street fairs. But bring some ink along and perhaps some paper when you expect to find one for sale, so you can determine whether you can write with it to your satisfaction. Prized pens do turn out at auctions but not often

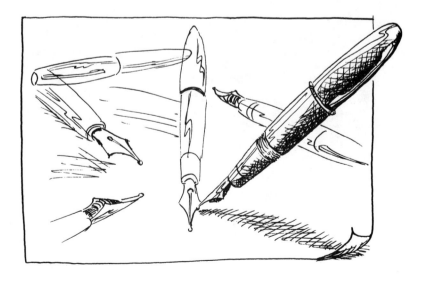

enough to give an accurate idea of going prices. Perhaps the best market for collectors is the one set forth in the monthly newsletter published by the Pen Fancier's Club (see below). In the newsletter, pens are often described and priced for mail-order purchase.

Clubs and Organizations
   The Pen Fancier's Club, 1169 Overcash Drive, Dunedin, FL 33528

Books Worthwhile for Collectors
   Lawrence, Cliff, *Fountain pens, History, Repairs and Current Values*, Collector Books, 1977
   Whalley, Joyce Irene, *Writing Implements and Accessories*, Gale Research Company, Detroit, 1975

FURNITURE

From 18th-century French ormolu-trimmed desks and cabinets (going at auction at a record $1.7 million for a single Louis XV cabinet by Dubois) to a simpler but elegantly-crafted Goddard-Townsend (U.S. 18th century) knee-hole desk selling at a record $250,000, the values achieved by fine furniture from selected craftsmen have continued to amaze collectors and dealers. Furniture is one of the most profitable of collectible categories, but the capital required can be considerable for fine items.

To wealthy U.S. collectors, French, English and U.S. furnitures of all periods have been favorites, although English and U.S. furniture has (until recently) lagged behind their French counterpart. Before the stock market crash of 1929, U.S. 18th-century furniture made by native craftsmen in the style of Chippendale, Hepplewhite and Sheraton enjoyed a small boom which quickly faded—until recent years, when interest revived. Collectors who had favored French furniture (parallel to the dominant interest in French art) found that their fine pieces of English and U.S. furniture had been neglected and were available at relatively lower prices. Prized pieces of U.S. furniture have tripled over the past ten years and will probably continue on an upward path.

As collectors and museums squirrel away the limited amount of prized 18th-century pieces, there is growing interest in more commercial pieces still available in larger quantities. In the U.S. this could mean furniture by Belter and Stickly, a whole swarm of mass-produced Victorian furniture, or typical Grand Rapids 20th-Century Plain, as well as more contemporary models from immigrant designers such as Saarinen or Breuer. In French furniture, this could mean Art Nouveau pieces by Majorelle or Galle. In Germany it could mean Hoffman and others; in England (Scotland, really) it could mean MacIntosh. All of these designers produced highly fashioned furniture in quantity for an affluent top-of-the-mass market. In not too long a time, most furniture manufacturers will undoubtedly sign or otherwise identify their products just as potters, utensil makers and other household-ware manufacturers capitalize on the growing fad—even rage—among U.S. families to spend money on good designs and high style for their homes, condominiums or apartments. These items are not only practical and useful, they are beautiful—and, as collectibles, valuable as well. If well chosen and maintained, furniture items do not depreciate in

Masterpiece from Massachusetts   *This mahogany bombé secretary/book-case in the Chippendale style might have brought more than the $100,000 it recently achieved at an auction at the William Doyle Galleries if it could have been attributed to a well-known cabinetmaker. As it is, this very rare Massachusetts piece (in fine condition) brought the fourth high-est price ever achieved at auction (as of November 1980) by an American-made piece of furniture. (Photo: courtesy of William Doyle Galleries.)*

value; they appreciate to become heirlooms—possibly the basis for funding one's retirement. They will eventually qualify as good collateral for loans, just as the basic U.S. single-family home has served as prime collateral for decades.

Where To Find Furniture—The Market

Market prices for very fine furniture have advanced so rapidly in the past several years that individual pieces have now broken the $1 million barrier at international auctions. At the Akram Ojyeh sale in Monaco in 1979, a ten-foot-tall Louis XV ormolu-mounted marquetry corner cabinet by Jacques Dubois was purchased by the J. Paul Getty Museum for $1.7 million. A Louis XVI ormolu-mounted marquetry commode by J.F. Leleu went for $983, 640 in the same sale. The Getty purchase far surpassed the highest previous record for a piece of French furniture ($585,500) and signaled a temporary topping out of the French furniture market which has led all other national and period furniture. Art Nouveau, Deco and Moderne furniture has recently enjoyed a run-up, and the excitement has been shared by many "name" pieces. Probably the best buy for beginning collectors is U.S.-manufactured furniture of the 19th and 20th centuries in first-class condition. You will buy best if you buy for looks and utility after brushing up on what is available and the going prices and trends.

You *can* find worthwhile pieces at estate sales, flea markets and garage sales. Collectible mass-produced furniture often goes unnoticed among other more nondescript pieces. If you can spot the prizes among the run-of-the-mill, they can often be yours at nondescript prices.

Museums Notable for Their Collections of Furniture
  The Metropolitan Museum of Art, New York, NY 10028
  J. Paul Getty Museum, Malibu, CA 90265
  Smithsonian Institution, Washington, DC 20560
  Greenfield Village and Henry Ford Museum, Dearborn, MI 48121
  The Brooklyn Museum, Brooklyn, NY 11238
  Henry Francis Du Pont Winterthur Museum, Winterthur, DE
    19735

Books Worthwhile for Collectors
  Grotz, George, *The New Antiques: Knowing and Buying Victorian Furniture*, Doubleday & Co, 1970

A Folk Art Craze   *Home craftsmen took to the hand and power-driven jigsaw during the latter part of the 19th century and early part of the 20th century, paralleling a similar hobby enthusiasm in France and England. This ungainly homemade étagère was expected to fetch between $500 and $700 but actually achieved only $300. It is limited in aesthetic appeal and design but was characteristic of jigsaw art, which grew very popular in the U.S. after demonstrations were given at the Philadelphia Centennial Exposition in 1876. (Photo: courtesy of Christie's.)*

Otto, Celia Jackson, *American Furniture of the Nineteenth Century*, The Viking Press, 1965

Because of the many worthwhile books on furniture, the collector will do well to go to a public library and simply browse in the fine and decorative arts section.

JAPANESE PRINTS

One of the minor (at first) benefits of the "opening" of Japanese international trade by Commodore Perry in 1853 was the discovery by Westerners of Japanese wood-block prints. According to a legend among collectors, the art's charm and value was first recognized by a Western printer who had acquired some of the block-printed paper used in packing Japanese export porcelain.

Wood-block prints had been a popular form of illustration and advertising for the merchant class of Japan that had been forbidden for two centuries to trade with the West.

Once the wood-block prints were discovered, they soon delighted such prominent French artists as Degas, Monet and the American expatriate James McNeil Whistler. These artists were early collectors of Japanese prints and showed the influence of the prints in some of their paintings. Their enthusiasm bestowed popularity and artistic recognition to the obscure Japanese artists who created the original prints.

Even with censorship for two centuries under a succession of shoguns, Ukiyo-e prints, translated as "pictures of a floating world," flourished. In variant forms they leave a graphic record of the interest and entertainments of the Japanese businessman from the 17th century onward. They began as illustrations of books that celebrated local people, popular actors, warrior heroes and courtesans who set the fashion. As advertisements, they even publicized the better brothels. (Brothels and the Kabuki theatre were probably two of the most popular amusements of the merchant class.) Seascapes, landscapes and other scenes also become popular and one of the most sought-after sets of prints, by Hiroshige, depicts the 53 way stations on the road between Tokyo and Kyoto.

From the very start the prints were published in great quantity and were thrown away as handbills are thrown away today. Still, hundreds of thousands remain available. Most of them are in the hands of U.S. collectors but a certain national pride has made them popular and sought after by the Japanese, who are some of the most avid customers of U.S. dealers and bidders for them at U.S. auctions.

Even 20th-century prints reproduced by machine have their collectors, but the most prized prints remain printed from wood blocks, mostly cherry wood, with a different block for every color applied. For the common black-and-white prints, of course, only one block was needed. The rarest prints are the early ones by such masters as Harunobu, Kiyonage and Utamaro, known for their portraits of women; Sharaku, famous for his portraits of actors; and Hokusai and Hiroshige, renowned for their landscapes. Prints in fine condition from these masters can easily exceed $100,000 in value but other of less quality or by lesser artists can go for as little as a few hundred dollars.

A confusing factor for print collectors is that reproductions have been made of famous old prints, both through the mechanical photoengraving process and through reproduction by the old woodblock technique. When the latter technique is used and sometimes passed off as an old print, you will have to rely on the apparent age of the paper to tell which is which.

Most of the artists, ancient and modern, identified their prints by plainly printed labels that gave the artist's name, the publisher and the government censor who had approved the publishing; often the special embossing of a collector's mark appears in one corner. When a print bears the seal of a noted collector, that very fact can raise the value of the print.

Many of the prints were creased down the middle so that they would fit into a book or portfolio and the creasing lessens the value; also staining or fading of the image on the paper, or an unusual amount of trimming of frayed margins, can reduce value.

Where To Find Japanese Prints— The Market

The place to find collectible prints in the United States today is through dealers who handle both old and new contemporary prints and their variations. Even Japanese collectors come to the United States to find the best specimens still available. You will not likely find many prints at local sales; you will find them at estate auctions and international auctions, as a special feature of a print sale, and often in a special sale arranged for Japanese print collectors. Recent prices at auction ranged from $150 to $63,000 (for a Harunobu of a young woman holding a lamp in the night).

Museums Notable for Their Collections of Japanese Prints
   The Art Institute of Chicago, Chicago, IL 60603
   Freer Gallery of Art, Washington, DC 20560
   Honolulu Academy of Arts, Honolulu, HI 96814
   Metropolitan Museum of Art, New York, NY 10028
   Museum of Fine Arts, Boston, MA 02115
   Philadelphia Museum of Art, Philadelphia, PA 19101

Clubs and Organizations
  Japan Group, 1818 Market Street, 33 Floor, Philadelphia, PA 19103
  Ukio-E Society of America, Inc., 1692 Second Avenue, New York, NY 10028

Books Worthwhile for Collectors
  Binyon, Laurence, and Sexton, J. J. O'Brien, *Japanese Color Prints*, Faber & Faber Limited, Salem, New Hampshire, 1960
  Narazaki, Muneshige, and Mitchell, C. H., *The Japanese Print: Its Evolution and Essence*, Kodansha International, New York, 1966

JAZZ RECORDS

Call it Dixieland, traditional or New Orleans jazz, blues, boogie-woogie, ragtime, swing, bop, bebop, or progressive, cool or free jazz (but not rock and its cousins), the recordings of these varying sounds make a reasonable, inexpensive and worthwhile collectible for beginners who love this sort of music.

The sound or beat itself is hard to define. Fats Waller, a great jazz piano performer—or was it Louis Armstrong, the jazz trumpeter; the anecdote is attributed to both—once told a lady who asked "What is jazz?" "Lady, if you gotta ask, you ain't got it."

Jazz has had floating centers for live performance: New Orleans, where it probably first started; New York, where it has flourished for decades; and Chicago, where it had great popularity in the 1930's. In addition, it is being excellently perpetuated in Europe and Australia.

It was first treated as a legitimate musical form by Europeans, particularly by French composers such as Satie and Poulenc, who borrowed its syncopated rhythms and habit of improvisation by leading instrumentalists for their serious music composed during the years right after World War II.

Down Beat, a U.S. magazine devoted to the sound, first came out in 1934, and since the mid-1930's jazz has enjoyed a continuing popularity in the United States and abroad. Most recently, as varieties of rock music have become more a matter of circus antics and costumes rather than skill in improvisation and composing, the big band sound of the 1930's and the World War II years has come back—to the delight of jazz record collectors.

The first jazz record was recorded in 1917, when the Original Dixieland Jass [sic] Band recorded the Darktown Strutter's Ball for Columbia.

Some of the early records are rare, a very few, and rarities can sometimes reach a value of several thousand dollars, but most jazz records still cost only a few dollars.

The controversy over what combos and bands produced the best jazz and who were the best instrumentalists and vocalists will probably go on indefinitely—just as it does with opera recordings; however, jazz is fortunate in that the greats *were* recorded with a fairly advanced technology that contemporary companies can improve further without too much difficulty as they reissue old records. Yet there *is* a difference between new and old issues in value.

The old ones that sound "good" have a higher value. For it is the "sound" that collectors want; there is only limited value in the record itself. (However, there are many "label" collectors who will pay dearly for the original recordings, be they 78 r.p.m. or long-playing.) In fact, the deep-down fan probably has modern tapes made from the old jazz classics, tapes that can be played over and over without causing deterioration of the original record, which remains the collectible sound of the master.

With interest increasing, it is only a matter of time and of royalties and right payments before most of the old performances are reproduced for modern stereo equipment. Then these, in turn, will be come collectible and achieve their own value level.

Where To Find Jazz Records— The Market

Jazz had a fairly limited audience in the United States during the 1920's and 1930's. Hence the recordings, though offered to a mass market, did not achieve great sales (or production) numbers. During the late 1930's and the big band/swing era, when the sound took over popular ballroom dancing and radio shows, the numbers of popular records produced multiplied greatly. And many of the records of the swing generation went into attics as teenagers and young marrieds put them away when they left home and the rock era took over. They are coming out of attics now as collectibles with the rebirth of interest in the big band sound.

Thus records appear at most of the popular outlets, at some specialty stores but seldom at fashionable auctions, except for the most rare and expensive examples.

Museums and Libraries Notable for Their Collections of Jazz Records

Duke Ellington Collection, North Texas State University, Denton, TX 76203

Institute of Jazz Studies, Rutgers University, Newark, NJ 07102

National Ragtime/Jazz Archive, Southern Illinois University, Edwardsville, IL 60026

William Ransom Hogan Archive, Howard Tilton Memorial Library, Tulane University, New Orleans, LA 70116

Stan Kenton Collection, North Texas State University, Denton, TX 76203

Smithsonian Institution, Washington, D.C. 20560

Clubs and Organizations
International Association of Jazz Record Collectors, 90 Prince George Drive, Islington, Ontario M9B 2X8, Canada
New Orleans Jazz Club of California, P. O. Box 1225, Kerrville, TX 78028

Magazines and Newsletters
Down Beat, Maher Publications, 222 West Adams Street, Chicago, IL 60606
Jazz Magazine, Stites-Oakey, Inc., 11 Bayview Avenue, Northport, NY 11768
The Jazzologist (a novel), Box 1225, Kerrville, TX 78020
Living Blues, Living Blues Publications, 2615 North Wilton Avenue, Chicago, IL 60614
Record Research, 65 Grand Avenue, Brooklyn, NY 11205

Books Worthwhile for Collectors
Case, Brian, and Britt, Stan, *The Illustrated Encyclopedia of Jazz*, Crown Publishers, New York, 1978
Chilton, John, *Who's Who of Jazz*, Chilton Books Co., 1970
Feather, Leonard, *The Encyclopedia of Jazz*, Bonanza Books, 1960
Rust, Brian, *Jazz Records 1897–1942*, Arlington House, New Rochelle, N.Y., 1978
Schuller, Gunther, *Early Jazz*, Oxford University Press, 1968
Stearns, Marshall, W., *The Story of Jazz*, Oxford University Press, 1968
Ulanov, Barry, *A History of Jazz in America*, Da Capo Press, New York, 1972

JEWELRY

Collectors of jewelry have a variety of periods and categories of value to choose from. Not all jewelry brings fancy prices but jewelry can also be one of the most expensive items to collect. The pain of paying for it is easier to bear if the collector genuinely *likes* to wear it as an adornment. However, with security against theft sketchy and insurance rates high, collecting jewelry is not for everyone.

Yet it is, if collected carefully a preserver of value. Jewelry usually is made of precious or semiprecious metals and stones, which give it intrinsic worth. In the case of Art Deco and Art Nouveau jewelry the material can be glass or plastic; then the value may depend more on the fame of the designer who has created an individual piece.

Collectible jewelry can be divided into several periods: Ancient jewelry with an archeological value; Georgian jewelry, produced in England from about 1714 to about 1830 in the fashion of the French 18th-century jewelry (much of it confiscated and melted down during the French Revolution); Victorian jewelry, promoted by the good Queen herself, who liked to wear opals and, later, the jet (black) that suggested her mourning for Prince Albert. (Queen Victoria also encouraged the Gothic (medieval) and Renaissance revivals.); Art Nouveau and Art Deco jewelry, from designers such as Tiffany in the U.S. and Lalique and Galle in France.

In recent times, American Indian jewelry—still being made in the Southwest of the U.S.—has provided a less expensive way to collect worthwhile artifacts. Items are made from native materials such as silver, lapis lazuli and turquoise.

Where To Find Jewelry—The Market

Because of the money involved and such intangible qualities as design and weight of precious stones or metals, jewelry probably requires the most expertise of all collectibles. You can find bargains because this challenge works both ways—specimens sometimes fall into the hands of non-specialized dealers or vendors at fairs and flea markets who do not realize what treasures they have in a mass of dross. *If you do,* you can pick up a bargain and sell it elsewhere at a profit.

But most valuable and significant jewelry (like valuable paintings and art in general) comes to market through specialized dealers, or at the best auctions featuring specific kinds of jewelry, or in the state of a prominent collector of jewelry (such as the recent sale by Christie's of Merle Oberon's jewelry). There you will find proper identification, a fair estimate of present values and a ready-made market for resale.

Museums Notable for the Collections of Jewelry
  The Metropolitan Museum of Art, New York, NY 10028
  Museum of the American Indian, Audubon Terrace, New York, NY 10032
  Smithsonian Institution, Museum of History and Technology, Washington, DC 20560
  The Walters Art Gallery, Baltimore, MD 21201

Magazines and Newsletters
  Ornament: *A Quarterly of Jewelry and Personal Adornment*, P.O. Box 24C47, Los Angeles, CA 90024

Books Worthwhile for Collectors
  Armstrong, Nancy, *Victorian Jewelry*, Macmillan Publishing Co., 1976
  Gere, Charlotte, *European and American Jewelry (1830–1914)*, Crown Publishers, 1975
  Goldemberg, Rose Leiman, *Antique Jewelry: A Practical and Passionate Guide*, Crown Publishers, 1975
  Hothem, Lar, *Collectors Identification & Value Guide: North American Indian Artifacts*, Books Americana, 1978
  Mason, Anita, *An Illustrated Dictionary of Jewelry*, Harper & Row, 1974
  Mourey, Gabriel, and Vallance, Aymer, *Art Nouveau Jewelry & Fans*, Dover Publications, 1973
  Rutland, E.H. *An Introduction to the World's Gemstones*, Doubleday, 1974

LALIQUE GLASS

Of all the master glass designers who flourished during the Art Nouveau period of the beginning of the 20th century, René Lalique is probably the most famous. Certainly his glass, which the firm of his descendants—Cristal Lalique—still manufactures today in limited quantities, has proven over the years highly collectible along with the art glass of Emile Gallé or Daum of Nancy.

It is claimed that Lalique products made before World War II (Laique died in 1945), under the master's direction, had a softness and a sensuousness that the products of the contemporary firm lack. Nonetheless both old and new pieces are collectibles. But, as often is the case with highly decorative collectibles, the older pieces bring higher prices, shape for shape.

Born in 1860, René Lalique became one of the leading designers of French jewelry by 1890. He was constantly innovating and during his middle years he immersed himself more and more in the making of glass.

In that early period, he made pieces with the "lost-wax" method of casting. Molten glass was poured or blown into a mold from an original wax or plaster sculpture or impression (much as your dentist today makes gold inlays for your teeth from wax impressions he trims and fashions to fit perfectly the drilled base). This method requires the breaking of the mold to free the finished object and makes it one of a kind. This scarcity contributes to the high prices of some Lalique glass. A green bowl, for example, with a frog motif, recently brought $23,000 at auction, a record high at the time for art glass.

Later, exploiting reusable molds, Lalique made bowls and vases that today bring $600 to $700 because of a greater supply of nearly identical pieces existing. In 1907, Lalique began a collaboration with the house of Coty, the French perfume maker, and opened the way for a flood of perfume bottles, bowls, vases, decanters, plates, paperweights, powder boxes and statuettes mass manufactured to delight the taste of an expanding and affluent market. As you might imagine, these items were popular as gifts for many occasions. Lalique also produced architecture glass and chandeliers on custom-order basis. His popularity put him in the forefront of designers as the Art Nouveau movement shaded into Art Deco in the 1930's.

Color plays a large part in the value collectors place on a piece of Lalique. Favorite colors are red, blue, green, amber and black.

Although shapes may be the same, Lalique often colored items differently. Sometimes the actual glass was of a different color. Other times it was hand-colored after molding; it could be stained, stippled or enameled.

All of these variants make a difference in value depending on beauty and scarcity and how the color, if applied, has held up. Because no Lalique these days is inexpensive or likely to be discovered at bargain prices, the collector simply has to know what he is buying if he is to avoid losing money on misrepresentation or fakery. There are imitators; some artisans imitated Lalique molds and then produced glass very difficult to differentiate from true Lalique. The situation is complicated by the fact that Cristal Lalique today sometimes issues a new version from the old molds it owns. Lalique signed almost all of his pieces "R. Lalique." The contemporary firm uses the trademark "Lalique," without the initial, except when the old molds are reused.

Where To Find Lalique—The Market

Do not count on finding bargains when collecting Lalique. You may, after you have educated your eye, find some pieces at estate auctions that may be underpriced as a result of the carelessness of executors and/or lawyers. But consider buying Lalique at the going prices at auctions or in shops specializing in Art Nouveau and Art Deco glass, for the market for Lalique has been going up and will continue to do so because so many pieces have great artistic merit and are highly decorative and appealing; collectors are scrambling after the limited supply. You might want to consider, at somewhat lower prices, the glass of such competitors as Gallé and Daum.

Start your collection, even if it will amount to only a few pieces of superb artistry, at auctions or with dealers who will stand behind the authenticity of the pieces you buy through them. Later you may find pieces elsewhere and will have educated your sensibility to know whether or not they are the real Lalique. Or you will have the common sense to show them to someone who does before you finally agree to buy. Keep your eye open for estate sales of upper middle class couples who were married in the 1920's when it was popular in the United States to give Lalique as a wedding present or as (fifteenth) Crystal Anniversary gifts.

Museums Notable for Their Collections of Lalique
  Art Institute, Chicago, IL 60603
  Calouste Gulbenkian Museum, Lisbon, Portugal

Chrysler Museum at Norfolk, Norfolk, VA 23510
Cincinnati Art Museum, Cincinnati, OH 45202
Corning Museum of Glass, Corning, NY 14830
Musée des Arts Décoratifs, Paris, France
New Orleans Museum of Art, New Orleans, LA 70179
Smithsonian Institution, Washington, DC 20560
Toledo Museum of Art, Toledo, OH 43697

Books Worthwhile for Collectors
McClinton, Katherine, *Lalique for Collectors,* Charles Scribner's
Sons, New York, 1975
Percy, Christopher Vane, *The Glass of Lalique, A Collector's
Guide,* Macmillan Publishing Co., Inc., 1978

MAJOLICA

Majolica makes an attractive collectible if you like a certain jaunty flair in design and color of relatively inexpensive earthenware. Majolica dishes, pitchers, urns and bowls are characterized by natural designs—fruits, flowers, leaves—often in garishly unnatural colors.

The name and the ware went through a variety of changes. It originates from an Italian way of saying "Majorca," an island in the Mediterranean from which Italians, during the Renaissance, first imported a colorful tin-glazed pottery. Then they began to make it themselves, and call it majolica. The French copied the Italians and called their ware faience; the Dutch did the same and called their creations delft.

But it was the English potter, Mintow and Company, known for its expensive porcelain and china, that introduced its version of majolica at the Great Exhibition in London in 1851 and began the boom in majolica. The display whetted the appetite of collectors in England, and competition from Wedgewood, George Jones and other English potters. On this side of the Atlantic, collectible potters were the Edwin Bennett Pottery Company of Baltimore, the Chesapeake Pottery Company of Baltimore, the Wannopee Pottery Company of New Milford, Connecticut, the Charles Reynolds Company of Trenton, New Jersey, Marley & Company of Needlesville, Ohio, and Griffen Smith and Hill of Phoenixville, Pennsylvania.

With collectors, English majolica has a slight edge in value because of the quality of the pieces and the English manufacturers' habit of marking almost all of the pieces they produced. American manufacturers were not as conscientious about these details. You will have to read carefully the recommended books on majolica in order to thread your way through the maze of marks and methods of dating. With majolica, you may want to start your collection by identifying a piece inherited from a Victorian grandparent and then build your collection around the production of that manufacturer. You can also collect vases or pitchers, or natural themes such as flowers or grapes and leaves.

Where To Find Majolica—The Market

You can find majolica in all the usual collectors' sources, up to the most fashionable auction houses where a single, rare piece in good condition, often called delft or American delft, can cost several thousand dollars. But prices for minor pieces in good condition are usually below $100 at auction and considerably less if you spot an odd piece at a street fair or attic sale.

The popularity of majolica as something for Victorian-style parlors, curiosity cabinets, mantelpieces and dining room sideboards assured that much majolica has been produced and bought. But its fragility has decreased the supply over the years.

When you find an unmarked piece, it is more likely to be British if it features parts of the human figure, more likely to have been made in the United States if its decorative theme features its function—icicles on an ice pitcher, an ear of corn for a corn syrup pitcher, asparagus on an asparagus dish and so on.

Since the rise of majolica in popularity as a collectible, it has become profitable to make it in the old designs and pass it off as classic Victorian pieces. Actually, they are contemporary fakes, usually marked by country of origin such as Italy, Japan and Germany. It is best to stick to marked pieces that identify the maker as a legitimate Victorian potter in the United States or in England. Later, when you know your majolica better, you will have developed confidence in your expertise in identifying unmarked pieces.

Museums Notable for Their Collections of Majolica
  Philadelphia Museum of Art, Philadelphia PA 19101

Books Worthwhile for Collectors
  Barber, Edwin Atlee, *The Pottery and Porcelain of the United States and Marks of American Potters*, Feingold & Lewis, 1976
  Rickerson, Wildey C., *Majolica: Collect It for Fun and Profit*, Pequot Press, 1972

MARBLES

For those who cannot afford or prefer not to collect paperweights or art glass, antique marbles make a good compromise. They offer the brilliant colors and sparkle of glass and are often objects of great artistry. And you can pick them up for just a few dollars each, though very rare sulphides might run as high as $400 or $500.

To make a profit in collecting marbles you have to know your marbles and keep ahead of the next collector or you may be conned into buying contemporary fakes made to imitate the authentic antique marbles, using old methods and tools. There is an increasing danger of this as the popularity of marbles swells.

Perhaps you massage a nostalgia when you collect marbles, particularly if you are a male who played marbles as a youngster. Who has not stood at a taw line and taken aim with a shooter at the circled prize some yards away? And lost or won a few marbles in the course of the game? If you want to collect marbles, examine first the contents of those old leather or cloth bags you put away when you put away childish things. Or perhaps the bag your father or grandfather put away.

Not all marbles are profitable to collect. You might as well read up on them first and then get rid of the worthless ones in the attic and get into the collectors' mainstream as soon as possible.

Almost all marbles were designed for either the ancient boy's game or for Chinese checkers and similar games that use them as playing pieces. Oddly enough, most marbles in history were not made of marble but of other, more available and workable, materials, primarily glass but also steel, porcelain, clay and semiprecious stones such as agate, onyx, rose quartz and carnelian. In the United States marbles have been made by machine since World War I and only unusual marbles or a full set of them have a value for collectors (such as marbles decorated with cartoons).

A set of marbles in their original flannel bag, for example, produced and marketed by the Arco company and sold in five-and-dime stores for 49 cents in the 1930's (according to one specimen examined with price still on the box), may retail through a marble dealer for $40. Of course, they are just glassies, not really antique marbles, but the fact that they are an entire set counts.

Most of the marbles that collectors seek most avidly were handmade and imported from Germany prior to World War I. Some were made in the United States by the Boston and Sandwich Glass Company. Some came in from countries throughout the world—but they were all handmade and some were of astonishing artistry, which gives them their primary value. Material also influences value; semiprecious stones are more valuable than clay but not always more valuable than artistic glass.

The most common old marbles are of ground stone, molded clay or crockery molded and fired. Some, called Benningtons, were of potter's clay that was glazed and fired to resemble Bennington pottery. Glass marbles, although the most common type of contemporary examples (they are, of course, still used for playing marbles as avidly today by every new generation of children), were not as prevalent as one might think before World War I. But those that were handmade were beautiful and thus are eagerly sought by collectors.

Most antique glass marbles were swirls made by rolling a clear glass rod across a grooved iron sheet containing rods of different colored glass. The colors adhered to the clear glass; the maker then covered the colors with more clear glass, reheated and twisted the rod and pulled it like taffy and then, with an instrument known as a marble scissors, cut the marbles into shape. This process leaves on each hemisphere a pontil mark that is a guarantee that the marble is handmade. They should never be polished off. Most rare of all are marbles cut from the end of a rod that have only one pontil mark. Depending on the patience and the skill of the maker, the small glass swirls can compete with those in paperweights in their color and the delicate designs buried within.

The most prized kind of marble, the sulphide, exhibits a technique also used by makers of paperweights—a small figure of lead sculpted of gypsum or clay, buried inside a clear or clear-colored glass marble. These usually were for display, not for playing. Bubbles around the figure suggest it is authentically antique and not a modern imitation where improved techniques have eliminated the bubbles.

Where To find Antique Marbles—
The Market

Even among the generations of boys who played marbles, bartering was an acceptable way of getting the beauties. The custom continues among collectors today. At fairs and at rummage sales, ask for marbles and when you are shown them, ask whether any of them are *antique marbles*. In the latter lies the profit potential for collectors. Collect machine-made marbles only if you have a game set of them or if they have an occasional distinction—for example, if they were associated with cartoon or comic strip characters or with celebrities. The rest? They may be pretty but they have little value and probably always will. Sulphides may cost several hundreds of dollars, particularly if the interior figure shows craftsmanship. *Never* have chipped and cracked marbles reground or repolished. Among the marbles collected, the veteran bears its wound proudly and its design—in the case of swirls—remains proportionally correct, with the pontil mark, like a navel, intact.

Yet, though dates are almost meaningless, condition does count. Marble for marble, between identical swirls, the one that is not chipped will bring more than the one that is.

Museums Notable for Their Collections of Marbles
  Children's Museum, Detroit, MI 48202
  Perelman Antique Toy Museum, Philadelphia, PA 19106
  Sandwich Glass Museum, Sandwich, MA 02563
  Smithsonian Institution, Washington, DC 20560

Clubs and Organizations
  Marble Collectors Society of America, P.O. Box 222, Trumbull
  CT 06611

Books Worthwhile for Collectors
  Baumann, Paul, *Collecting Antique Marbles*, Wallace-Home-
  stead, 1970
  ———, *Price Guide to Collecting Antique Marbles*, Wallace-
  Homestead, 1976
  Ferretti, Fred, *The Great American Marble Book*, Workman Pub-
  lishing Co., New York, 1973
  Ingram, Clara, *The Collector's Encyclopedia of Antique Marbles*,
  Collector Books, 1972

MECHANICAL BANKS

Toy banks came to the United states when its own coins were created, shortly after the Revolutionary War. But these were "still" banks, decorative or amusing containers intended to stimulate thrift, particularly among children.

The first mechanical banks appeared in the 1860's and flourished after the Civil War until the 1930's. Some are still made for savings promotion programs. Since World War II the collecting and display of mechanical banks has enjoyed an unusual upsurge, spurred in part by the publicity savings and commercial banks give this collectible.

There are about 400 different types of these banks and each has its variation in action, materials and color. If one manufacturer came out with a new type, often based on current events, politics or ethnic stereotypes, other manufacturers came out with variants that exploited the popularity of the type but avoided direct patent infringement.

In general the action of the mechanical bank is caused by a coin inserted and/or a lever pressed to set a spring-powered or counterweighted mechanism into motion. Most of the banks are made of cast iron (though some of the more modern models are made of lithographed tin and now, of plaster) and painted gaily to delight children. The original audience consisted of children, in whom these toys were supposed to develop habits of thrift. The banks' themes, though sometimes political and satirical, were more often based on games of skill, folk legends, fairy tales, the circus, Bible stories or children's pastimes such as skipping rope, dancing or roller skating. Because they were children's toys, unfortunately, the examples available today are often banged up and only in fair condition.

By and large, the highest prices are paid for banks that work and that still have their original paint (as with most toys). A lesser price is assigned to banks skillfully restored and/or repaired. Rarity also increases value. Mechanical banks by any one maker or distributed by any one sponsor were usually not made in a large quantity and thus the best specimens are not often accessible to the beginning collector even if the price can be met.

Where To Find Mechanical Banks— The Market

The market for mechanical banks is specialized because some of the most original and prized banks were produced in small volume and the best specimens are tightly held by collectors. While you may find one good bank in your attic, you are not likely to find many more. Nor do they turn up in quantity at garage sales or street fairs. Many of them are already in the hands of devoted collectors and dealers/specialists. They do appear regularly, however, in Americana or special collectors' sales and auctions. Prices are not extremely high except for rare specimens in excellent condition, for which the price tag may run $1600. More likely to be found is an Uncle Sam made by the Shephard Hardware Co., with paint in fair to good condition, at $475; a popular Tammany tiger by J. E. Stevens Co. at $200; a Jolly Nigger at $125; and a Jonah and the Whale by Shephard Hardware Co. at $450.

Museums Notable for Their Collections of Mechanical Banks
   Museum of the City of New York, New York, NY 10029
   Perelman Antique Toy Museum, Philadelphia, PA 19106
   Seaman's Bank for Savings, New York, NY 10005

Books Worthwhile for Collectors
   Meyer, John D., *Old Penny Banks: Mechanicals, Stills by Larry Freeman*, Century House, Watkins Glen, N.Y., 1960
   Warman, Ewin G., *Mechanicals and Stills Price Guide*, E. G. Warman, 1975

MODEL SOLDIERS

Is there an American boy who has not played with lead soldiers? Maybe they were his own, received on a preteen birthday, or perhaps they were the soldiers of a friend. How many "wars" were staged with armies of soldiers and battlefield equipment carted from house to house?

Now these toys have become popular collectibles, prized for their vivid detail and good condition—if they managed to survive the many skirmishes of play.

An offshoot of that interest is the "connoisseur" figure that has the same general size, usually about 1.25 to 2.25 inches in height, but has poses, uniforms and weapons researched and reproduced in such meticulous and dramatic detail that they become documentary likenesses and were never really made as toys. Richard Courtenay, an English historian, created many of these and those that remain bring high prices today. Others have imitated Courtenay and expanded his range. Today the connoisseur figures are usually available as a kit with soldiers carefully cast. The collector, however, paints them as directed. The most highly valued of these—at several hundred dollars each—are those finished by Courtenay himself.

But *most* collectors today seek the toy variety manufactured during the 19th and early 20th centuries by such firms as W. Britain, Ltd. (in England) and McLoughlin Brothers of New York.

Some of the earliest model soldiers were of paper. The player was supposed to cut them out and paste them on thin wood or cardboard. Some of the oldest soldiers collected were cast by Johann Gottfried Hilpert in Germany. His soldiers bore a varying combination of his initials on the bottom and they were sometimes dated. Actually, a date is not very important to collectors except to suggest when a particular model was first cast. Soldiers may have streamed from a basic mold for years thereafter. Condition *is* important and if you find a troop of soldiers in their original box you are indeed fortunate. Leave them there with their fastening strings intact. They are most valuable that way.

From O. A. D. Hausser of Germany came remarkably realistic three-dimensional figures made of "Elastolin."

Of the various kinds of material used, *metal* soldiers are valued most highly. They come in a variety of casting modifications—two-dimensional, semi-round or semisolid, and three-dimensional soldiers, and those that are hollow-cast, which are three-dimensional and lightweight because hollow.

Lucotte in France specialized in three-dimensional soldiers and was later succeeded by other firms, including Henry Mignot. W. Britain, Ltd., in England, specialized in hollow casting; Heyde in Germany made solid soldiers.

In the United States McLoughlin Brothers of New York used a hollow-cast method and tended to copy the British figures. The Barclay Manufacturing Co. of New Jersey and the Manoil Manufacturing Co. of Waverly, New Jersey, produced hollow-cast figures also.

Louis Marx & Co. of New York manufactured colorfully lithographed tin flats, taller than most, about 3.5 inches high. They were highly popular and were distributed by such mail order houses as Montgomery Ward. Some U.S. collectors claim, though, that the solid figures made by Comet Metal Products, using the trademark "Authenticast," have the highest quality.

Where To Find Model Soldiers— The Market

There are specialty and hobby shops that cater to model soldier enthusiasts. You can also find scattered examples at flea markets and attic sales. The Louis Marx figures, which cost $0.98 for a set of 36 in the Montgomery Ward catalog for Christmas of 1941, are currently bringing about $1 to $2 each at such sales. At a special London auction for collectors, a complete 21-man Royal Marine band, made by W. Britain, Ltd., which cost $1.50 in 1938, brought $1,400 recently. It had a special provenance; it once belonged to a famous movie star, Douglas Fairbanks, Jr.

Clubs and Organizations
  American Model Soldier Society, American Military Historical Society, 1528 El Camino Real, San Carlos, CA 94070
  Miniature Figure Collectors of America, 813 Elliston Drive, Wynmoor, PA 19118
  National Capital Military Collectors, P.O. Box 166, Rockville, MD 20850

Magazines and Newsletters
  Old Toy Soldier Newsletter, 209 North Lombard, Oak Park, IL 60302

Toy Soldiers Rally   When sold by Phillips in London for $10,400 (£5,200), this battalion of 666 toy soldiers made a record as the most expensive set sold at auction. The soldiers are modeled after the London Scottish Regiment, which was in active service in France in 1916. (Photo: courtesy of Phillips.)

Books Worthwhile for Collectors

Barratt, John G., *Collecting Model Soldiers*, Arco Publishing Co.,
New York, 1975

McKenzie, Ian, *Collecting Old Toy Soldiers*, Hippocrene Books,
Inc., 1976

Richards, L. W., *Old British Model Soldiers, 1893–1918*, Tricorn
Press, 1970

MUSICAL BOXES

Enthusiasts of musical boxes collect with their ears as well as their eyes. Recently they have had to have ample cash, too, for the pleasure of possession. For those who love the sounds created by vibrating teeth on metal combs, the neat rat-tat-tat of mechanically beaten percussion instruments or the huff and puff of a bellow blowing through pipes, automated musical machines are ideal collectibles. They include musical boxes and automata, player pianos, and calliopes. The most valued of these specimens predate Edison's phonograph (1910) and radio and are no longer manufactured—only restored, repaired or reproduced for the growing number of antique musical box collectors.

The musical box and its larger relatives flourished in the 19th century until Edison's phonograph upstaged it by *reproducing all* the sounds of an orchestra and voice. The musical box has always made its *own sound*. It evolved from an invention of a tuned steel comb by Antoine Fabre, in Geneva, Switzerland. Then the Swiss, with their genius for watchmaking and other small precision machinery, adapted the simpler comb to a boxed mechanism that managed to twang a whole tune. Boxes grew in size and sound until the end of their Victorian golden age. They came in beautifully inlaid chests with matching tables or even more grandly as upright, highly styled pieces of furniture that required several people to move them about. The more elaborate examples contained bells, a reed organ, drums and castanets, as well as one or more tuned steel combs that were twanged by a cylinder powered by a wind-up spring.

Today you can buy a tabletop-sized musical box manufactured by Gautschi with eight 14-inch six-tune cylinders installed in a protective compartment in a matching table. The box is of burled walnut with delicate inlay work. The mechanism is powered by two large springs with gleaming brass and chrome cylinders and parts, the whole, as it works, producing a remarkable, rich sound; it sells for $27,000.

Paul Lochmann of Leipzig, Germany, produced an improvement on the familiar cylinders with pins. He created a more versatile flat disc for a machine he called the Symphonion. He was soon competing with a similar disc from Polyphon Works, also in Germany, and later with many others, including the Regina made in the United States.

Although the phonograph cylinder, record disc and tapes have now superseded the musical box in the production of music, some musical box makers in Switzerland and Japan continue to make relatively modest musical novelties based on the old mechanisms. Yet, with the resurgence of interest in *collecting* old musical boxes, particularly the famous makes such as Symphonion, Polyphon, Regina, Gautschi, Nicole Freres and Troll & Baker, most of these large machines, in working condition, can easily cost from $20,000 to $30,000.

On the other hand, a handsome contemporary box finished with hand-tooled leather with six tunes of Stephen Foster and Swiss works could cost $165 or more, depending on ornamentation and inscription. Such a handsome box is still popular to present as a gift on state occasions and, of course, when associated with a historic figure, it can have added value for the collector if it should later come to market.

Where To Find Musical Boxes— The Market

You are most likely to find the large collectible musical boxes at specialized auctions; the smaller variety and novelties can crop up at street fairs, flea markets and dealers. It is worthwhile, too, to follow prices in the *Musical Box Society News Bulletin*, which keeps collectors up-to-date on sales, repair services and prices. At auction recently a Regina metal disc mechanism in a wood case with 27 discs, manufactured about 1880, went for $1,000. A Swiss interchangeable cylinder mechanism, in a veneered wood case with 3 cylinders, manufactured about 1900, went for $2,000.

Museums Notable for Their Collections of Musical Boxes
Bellm's Cars and Music of Yesterday, Sarasota, FL 33580
Lockwood-Mathews Mansion Museum, Norwalk, CT 06850
Miles Mountain Musical Museum, Eureka Springs, AR 72632
Musical Museum, Dansboro, NY 13328
Musical Wonder House, Wiscasset, ME 04578
Tom's Musical Wonderland U.S.A., Manly, IA 50456

Clubs and Organizations
Automatic Musical Instrument Collectors Association, State Road and Broadview Street, Springfield, PA 19064
Musical Box Society International, Box 202, Route 3, Morgantown, IN 46160

Books Worthwhile for Collectors

Bowers, Q. David, *Encyclopedia of Automatic Musical Instruments*, Vestal Press, 1974

Ord-Hume, Arthur W. J. G., *Collecting Musical Boxes and How to Repair Them*, Crown Publishers, New York, 1967

Tallis, David, *Music Boxes: A Guide for Collectors*, Stein & Day, New York, 1971

Wiess-Stauffacher, Heinrich, *The Marvelous World of Music Machines*, Kodansha International, New York, 1976

MUSICAL INSTRUMENTS

Musical instruments make good beginners' collectibles for a variety of reasons. For one thing, they are plentiful; for another, they are often playable and hence have an aesthetic use and pleasure for the ear as well as the eye. For a third reason, musical instrument makers changed materials and design many times so that the collector can specialize in instruments in a number of ways: by size, by famous manufacturers or simply by a single instrument—a flute for example, as it metamorphosed through the hands of European and/or U.S. manufacturers.

And one can specialize in voices of the orchestra—strings, woodwinds, brass, percussion or peripheral solo instruments—or in small groups of "social" instruments such as the ocarina, Jew's harp, harmonica or piano and its ancestors.

The range is almost infinite but the beginner should be careful in considering the storage space required. A double B-flat bass horn (or sousaphone) in brass or fiberglass from a marching band is a marvelously shaped contraption; its plumbing is at once precise and ornate. But it is heavy and requires a lot of space. Piccolos and flutes are small and refined, often made of precious or semiprecious metals such as silver, gold or even platinum, or of the finest woods with a key system featuring mother-of-pearl finger rests. They have the advantage of being small with working parts displaying jeweler's precision and micromeasurement.

In general, brass band instruments are the least expensive; they are often beautifully crafted in lacquered metal. Whether you wind up with seventy-six trombones or one thousand and one piccolos, you will find yourself in the midst of American folklore and popular culture, a field as resonant in nostalgia as it is wide and abundant in objects.

You will probably find the famous Italian violin makers—Amati, Guarneri and Stradivarius—out of your reach. They made superb instruments during the 18th century and a single instrument can today bring easily more than $100,000 at auction.

But you can collect guitars, such as those of C. F. Martin, which has put out a variety of these instruments since its founding in 1833. Through 1867 these instruments were identified "C. F. Martin, New York." During the period 1867–1898 the guitars were identified "C. F. Martin & Co., New York." After 1898 the guitars bore serial numbers and after 1929 they carried model designa-

Attic Treasure Brings Music to Owner's Ears *Attics do not often reveal found treasures as valuable as this violin. The owner found it in his attic, encrusted with dirt and loosely wrapped for protection in a pair of old bloomers. An expert at Phillips identified it as a fine instrument by Guadanini, an 18th-century Italian maker. It sold for $40,000 (£20,000). (Photo: courtesy of Phillips.)*

tions. Guitar players prize the Martin Model D guitars made after 1898. Nonplaying collectors value most highly the oldest Martin guitars. Other manufacturers of sought-after guitars are Gibson, Epiphone, Bruno, American Conservatory, Washburn and Maurer.

Also collected avidly are mandolins made by Gibson and Washburn, particularly the Gibson F-5's, which were signed by acoustic designer Lloyd Loar who created in the 1920's some of the pioneering electronic guitars, banjos and basses.

Other instruments for the band and orchestra often came from Europe where they were perfected over centuries. Collectible European manufacturers are Adolphe Sax, who created the saxophone; Thomas Stanesby, Sr., well-known for his oboes and flutes; his son, Thomas Stanesby, Jr., who made flutes, recorders and bassoons; and Johann Christof Denner, who made clarinets.

Collectible pianos include the Steinway, Knabe, Baldwin, Bechstein-Moor, Chickering and Pleyel. They are usually repaired and can be played but are most highly valued when decorated by a well-known artist, playable or not.

Collectors have to decide whether they want to play their instruments or merely display them. Expert repair is still available for restoring an instrument to playing condition. An antique should *not* be restored or repaired *if it will not be played*; it loses its historic value and often its value to collectors.

Where To Find Musical Instruments— The Market

Playing musical instruments was so popular in U.S. families up to about the time of World War II that most attics still will yield a guitar, mandolin, French horn, trombone, cornet or drum. Thus local sales are a good source, as are pawnshops. The rarer and most famous instruments will turn up at specialized sales of the major auction houses. At recent sales, a Gibson flat-back mandolin went for $875; a Pourcelle clarinet with 10 brass keys sold for $350; a Klemm & Brother cornet in brass with nickel mounts went for $1,500; a slightly repaired Stradivarius violin went for $33,000; an Amati violin in fine condition went for $46,000. Decorated pianos have been rising rapidly in value since the sale of an ornately carved Steinway grand decorated by Alma-Tradema that went for $390,000 in 1980.

Museums Notable for Their Collections of Musical Instruments
   Metropolitan Museum of Art, New York, NY 10028
   Smithsonian Institution, Washington, DC 20560
   Stearns Collection of Musical Instruments, University of Michigan, Ann Arbor, MI 48105

Clubs and Organizations
   American Musical Instrument Society, University of South Dakota, Box 194, Vermillion, SD 57069

Magazines and Newsletters
   Mugwumps, Michael Il Holmes, 1600 Billman Lane, Silver Spring, MD 20902
   Pickin', North American Publishing Company, Philadelphia, PA 19108

Books Worthwhile for Collectors

Baines, Anthony, *Musical Instruments through the Ages*, Penguin Books, Baltimore, 1976

Marcuse, Sybil, *Musical Instruments: A Comprehensive Dictionary*, W. W. Norton & Co., New York, 1975

Willcutt, J. Robert, and Ball, Kenneth R., *The Musical Instrument Collector*, J. Robert Willcutt, 1977

NAVAHO BLANKETS AND RUGS

Beauty and practicality unite in Navaho blankets and rugs. Although the history of their weaving includes changes dictated by commercial interest, these works of art continue to flow from Navaho looms in the Southwest. Collectors seem willing to pay many thousands of dollars for the old creations and almost as much for new ones.

One of the traditions of hand weaving is to make each rug an individual art object. No two are the same in design, although they may bear close resemblance to one another.

Their qualities caught the attention of early white pioneers in the West. Because they were of tightly woven wool, they served as protection as well as warmth. They could shed or absorb water without its leaking through and they maintained body warmth. They could be fashioned into tube skirts or ponchos—garments uniquely suited to the dry-hot-cold Southwestern climate.

The blankets and later the rugs came East through the enterprise of traders such as Juan Lonzo Hubbel, sheriff of Apache County, Arizona, during the range wars of the 1880's. Traders like Hubbel encouraged the Indians to sell their blankets and to weave them of heavier material for use as rugs. They also supplied their home workers with bright wool that had been commercially dyed.

As a result of this commercial nudging, the collectors of Navaho blankets or rugs generally recognize four stylistic periods:

1. Blankets made before 1870 are now generally the most valuable. They are woven from hand-spun yarn in undyed white, gray, brown and black of natural sheep wools. Sometimes they also contain blue yarns, dyed with indigo obtained from inter-Indian trading with the Pueblo tribe. Or they might have bits of red yarn obtained from bayeta—a red commercial flannel the Indians got from white traders. The Indians then unraveled the cloth and wove the red threads into their blankets.

2. After the 1870's this bayeta was replaced by a red aniline-dyed flannel, the same that was used for long underwear. This, too, was unraveled and woven into blankets. But it faded more quickly than the darker red Indian dye; the dating of rugs can depend on the use of one or the other of these dyes.

The designs of these early blankets were mostly horizontal stripes or bands. After a while, at the suggestion of traders, the weavers added rectangles, zig-zags, crosses and diamonds that they saw on Mexican serapes.

3. A third style was prevalent between 1875 and 1890. It used complex geometric designs and many colors of commercial, machine-spun aniline-dyed "German" yarns. A great quantity of these dazzling carpets were produced and make a large supply still available to collectors.

4. In the 1890's, Victorian taste changed and "civilized buyers" wanted more subdued colors, heavier weaving and foreign designs on rugs. This meant adding borders in the manner of Oriental rugs. In turn, these modifications gave way in the 1920's to a "reform" movement and a return to original styles; weavers continue in this "reform" tradition today.

Where To Find Navaho Blankets and Rugs—The Market

You can find them on the loom, still, in the Southwest. But the earlier blankets of the first two styles generally bring much higher prices, rug for rug, than intermediate styles (which were produced in great quantity). Still, a noted weaver, today, can ask for and will get thousand of dollars for a new rug—a rare example of a collectible in which the entirely new rivals the old in value. To buy the older versions, you will have to go to dealers who specialize in Indian art. Also try the leading auction houses that feature auctions of Indian crafts or Indian artifacts from time to time. Prepare

to pay $10,000 to $20,000 for rare and highly prized Navaho blankets or rugs in fine condition, a few thousand for lesser rugs in fair condition.

The blankets and rugs are remarkably strong and sturdy. They need protection against moisture and the sun. If hung on a wall, they need a textile sleeve sewn to the reverse so that a rod can enable them to hang evenly. There *are* attractive contemporary Belgian and Mexican imitations but there is usually a less difficult weaving technique used—with knots and noncontinuous threads—the knot lumps give away the spurious origins.

Museums Notable for Their Collections of Navajo blankets and Rugs
   Denver Art Museum, Denver, CO 80204
   Field Museum of Natural History, Chicago, IL 60605
   Hoard Museum, Phoenix, AZ 85004
   Museum of the American Indian, Heye Foundation, New York, NY 10032
   Museum of Northern Arizona, Flagstaff, AZ 86001
   Southwest Museum, Los Angeles, CA 90065

Magazines and Newsletters
   American Indian Art Magazine, 7333 East Monterey Way, No. 5, Scottsdale, AZ 85251
   The Indian Trader, P.O. Box 31235, Billings, MT 59107

Books Worthwhile for Collectors
   Amsden, Charles Avery, *Navajo Weaving: Its Technic and History*, Rio Grande Press, Glorieta, N. Mex., 1972
   Berlant, Anthony, and Kahlenberg, Mary Hunt, *The Navajo Blanket*, Praeger Publishers, New York, 1972
   Dedera, Don, *Navajo Rugs: How to Find, Evaluate, Buy and Care for Them*, Northland Press, 1975
   Mera, H. P., *Navajo Textile Arts*, Peregrine Smith, Inc., 1975

NETSUKE

Copies of netsuke (pronounced as if spelled netzkay), to the frequent consternation of collectors, are being produced by the thousands every week in Hong Kong. Carvers, with varying degrees of skill, turn them out on an assembly line system whereby several artists contribute their specialty to popular shapes and themes.

Most of this prodigious production flows, via export, to Western Europe, the United States and, ironically, to Japan where the art form originated centuries ago as part of the clothing of aristocrats. Because the traditional Japanese kimono had no pocket, the wearer carried a lacquer box, or inro, that served as a kind of purse. The inro was fastened to the Japanese sash or obi with a cord that had a netsuke as a fastener or button. It acted as a toggle at the top of the cord; the tightness of the sash binding the cord to the wearer's body prevented the toggle-tipped cord from slipping through.

Sometimes netsuke are mistaken for large carved ivory buttons or small statues, also carved from ivory, that were used to adorn the Japanese home. The traditional netsuke, however, had two holes or *himotoshi*, through which passed the cords holding the inro. Another distinctive characteristic of the netsuke was its smooth shape—no matter how intricate the three-dimensional carving, it was designed with fairly smooth surfaces and with nothing protruding that would catch and scratch the fabric of a kimono.

Mass-produced netsuke, some well carved, some not, usually do not have the delicacy and the worn, warm feel of old netsuke. And the stain may be applied more liberally to cover up flaws.

When the Japanese Westernized their clothing, they tended to forget about netsuke and inro but Western collectors did not and a large trade developed. It continues today. Commercial copies of netsuke are made and bought purely as decorative objects.

When the U.S. armed services occupied Japan during the years following World War II, G. I.'s bought many contemporary and old netsuke put on the market by Japanese families who needed the money. The G. I.'s took them home as souvenirs. There may now be hundreds of thousands of these in drawers and attics of families who had servicemen in the Pacific area of the war. Oddly enough, most American families do not know a netsuke from a piece of costume jewelry or a cuff link. But they are learning fast from the publicity given recent auction records of prices.

Where To Find Netsuke—The Market

You can find contemporary netsuke and other ivory sculpture at any store featuring imported decorations. Look for those fascinating Buddha figures in ivory or the bridges of elephants, and eventually you will find some netsuke nestled somewhere in the vicinity. What you pay for them should vary with the quality of the carving. A few contemporary carvers do better work than *some* of the artisans of long ago and prices reflect this; prices for contemporary pieces may exceed those for old netsuke. You will usually find genuine netsuke at Oriental fine art dealers or at auctions that now specialize in Japanese lacquer ware, inro and netsuke. One fine 18th-century netsuke portraying a deer and its fawn, executed by the master carver Tomofoda, brought $24,000 at auction in the mid-seventies. Recently a prized figure of a horse went for $78,000 in a Honolulu auction. At the same time, run-of-the-mill commercial copies of netsuke made in Hong Kong are still available for $25 to $35.

Since the great majority of netsuke produced through the centuries were not signed, you have to take your chances on authenticity. Clever modern carvers, unfortunately, have imitated celebrated designs of the past and have even faked the names of famous carvers. You probably will not want to risk large sums of money on netsuke unless you buy them through expert dealers or an international auction house with statements of authenticity. Once you become an expert collector, however, you can compare a true Tomofoda, with its three-dimensional finesse of detail, to a modern Hong Kong version, and you will probably see that the imitation shows its inferiority in detail and stain and lack of what you would recognize as real patina. With netsuke you have to use what is known to be genuine as a touchstone to detect fakes and imitations. It is not easy to develop this detective sense. It requires much viewing and touching but it is a skill that is worthwhile to develop when you collect these diminutive objects of sculptors' genius.

Museums Notable for Their Collections of Netsuke
Asian Art Museum of San Francisco, San Franciso, CA 94118
Joslyn Art Museum, Omaha, NB 08102
Museum of Fine Arts, Boston, MA 02115

Clubs and Organizations
International Netsuke Collectors Society, P.O. Box 10426, Honolulu, HI 96816

Magazines and Newsletters
Journal of the International Netsuke Collectors Society, P.O.
Box 10426, Honolulu, HI 96816

Books Worthwhile for Collectors
Bushell, Raymond, *Collectors' Netsuke*, John Weatherhill, New
York, 1971
————, *Netsuke Familiar and Unfamiliar*, John Weatherhill,
New York, 1975
————, *Netsuke Handbook of Ueda Reikichi*, Charles E. Tuttle
Co., Rutland, VT , 1976
Davey, Neil K., *Netsuke*, Sotheby Parke Bernet Publications,
Ltd., 1974
Hurtig, Bernard, *Masterpieces of Netsuke Art*, John Weatherhill,
New York, 1973
Jahss, Melvin and Betty, *Inro and Other Miniature Forms of
Japanese Lacquer Art*, Charles E. Tuttle Co., Rutland, VT ,
1971
Kinsey, Miriam, *Contemporary Netsuke*, Charles E. Tuttle Co.,
Rutland, VT , 1977
Newman, Alexander R., and Ryerson, Egerton, *Japanese Art: A
Collector's Guide*, A. S. Barnes & Co., Cranbury, N J , 1966

ORIENTAL CERAMICS

The prices of the finest Oriental ceramics, Chinese porcelain of the Sung (960–1279), Ming (1368–1643) and Ching, (1644–1912) periods (dynasties of Chinese rulers during the 10th through 19th centuries) are out of reach of most U.S. collectors. A delicately colored porcelain cup from the 15th century—3.5 inches in diameter—and decorated with a rooster, hen and three chicks, and small enough to examine in the palm of one's hand, recently was bought by a Hong Kong collector for $1 million.

At present, the most highly valued Oriental ceramics are those from China, made for *domestic* use in aristocratic houses. Chinese porcelain made for *export* is less delicate and has its own enthusiastic collectors but at much lower prices.

The investment values of the finest chinese porcelain have consistently moved upward by double-digit percentages each year for the past decade and have incited interest in all manner of other Oriental art: the porcelain of Japan and Korea, bronzes, lacquer ware, prints, netsuke, and sculpture in many materials including ivory and jade.

Because there has been a collectors' interest in Oriental objects by Western collectors for at least three millennia (3,000 years), the kinds and quality of Oriental ceramics are many and varied and require an expertise beyond the capabilities and pocketbooks of most U.S. collectors. They have left the field in large part to wealthy Japanese or to the billionaire internationals of Hong Kong.

Nonetheless, the ceramics can be studied and admired through books and in museums, and related minor objects are accessible to the average collector.

Where To Find Oriental Ceramics— The Market

Most Oriental ceramics worth collecting are so prized and expensive that they appear only at special auctions where dealers (frequently on the behalf of wealthy collectors who want to retain their anonymity) and museums compete for them.

Since the 1949 Revolution, hardly any works of ancient art have come out of China and active museum purchases throughout the world deplete the supply. At present Ming ceramics command the highest prices, followed by ceramics of the Ching and the Sung periods. There is growing interest, too, in the brilliant glazes of an even earlier period, the Tang Dynasty (618–907). A Tang pottery camel, for example, recently brought $17,000 at auction; a Ming Dynasty altar vase brought $12,000; a *blanc de chine* figure from the Ching period of Kuan Yin brought $101,500. And these were minor pieces.

Museums Notable for Their Collections of Oriental/Chinese Ceramics
   Asian Art Museum, San Francisco, CA 94118
   Cleveland Museum of Art, Cleveland, OH 44106
   Metropolitan Museum of Art, New York, NY 10028
   Museum of Fine Arts, Boston, MA 02115
   Nelson-Atkins Museum, Kansas City, KS 64111

ORIENTAL RUGS

The Oriental rug market operates on several levels and all of them offer challenges to the collector. Oriental rugs have become popular because they offer the collector a fine art that is also practical; most Oriental rugs can be used as floor coverings. They have utility, endurance and beauty. They are a delight for collectors who like to display their treasures.

Authentic examples of certain prized kinds of Oriental rugs, in good condition and aesthetically pleasing, such as a Kirghiz rug 20 feet × 20 feet, can easily bring more than $100,000 at auction. But most rugs at auction bring prices of from $5,000 to $90,000.

If well chosen and given reasonable care (not too much foot traffic, not too much exposure to the sun, not too vigorous treatment with a vacuum cleaner), they will last a lifetime or more. Treatment varies, of course, with the condition and the toughness of the rug.

The term "Oriental rug" can cover a multitude of products handmade in any number of countries at different times. Today, good handmade Oriental rugs are coming into the United States from India, Pakistan, Turkey, China, Nepal, Tibet, Rumania and parts of Russia. Until the recent troubles, they were also coming in from Iran. There is a reason for this—skilled labor for making the hundreds of thousands of knots in each rug is inexpensive in these countries and so they continue in the age-old handcraft tradition.

Authentic examples *are* a worthwhile investment as well as objects to give pleasure over many years to many generations of owners.

The usual way to start collecting Oriental rugs is with an inherited item from a family living room or a runner from a hall. Affluent Victorian households in the United States and in England bought these rugs as serviceable and attractive floor coverings with little thought of their potential gain in value.

Dealers will still emphasize their durability and decorative value rather than their investment value because Oriental rugs have been hawked as "investment" at hotel auctions and in a bazaar-like atmosphere that makes the public suspicious of prices bid, asked and achieved.

Where To Find Oriental Rugs—
The Market

It is best to begin collecting Oriental rugs with a reputable dealer. The dealer may specialize in such rugs; you may also begin with the Oriental rug department of a fine furniture and furnishings store. Get to know the kinds of contemporary rugs and antique rugs and the typical asking prices for each kind. Develop an eye for beauty and condition.

After you feel confident as a buyer you can try the auctions. There are three levels of these. One is the itinerant auction, often held in hotels of large cities or at country fairs. Be doubly wary of these movable dealers; they will not be there the next week when you may find your rug defective in some way. They often handle rugs that they buy wholesale from dealers who have an oversupply of unpopular designs; there may be a number of culls or rugs stained with mildew or rot or defective in one way or another. But in all this questionable merchandise there are usually also some worthwhile specimens. You will have to learn which is which. In estate sales, too, the auctioneers have been known to bulk out existing rugs from the estate with other rugs from other sales, those they have picked up from wholesalers, those that did not sell at previous auctions and so forth.

The popularity of Oriental rugs is such that Sotheby's, Phillips, Christie's and William Doyle, all in New York City, and leading auction houses in other major cities have special Oriental rug auctions where you can buy authentic contemporary and antique Oriental rugs. But *you* will have to be the ultimate judge of quality and condition.

At a recent auction a Karatchoph Kazak (from Caucasia) with an octagonal medallion and blue border, 99" × 69", fetched $10,000. A Chinese beige field with birds, urns and a lotus border, 216" × 144", brought $2,400. A Manchester Indo-Kashan rug with a flower-filled border, 258" × 117", brought $4,500; a Tabriz medallion rug of silk with ivory field and polychrome medallions, 69" × 49", brought $4,500; a Turkish Bergamo prayer rug with diamond design brought $5,500.

Museums Notable for Their Collections of Oriental Rugs
   Metropolitan Museum of Art, Fifth Avenue at 79th Street, New
      York, NY 10028
   Cooper Hewitt Museum, the National Museum of Design, Fifth
      Avenue at 91st Street, New York, NY 10028
   Fogg Art Museum, Boston, MA 02115

Books Worthwhile for Collectors

Denny, Walter B., *Oriental Rugs*, Cooper-Hewitt Museum, 1981

Formentor, Fabio, *Oriental Rugs and Carpets*, McGraw-Hill Book Co., New York, 1972

Franses, Jack, *European and Oriental Rugs*, Arco Publishing Co., New York, 1970

Herbert, Janice Summer, *Affordable Oriental Rugs*, Macmillan Publishing Co., 1980

————, *Oriental Rugs: The Illustrated Guide*, Macmillan Publishing Co., 1978

Kokker, Nicolas, *Oriental Carpets for Today*, Doubleday & Co., Garden City, N.Y., 1973

PAINTINGS AND DRAWINGS

Oil paintings have probably been the most publicized inflation hedges and profitable investments in the whole field of collectibles. They make ideal collectibles. With proper care paintings can last several lifetimes; in fact, famous paintings, through modern techniques of conservation and restoration, can last almost forever—even though the original pigment and canvas are, in reality, replaced.

Paintings have the great advantage of being decorative, easily displayed and, except with some of the most modern artists with a flair for sheer gigantism (very large panels for minimal subject or color), available in many sizes to suit the collector's need for display as well as investment.

Before investing in paintings you should set up strict priorities of price, period and eventual goal of your collection.

Price.   Most good oil paintings today are priced out of the range of the beginning collector. (If you can't afford even to begin to collect oil paintings, you can't afford to amass a meaningful collection. If you do have the money, of course, you should buy true quality as well as current reputation, which may or may not be inflated for reasons irrelevant to quality. You can expect oils by painters of reputation to cost at least several thousands of dollars each; auction records show that several millions were recently paid for paintings by W.M.J. Turner, Velasquez, Church and Picasso.

Reputation.   Many European painters of the last three centuries—the golden age of the pictorial arts—have reached high price levels. This publicized achievement sometimes has given painters, particularly modern expressionists, a higher reputation than deserved over the long run. Some artists (like Vermeer) painted extremely well but had a small output; that makes them virtually untouchable today by individual private collectors because of price and reputation. *Such paintings are rightly appreciated in museums.*

Other painters, such as Rembrandt, are museum-bound in oils but have left etchings and drawings of high quality that can still be collected (although also at increasingly high prices).

The tendency is to try to collect other paintings of the same period by painters imitating the great names. Sometimes these lesser artists were pupils or at least followers of the greater painter. A painting attributed to a pupil has been known to be later authenticated as painted by the master himself. However, the reverse also

Celebrity Artist and Model *Portraits, even of celebrities, do not always do as well as a celebrity artist's main body of work. This painting of opera star Lawrence Tibbett exhibits Howard Chandler Christy's usual flair with a society portrait. Apparently Tibbett did not buy the portrait; it remained in the Christy family's possession. It sold a few years ago for $1,600 at a William Doyle auction—below estimates and less than an oil by the artist would usually achieve at the Doyle gallery, which makes a market in Christy's works. (Photo: courtesy of William Doyle Galleries.)*

happens, particularly as curators in museums pare away treasures obtained in an age more blithe and less analytical.

While it is intriguing to read about the collections that bring record prices at auction today, the news brings an underlying sadness, too; for such noteworthy collections will appear less and less frequently. There just is not the quantity of money available for amassing such treasures today, even if they could still be found *outside* of museums.

Paintings of unknown painters (both living and dead) can each cost a few thousand dollars with almost no potential for resale. Aggressive collectors of contemporary works may be lucky with their choices—but the odds are against it. Nonetheless, you may want to collect paintings by young unknowns of various styles simply because you like the way they paint. But do this *after* you have made an educated investment in a work by a well-known painter. You will carry less risk if you form a limited partnership of friends (with a dealer in the field as a general partner) in the acquisition of a single major painting worth several hundred thousands of dollars—or more—than you will by buying 100 paintings of unknown artists for $1,000 each.

Period or Source.   Paintings have their changes of fashion just as clothes do, although the changes are mercifully less frivolous with paintings. Perhaps it is somewhat daring to say it, but *every* good painting by a painter with an established reputation *will have its day* as interest revives in various periods. Who would have thought that academic European paintings of the 19th century would ever regain collectors' interests after their trouncing on the markets for so long by French Impressionists and their successors? Or who would have thought that a huge, offbeat landscape of icebergs (*Icebergs* by the American painter Frederick Church) would bring an auction price of $1.5 million and become the holder— probably temporarily— of the record for the most expensive American painting ever sold at auction and the sixth most expensive work of art sold at auction in the world?

The surprising sale of *Icebergs* at such a price has raised the potential value of *all* American paintings which had not kept pace with earlier price trends. Another neglected area (still not reviving) is 18th-century English portraiture. This includes works by Reynolds, Gainsborough and even Sir William Beechey, who presided over a "factory" of pupils and relatives in an effort to catch the likenesses of the nobility and the newly-rich at a time when there were no photographs.

Other neglected areas have been drawings and paintings of the Art Nouveau, Art Deco and Art Moderne periods, although the

Values of American Paintings Surge *"Going West," an oil on canvas done by Thomas Hart Benton in 1926, recently brought $200,000 at auction—a record for the artist, who specialized in Midwestern subjects. American paintings, long neglected in favor of European art, have come into their own during the past decade. (Photo: courtesy of Christie's.)*

furniture, jewelry, glassware and other decorative pieces have possibly peaked—for the time being—in value. All work in the Art Nouveau and related styles had been neglected for decades; the small pieces were relegated to the state of "old wedding gifts stored in the attic." Posters of the period have had their play and now related paintings and drawings begin to have theirs.

The trends in collecting paintings are so complex and the prices so often surprising on the upside that profits in the field are probably not accessible to any but the most lucky beginners. If you have the kind of money (say, $50,000 to $100,000 or so) to begin a serious collection, hitch yourself to a reliable dealer in the period of your choice who will help you choose investment quality paintings. Perhaps the dealer will introduce you to like-minded investors who can club together to buy an unusual item that comes to market.

Look at paintings and then more paintings, to educate your eye to what is "good" as art as well as what pleases you. After all, a major part of the pleasure of collecting paintings and drawings is the joy in looking at them at leisure in your own home.

Where To Buy Paintings—The Market

For fine paintings, drawings, watercolors and graphics, the best place to collect is through dealers who specialize in periods and well-known painters. They are also in touch with collectors who might be persuaded to relinquish certain specimens, also with mu-

Highly Prized Pastel by Mary Cassat *"Baby Charles Looking Over His Mother's Shoulder," signed by Mary Cassat, recently brought $120,000 at an auction of American paintings and drawings. It was a record price for a pastel by Cassat, whose drawings and oils are also in great demand among collectors. (Photo: courtesy of Christie's.)*

seums that are ready to weed out their collections and make lesser works by well-known figures available to the public once more. Dealers can also provide invaluable educational help along the way and act as buying or selling agents for you once they know your specialty.

The auction houses form the other marketplace; there is a definite advantage in following auctions to get an idea of the quality and prices achieved by individual items. It is unlikely that you will find bargains at these widely-publicized sales, but occasionally the quality and quantity of paintings offered is so high that only rare museums collections can compete with the show.

Museums Notable for Their Collections of Paintings
   Metropolitan Museum of Art, New York, NY 10028
   Chicago Art Institute, Chicago, IL 60603
   Museum of Modern Art, 11 East 53 Street, New York, NY 10019
   The Frick Museum, 1 East 70 Street, New York, NY 10021

The Guggenheim Museum, 89 Street & Fifth Avenue, New York,
  NY 10028
The Brooklyn Museum, Brooklyn, NY 12034
Whitney Museum of American Art, 945 Madison Avenue, New
  York, NY 10021

Check also the art museums of any major U.S. city. Books on
paintings, drawings and prints are legion; ask for them at any
public library and simply browse your way to a general orientation.

PAPERWEIGHTS

No one knows who first created a prismatic prison for the bright meadows of color one discovers in paperweights. Millefiori (or thousand flowers) globes of glass using colored canes set side by side in a base to form patterns of color were produced by the Egyptians as early as 1500 A.D. Others have been found on the site of a Greek temple from the 4th century B.C. And Venetian Millefiori glass was famous all over Europe during the Renaissance.

Technology for the manufacture of paperweights developed over the centuries but it was only about 1842 that the elements of what are now regarded as classic paperweights created something beautiful and sought after by the 19th-century collector. Perhaps it was the delight in bric-a-brac, perhaps the increased use of steel-nibbed pens and the rise in the number of letters sent after the creation of the inexpensive penny post in England. Paperweight collecting suddenly became a mania during the decade 1845–1855 in France, England and the United States. The great Exhibition at the Crystal Palace in London in 1851 had glass paperweights on display. They were made by the great French glass factories of Baccarat, Clichy and St. Louis, and by the English firm of Bacchus. The craze spread to the United States through New York's Crystal Palace exposition in 1853, which featured Clichy weights. The U.S. market was supplied by such native firms as the New England Glass Company and the Boston and Sandwich Glass Company.

In those days nearly everyone could afford to collect paperweights. Even the finest Baccarat paperweights in 1849 cost about $10 (now easily worth $1,000 or more) while in the United States a fancy weight was listed at 75 cents. The craze subsided almost as quickly as it began as the public turned to other baubles and the glass manufacturers catered to other fashions. Weights went "underground" to the back shelves of dealers who hoped for a revival. They had to wait until after World War II, when a few of the people who had persisted as collectors began to offer their treasures at auction. The Applewhaite-Abbot sale in 1952–1953 at Sotheby's in 537 lots, over four auctions, stimulated a resurgence, which developed further with the sale of the former King Faruk's collection in Cairo in 1954. It featured 252 weights. The quantities in those two collections were considered large for the time. In the 1950's, Arthur Rubeloff, a Chicago builder, began his collection. When he recently gave the Art Institute of Chicago 1,200 fine weights, his collection was regarded as the world's largest.

Paul Hollister, an expert in the field, estimates that there are between 15,000 to 20,000 antique classic paperweights remaining on the market, and they are not all of collectible quality. Wear and tear cuts into the limited supply. For a paperweight to perform at its best the domed surface must retain its original curve and the facets their original cutting. Only in this way can the original design, proportion and refractive magic work. Minor scratches and chips do not much bother the seasoned collector, though the more perfect the condition the better. Unfortunately many dealers and neophyte collectors have not understood this; perhaps half of all the weights left to collect have been "repolished." This usually means they have been reground to a depth beneath a defect. Too many slightly damaged paperweights have been reground and almost ruined in the process.

In today's markets you can buy for about $125 the weights made by one of the great 19th-century U.S. companies: the New England Glass Company or the Boston and Sandwich Glass Company. These seldom have dates and they feature scrambled designs. This price compares to a classic Clichy weight sold at Sotheby's for $51,000 in 1977. Most weights sell for several hundred dollars apiece and the best ones that find their way to auction catalogs can run as high as $1,500 and more. A rare Baccarat paperweight containing an unusual flower bouquet—estimated to sell for $750 to $1,000—actually sold for $5,750 at the recent auction of the Bill Hahn collection at the William Doyle Galleries in New York.

Contemporary Paperweights Also Collectibles

Modern paperweights, made in the classic manner, are produced by the St. Louis and Baccarat factories in France; by Perthshire Paperweights Ltd. in Scotland; and by such individual artisans as Charles Kaziun, Paul Stankard, Ray and Bob Banford, Francis Whittemore, Delmo and Debbie Tarsitano (a father and daughter pair) and Rick Ayotte—all in the U.S.—and by Paul Ysart in Scotland.

Where To Find Paperweights— The Market

The best way to begin collecting weights is to view them in a store, museum or auction. Flea markets and fairs often carry inferior weights recently manufactured in the Far East.

Scarcity of Design Influences Prices of Paperweights *From left to right, the first example is a scatterweight millefiore paperweight created by the French firm of Clichy in about 1850. Its characteristic Clichy rose (in the center) gives it added value because not all Clichy weights have the rose included. Today this piece is worth about $500. (If it had been signed on the bottom, it would be worth a few hundred dollars more.) The second is a Baccarat wheat flower weight, yellow with brown spots, which is a rare treatment of an otherwise typical flower design. It recently sold for $2,500 but could run about $4,000 at auction today. The third weight is a Baccarat created about 1850; it features a white primrose and is not at all as rare as its neighbor. The value of this piece is about $1,000. (Photo: courtesy of Gem Antiques.)*

Museums Notable for Their Collections of Paperweights
  Art Institute of Chicago, Arthur Rubeloff Collection, Chicago, IL
    60603
  Bergstrom Art Centre, Collection Evangeline Bergstrom, Neenah,
    WI 54946
  Corning Museum of Glass, Corning, NY 14830
  Old Sturbridge Village, J. Cheney Wells Collection, Sturbridge,
    MA 01566
  Sandwich Glass Museum, Sandwich, MA 02563
  Smithsonian Institution, Washington, D. C. 20560

Organization and Clubs
  Paperweight Collectors Association, Inc., Mr. Paul Jokelson,
    President, P.O. Box 128, Scarsdale, NY 10583

Books Worthwhile for Collectors

Hollister, Paul, *Encyclopedia of Glass Paperweights*, Bramhall House, 1969

Jokelson, Paul, ed., *Annual Bulletin of the Paperweight Collectors Association*

Melvin, Jean S., *American Glass Paperweights and Their Makers*, Thomas Nelson Inc., 1951

Selman, Lawrence H., *Collectors Paperweights, Price Guide and Catalogue*, Paperweight Press, 1979

————, and Pope-Selman, Linda, *Paperweights for Collectors*, Paperweight Press, 1975

PEWTER

Pewter, an alloy of tin and usually of lead but sometimes copper, bismuth or antimony, or mixtures thereof, has been around since the Bronze Age—that is, before recorded history. Pewter was useful because of its relatively low melting point and the fact that lead gave the mixture heft and tin a certain shine resembling silver.

Because it could be melted easily and molded rather than hammered, as was necessary with harder metals such as bronze or iron, pewter has been used since early times to make household containers and for inexpensive ornamentation.

For U.S. collectors, however, pewter produced during the 19th century has the most appeal. United States colonial pewter, still extant, is highly prized. But there is little of it because of a curious restriction on tin imports by the English during the Colonial period. Colonial craftsmen customarily melted down worn-out or broken pieces to fashion new pieces.

After the Revolutionary War, tin ore imports grew and gradually a large supply of pewter ware accumulated. It is now sought after by collectors who give U.S. ware a slight edge in value over objects made (and still made) in England or France. As it happened, U.S. family tastes turned to ceramics and glass after the Revolution and pewter makers, to compete, upgraded their metal by substituting antimony or lead to give the finish a brighter luster, more like silver. Pewter had always imitated the shapes of silver household plates, porringers, spoons, tankards and ladles and for many centuries was known as "the poor man's silver," even though it was never inexpensive and was desired in the best of houses as a kind of second service, somewhat in the position of today's stainless steel as everyday ware. It was produced (as is stainless steel today) in richly tooled patterns as elegant as sterling silver.

Finally, pewter was electroplated with actual silver. During the latter part of the 19th century, the affluent Victorian household turned to sterling silver and silver plate and put pewter in the shade. Then, after World War I and the Depression, new designs and the price differential between pewter and silver made the former more attractive once more.

Pewter is prized primarily by condition. Early Colonial pieces are so scarce that they cannot be considered collectible by most people. Nineteenth-century pewter is most prized if the piece is intact, shows some age, exhibits a maker's "touch" mark, is clean

American Pewter Tankard at World Record Price   *This American pewter flat-top quart tankard was crafted by William Bradford, Jr., of New York City during the 18th century. It brought $15,000 at a recent auction. The price set a world record for a piece of pewter. (Photo: courtesy of Christie's.)*

without the discoloration of oxidation and has not been overpolished. It is a relatively soft metal and details can be polished away, somewhat like oversanding of soft wood.

Where To Find Pewter—The Market

You can find pewter, with the exception of rare pieces from the Colonial period, at most local sales, even at flea markets and garage sales. Most families that had substantial households in the Victorian period have handed down pewter pieces for generations and these pieces now appear at estate sales.

Typical pieces, makers and recent prices of American pewter are as follows: a basin by Daniel Curtiss, dated about 1830, $350;

basin by Spencer Stafford, dated about 1794–1800, $1,000; baptismal bowl by Oliver Trask, dated about 1835, $2,900; candlesticks, a pair by Thomas Wildes, dated about 1833, $1,500; drinking mug, pint size, by Robert Bonynge, dated about 1760, $1,600; plate marked on the reverse, Bassett, measuring 8.5 inches, dated about 1770, $2,400; porringer with scroll, made by Samuel Hamlin about 1800, $1,050.

Museums Notable for Their Collections of Pewter
  Art Institute of Chicago, Chicago, IL 60603
  Colonial Williamsburg, Williamsburg, VA 23185
  Greenfield Village and Henry Ford Museum, Dearborn, MI 48121
  Henry Francis du Pont Winterthur Museum, Winterthur, DE 19735
  Historic Deerfield, Inc., Deerfield, MA 01342
  Metropolitan Museum of Art, New York, 10028
  Museum of Fine Arts, Boston, MA 02115
  Shelburne Museum, Shelburne, VT 05482

Clubs and Organizations
  Pewter Collectors Club of America, Old Bull House, Main Street, Centerbrook, CT 06409

Books Worthwhile for Collectors
  Cotterell, Howard H., *National Types of Old Pewter*, Pine Press, 1972
  ———, *Old Pewter, Its Makers and Marks*, Charles E. Tuttle Co., Rutland, Vt., 1963
  Kauffman, Henry J., *The American Pewterer, His Techniques and His Products*, Thomas Nelson, Camden, N.J., 1970
  Kerfoot, J. B., *American Pewter*, Gale Research Co., Detroit, 1976
  Laughlin, Ledlie Irwin, *Pewter in America: Its Makers and Their Marks*, Barre Publishers, Barre, Mass., 1970
  Montgomery, Charles F., *A History of American Pewter*, Praeger Publishers, New York, 1973
  Real, Christopher, *British Pewter and Britannia Metal*, Peebles Press, 1971
  Rainwater, Dorothy T., *Encyclopedia of American Silver Manufacturers: Their Marks, Trademarks, and History*, Crown Publishers, New York, 1975

PHOTOGRAPHS

The attention given to photographs as a collectible is recent and intense, and has catapulted prices to levels that would have seemed incredible in the 1960's.

There are really two levels of collectible photographs. One is those taken by professionals such as the pioneering Edward S. Curtis, Mathew Brady, Julia Margaret Cameron and Charles Lutwidge Dodgson (Lewis Carroll) in the 19th century, and Alfred Stieglitz, Jacques-Henri Lartique, Ansel Adams, Cecil Beaton, Alfred Eisenstaedt and others in this century. There are lesser "famous" names, of course, which become household words with collectors once they plunge into their hobby. Highly valuable prints of certain subjects can bring more than $20,000 at auction today.

Then there is a second kind of photographs, those taken by amateurs—sometimes with considerable talent—which record landscapes, buildings and typical people, like familiar snapshots do today, scenes that would be lost to memory except for the roving and recording eye of the photographer.

Old pictures from the 19th century by virtually anonymous photographers depend for their value on dating and subject matter, and sometimes on the medium or photographic process used. The majority of these old photos are paper prints made similarly to the familiar color print of today (a negative to produce one or more positive prints). The "old" variety, in contrast to contemporary black-and-white prints, may look brownish or silvery and may seem more blurred.

As it happens, however, the most valued collectible photographic prints were produced in other ways that are now obsolete. These are colored transparencies on glass or negative images in glass or metal that look like positives when viewed at certain angles. Of these kinds, the most valued is a daguerreotype, named after the creator of the process, Louis Daguerre. They were created by a master photographer who used iodine and mercury vapors and silver-coated copper plates as his chemical process. Most daguerreotypes are portraits. If you find landscapes or cityscapes, you have probably found rarities worth more than the usual portrait— for both historical and sometimes aesthetic reasons.

A variation on the daguerreotype process was the ambrotype, a glass plate negative mounted over a black backing to display a positive image. Another variation, called tintype, had a light-sensitive emulsion on a black-lacquered metal. Ambrotypes enjoyed a brief

Early Photo of San Francisco *This very early daguerreotype, perhaps the earliest surviving view of San Francisco and the oldest made in the Far West, is attributed to the photographer Pierpont of San Francisco. It was dated about 1850 by reference to news items of the recently constructed buildings pictured and fires that destroyed other buildings. Because of its extreme rarity and identification with a pioneering photographer, this print—despite visible surface abrasions—sold for $7,000 at a Christie's auction in May 1980. (Photo: courtesy of Christie's.)*

popularity at about the time of the Civil War. Tintypes continued into the 1930's and were used at fairs and other public, open-air events where being photographed was fashionable. The quality of these variations was less than that of the daguerreotypes and they are less prized as collectors' items unless they have an unusually rare subject.

Interesting as these early experimental photographs may be, the bulk of collectible photographs are paper prints. Many early commercial paper prints were of famous people. They were done up as *cartes de visite*, calling cards, but seldom were actually used for that purpose.

In general, 20th-century amateur snapshots are of only minor interest to collectors unless they record and document a special subject that would otherwise be lost. Prints by professional photographers are entirely another matter and they continually bring higher and higher prices at auction.

Favorite Subject by a Well-Known Artist/Photographer   *This handsome gelatin silver photographic print, taken about 1917 by Charles Sheeler, achieved a world record for this photographer: $15,000, in May 1980. Enhancing its value was the fact that Sheeler painted the same* Bucks County Barn *ten years later; the painting is part of the Abby Aldrich Rockefeller Collection at the Museum of Modern Art. (Photo: courtesy of Christie's.)*

Where To Find Photographs—
The Market

If you had a photographer in the family in the latter part of the 19th century, try to locate some of the prints that might have survived. You may also discover some negatives from which new prints can be made, even enlarged. Both old and new could be collectibles if the subject matter is particularly interesting.

When you have settled down on a special subject, try to get positive identification through comparison with pictures of buildings, people or landscapes that have identifications. Then carefully identify the image you own. Be careful when writing directly on the rear of a photograph. Ink sometimes goes through the dry paper and a ball-point pen or a pencil can dig disastrous ridges. Perhaps best is a self-adhesive label on which you can type the information before peeling it from its waxy carrier and affixing it to the photograph.

You will find photos, usually of local people and landscapes, at street fairs, local auctions and flea markets. You may also find there the souvenir collections of travelers who collected commercial photos of places they visited—like today's tourists collect and send picture postcards. Thus attics may yield whole or fragmented collections of photographs brought back from the ends of the earth.

Museums Notable for Their Collections of Photographs
   International Museum of Photography, George Eastman House, 900 East Avenue, Rochester, NY 14607
   Museum of Modern Art, New York, NY 10019

Clubs and Organizations
   Photographics Historical Society, P.O. Box 1839, Radio City Station, New York, NY 10019

Books Worthwhile for Collectors
   Blodgett, Richard, *Photographs: A Collector's Guide*, Ballantine Books, New York, 1979
   Dennis, Landt and Lisl, *Collecting Photographs*, E. P. Dutton & Co., New York, 1977
   Haller, Margaret, *Collecting Old Photographs*, Arco Publishing Co., New York, 1978
   Weinstein, Robert A., and Booth, Larry, *Collection and Use of Historical Photographs*, American Association for State and Local History, 1977

Scarcity of Certain Sizes of Prints Can Affect Auction Price   *This famous photograph in silver print,* Moonrise, Hernandez, New Mexico, *by Ansel Adams, has achieved ever higher prices at auction. Not every collector, however, realizes that it is available in several print sizes. The most usual is 16″ × 20″, which sold for a world record of $16,000 at Christie's in May of 1980. A scarcer size is 21.5″ × 26.5″; a print of this dimension sold for $22,000 at Sotheby's in 1979. Even more rare are the 40″ × 60″; only a dozen or fewer are known to exist. One was sold by a dealer to a private collector for $71,500 in early 1981 but another, offered at auction, did not reach its reserve of $45,000 and was bid on by the house. (Photo: courtesy of Christie's.)*

Welling, William, *Collectors' Guide to Nineteenth Century Photography*, Macmillan, 1976

———, *Photography in America: The Formative Years 1839–1900*, Thomas Y, Crowell Co., New York, 1978

Witkin, Lee D., and London, Barbara, *The Photograph Collector's Guide*, New York Graphic Society, Ltd., Greenwich, Conn., 1979

POSTERS

Poster fans use the date 1869 as the birth of the modern illustrated advertising poster. In that year Jules Chéret, a Frenchman, served as father for a flood of colorful progeny. The lusty child attracted a prospering industry of producers, artists and printers—and collectors—from the very start.

Artists such as Pierre Bonnard and Toulouse-Lautrec designed popular posters *before* their paintings became famous. And in recent years the posters of Picasso, Chagall and many other international artists were often designed to advertise their own current exhibitions of oils or drawings.

So fierce was the mania for posters at the turn of the century that they were often stripped from public places almost as soon as they were pasted up. Printers caught on to this popularity quickly and began to print enough posters to satisfy both advertisers and collectors. For a time collectors even staged poster parties, for which owners were supposed to masquerade as one of the poster's character illustrations.

Most posters are rectangular rather than square. They tend to measure 4 feet high and a yard across and they usually advertise a product or entertainment such as a theater piece, a cabaret, cigarettes, liquor, a cause (such as soldier recruitment), a charity appeal or an art exhibition. The Metropolitan Opera, the New York Shakespeare Festival and the Metropolitan Museum of Art regularly issue posters to advertise special attractions and sell a good quantity of each run to collectors. An illustration, for example, by Marc Chagall to celebrate the opening of the New Metropolitan Opera House in 1966 was sold at the time for $20. Today, examples in good condition can fetch $700 or more.

Very early posters, particularly from French artists such as Jules Cheret, Toulouse-Lautrec, Pierre Bonnard and Alphonse Mucha (who did all of Sarah Bernhardt's later posters), can bring more then $20,000 today, though you were able to buy them for $50 to $100 shortly after World War II before the current poster boom got under way.

Posters are popular because they are bright, brash and often extremely well-designed and good examples of contemporary art fashions. For instance, Jean Dupas' posters for the London Transit System are highly prized as representative of Art Deco graphics. Posters participate in the general boom for art among collectors and in comparison to paintings, drawings and limited edition prints, most posters are relatively inexpensive. Still, they were printed, *as originals, in limited quantity*, and many were lost or destroyed as mere advertising of the day. Some early posters are very scarce today and, if by a famous artist such as Toulouse-Lautrec, can bring more than $50,000 for a rare example in good condition. Condition is most important.

Collectors insist on *originals* for their collections. Hence the need to distinguish between originals of the first limited edition and later reproductions. Before 1920 this was easy because most originals were printed one by one by hand and by color lithography. Each color required a separate run or impression on the sheet of poster paper. This meant solid masses of color, not the tiny dots that characterize the photoengraver's later reproductions. After 1920 it is more difficult to separate originals from reproductions because both were printed by photoengraving processes. You will have to compare the color intensity of a known original with that of an uncertain specimen. In general, the reproduction will have duller colors and thicker paper, and often measures smaller in size than the original.

The value of individual posters varies with the artist (known or unknown), the subject or place (unknown or celebrated) and the aesthetic achievement.

In addition to the artists already mentioned, some of the more valuable names to collect are the Americans Will Bradley, J. J. Gould, Will Carqueville, Edward Pensfield, James Montgomery Flagg and Norman Rockwell. In England the work of John Gilroy for Guiness Stout and Aubrey Beardsley for theatrical productions are much sought after. Capiello, in France, designed for Cinzano and Campari. Other French poster celebrities are A. M. Cassandre and Paul Colin.

Where To Find Posters—The Market

Posters by famous artists are available today almost entirely through dealers and auctions. Bright posters by anonymous or little-known commercial artists crop up at flea markets, antique shops and estate sales and all manner of lesser local sales.

Occasionally quantities of unsold posters emerge from store-rooms of companies that used them in advertising, or from advertising agencies and/or printers involved in the process. If you uncover such a cache you will certainly not want to keep all of them. Use them for bartering.

Museums Notable for Their Collections of Posters
  Art Institute of Chicago, Chicago, IL 60603
  California Historical Society Library, San Francisco, CA 10029
  New York Public Library and Museum of the Performing Arts at
    Lincoln Center, New York, NY 10023
  Warsaw Collection of Business Americana, Museum of History
    and Technology, Smithsonian Institution, Washington, DC
    20560

Books Worthwhile for Collectors
  Barnicoat, John, *A Concise History of Posters, 1870–1970*, Harry
    N. Abrams, New York, 1972
  Fern, Alan, *Word and Image*, Museum of Modern Art, New
    York, 1958–1968
  Gallo, Max, *The Poster in History*, American Heritage Publishing
    Co., New York, 1974
  Marx, Roger, ed., *Masters of the Poster, 1896–1900*, Images Gra-
    phiques, 1977
  Renner, Jack, *One Hundred Years of Circus Posters*, Darien
    House, 1974
  ———, and Terry, Walter, *One Hundred Years of Dance Posters*,
    Darien House, 1977

PRESSED GLASS

Still another variation of collectible glass, *pressed glass*, was the darling of our Victorian grandmothers who could buy it in quantity—it was manufactured by machine. It was decorative in its own right and much less expensive than cut glass or crystal, which it often attempted to imitate. Manufacturers still produce pressed glass today and continue some of the oldest and most popular designs. It makes a fine collectible for beginners; it can be admired as well as *used*.

Tried and true collectors, however, chase the old pieces, those made from about 1825 through 1900.

Of the mass of collectible pressed glass that remains from this period, there are two kinds based on the manufactured finish: *lacy pressed glass* and *pattern glass*. Lacy glass was covered with small dots called stippling (created to hide imperfections in the early pressing process) except where it was actually molded into a form. This kind of glass was generally sold as individual pieces and flourished until the middle of the 19th century. As it diminished in popularity, pattern pressed glass (taking advantage of improved pressing techniques) took over. It was generally clear or colored but not stippled, and was made to be sold in sets of the same pattern, much like table settings of china.

Today the price of lacy or pattern pressed glass is influenced by the size of the piece (larger is more valuable) and the age (older is more valuable). But most important is the *rarity* of the design and/or the form.

Among the large variety of designs (there are more than 3,000 different designs of lacy glass, for example), the Roman Rosette and several heart designs are the most prized. In pattern glass, collectors search eagerly for the Bellflower and Westward Ho designs.

Among the rarer forms in lacy glass are large serving dishes and decorative door panes, of any form and color. In pattern glass you will have a treasure if you find a wine jug or a punch server. Color in pattern glass came gradually and at first the shades were soft and gave the impression of a tint. After about 1880 brighter, harsher colors came on strong. After approximately 1870, pattern glass carried more complex designs.

Another way of telling the age of old glass lies in the random and various scratches that come with moving and handling it over the decades. Some more recent products have been artificially aged, to give them the signs of wear, but this mechanical aging tends to produce regular and/or parallel scratches and not always at the obvious points of wear. The earliest glass also is likely to have imperfections where molds did not match exactly or leaked and left a ridge at the mold's joining line. Modern reproductions do not have these defects, which authenticate old glass.

Where To Find Pressed Glass—
The Market

It was rare when a manufacturer marked its products but it is known in the glass industry that the earliest producers of pressed glass were Boston and Sandwich on Cape Cod in Massachusetts, Blakewell (also later known as Blakewell, Pears & Company) in Pittsburgh and the New England Glass Company of Boston. Though other manufacturers sprung up in other parts of the country, collectors still find their earliest examples of pressed glass in the Northeast in the vicinity of the three pioneering firms. It comes out of attics and can be found at all manner of local sales as well as at the international auction houses at special glass or Americana sales. A rare deep dish of lacy glass from Boston and Sandwich Glass Company, in its tapestry pattern, recently sold for $175; a set of four plates of campaign contenders in the 1884 presidential election in pattern glass recently sold for $1,100 the set.

Museums Notable for Their Collections of Pressed Glass
   Bennington Museum, Bennington, VT 05201
   Carnegie Institute Museum of Art, Pittsburgh, PA 15213
   Corning Museum of Glass and Glass Center, Corning, NY 14830
   Ford Museum, Dearborn, MI 48121
   Historical Society of Western Pennsylvania, Pittsburgh, PA 15213
   Sandwich Glass Museum, Sandwich, MA 02563
   Study Gallery, A Center for Glass and Ceramics, Douglass Hill, ME 04024
   Toledo Museum of Art, Toledo, OH 43601

Clubs and Organizations
   National Early American Glass Club, 55 Cliff Road, Wellesley Hills, MA 02181

Books Worthwhile for Collectors

Barret, Richard Carter, *A Collector's Handbook of Blown and Pressed American Glass,* Forward's Color Productions, Inc., 1971

DiBartolomeo, Robert E., ed., *American Glass II: Pressed and Cut,* Pyne Press, Princeton, N.J., 1974

Innes, Lowell, *Pittsburgh Glass 1797–1891: A History and Guide for Collectors,* Houghton Mifflin Co., Boston, 1976

Lee, Ruth Webb, *Early American Pressed Glass,* Lee Publications, 1967

————, *Sandwich Glass,* Lee Publications, 1966

Metz, Alice Hulett, *Early American Pattern Glass,* Heritage Antiques, 1977

————, *Much More Early American Pattern Glass,* Heritage Antiques, 1977

Revi, Albert C., *American Pressed Glass and Figure Bottles,* Thomas Nelson, Camden, N.J., 1964

Rose, James H., *The Story of American Pressed Glass of the Lacy Period, 1825–1850,* Corning Museum of Glass, Corning, N.Y., 1954

Wilson, Kenneth M., *New England Glass and Glassmaking,* Old Sturbridge, 1972

SATIRICAL CARTOONS

Born in Italy, cartoons emphasizing caricature found their heyday in 18th-century London where a venting of spleen took this hilarious and acid form and reached sublimity, perhaps, in Hogarth's several series. The genre of caricature (from the Italian *caricatura*, or exaggerated portrait) stems from 16th-century Italian artists as a kind of a play after their more serious work and portrait commissions.

It is hard to define the difference between cartoon and caricature because cartoons very often use the caricature technique. They are a comic art; contemporary comic strips are a descendant of both even though they do not usually spoof specific people: Blondie and Dagwood are types; in Doonesbury, however, real political figures are spoofed in the midst of imaginary characters that put them down. In Doonesbury, the person's face is often not seen but the figure is satirized by what others say and within the context of the drawing.

Satirical drawings in the 18th century were not as veiled. By word, dress or face, the viewer *knew* who was being satirized just as the one-frame political cartoon of today's newspapers makes the target evident either by labels or by an obvious likeness of a well-known person.

Drawings of these kinds were highly collectible in late 18-century London and have remained very popular to this day. The mania for them, then, caused printing presses to use various processes—etching, engraving or lithography—to mass-produce the original drawing or painting. There was a great spewing out of various editions depending on how popular the satire became. Thus there is a plentiful supply of the most popular drawings and at surprisingly modest prices—a few hundred dollars per print at the most.

Where To Find Cartoons and Satirical Prints—The Market

If you know what you are looking for, you can pick up bargains from dealers and at flea markets and fairs where vendors know considerably less about this specialized art form than you should know if you are to become a serious collector. Do not overlook descendants of famous cartoonists or their estates, which may be trying to create a market for the myriad drawings left behind by a great cartoonist.

You will naturally want to specialize in either a specific cartoonist or a political target such as Churchill or an American president as seen by various artists. This will give your collection a theme and added value if you manage to reach your goal in a comprehensive way.

Some leading names of artists who did satirical cartoons are: *from England*, George Woodward, Thomas Rowlandson, James Gilray, John Kay, William Hogarth, George Cruikshank, Sir John Tenniel, Leslie Illinsworth, David Low and Max Beerbaum; *from the United States*, Eugene Zimmerman, Thomas Nast, Al Hirschfield, Matt Morgan, William Norman Ritchie and David Levine; *from France*, Honore Daumier, Jean Louis Forain and Andre Rouveyre; *from Italy*, Pier Leon Thezzi and Carlo Pellegrini (who later came to the United States).

The possibilities are many, the limits few. The hazards come in selecting prints or originals (very few still exist) and in the condition of the print. A cartoon printed in *The New York Times* is not nearly as valuable as the original studies the artist may have made for it. The final original art as submitted and signed by the artist has the most value of all other versions.

Museums Notable for Their Collections of Cartoons
> Chicago Public Library Cultural Center, Fine Arts Division, Chicago, IL 60602
> New York Historical Society, New York, NY 10024
> New York Public Library, Print Division, New York, NY 10018

Books Worthwhile for Collectors
> Hess, Stephen, and Kaplan, Milton, *The Ungentlemanly Art*, Macmillan Publishing Company, 1968, 1975
> Hill, Draper, *The Satirical Etchings of James Gillray*, Dover Publications Inc., New York, 1976
> Hoff, Syd, *Editorial and Political Cartooning*, Stravon Educational Press, New York, 1976
> Nevins, Allan, and Wietenkampf, Frank, *A Century of Political Cartoons: Cartoons in the United States from 1800 to 1900*, Charles Scribner's Sons, New York, 1944
> Vinson, J. Chal, *Thomas Nast, Political Cartoonist*, University of Georgia Press, Athens, Ga., 1967

SILHOUETTES

Perhaps, as a child, you had your silhouette made by an artist at a state fair, a department store or a community social. Or in grade school perhaps your teacher used the old "shadow" method of casting your profile on paper, tracing it, reducing it via pantograph and mounting the black paper cutout on a white folder, as a Christmas present to your mother.

Until photography became popular after 1840, the silhouette was the popular and inexpensive form of portraiture. Thousands of itinerant silhouettists roamed Europe and the United States during the 18th and early 19th centuries and a respectable number of them still cut pictures today.

The silhouette, as all collectors know, was named after Etienne de Silhouette, controller of finance for King Louis XV of France. He was so renowned for his frugality that people named inexpensive paper portrait cutouts after him—portraits "à la Silhouette"; the phrase shortened eventually to his name only. It would be interesting to discover a silhouette of M. de Silhouette, but none has yet emerged though, in theory, one certainly ought to exist.

In Europe, the silhouette generally was made from black paper and the cutout head was then pasted on light paper. In the United States, the reverse, or hollow-cut method, became most popular. The paper actually cut was light in color, the head was removed and the remaining "frame" was pasted on dark paper, usually black or brown.

The value of a silhouette increases with its artistry and documentation. Some artists added clothing details in watercolor and signed their work, and named the person, the date and perhaps the special event such as a wedding, birthday or anniversary.

The popularity of the silhouette in the United States was such that professional artists set up museums of famous people in silhouettes cut from life or from engravings and would travel with their museums from city to city to encourage customers to see and to sit for a likeness. The most famous of these museums was opened and run by Charles Wilson Peale, of the celebrated family of artists. His name embossed or stamped on a silhouette can increase its value substantially, and his "signature" has been widely faked.

More than 24,000 well-made silhouettes were cut by one "Jean

Millette." Many of them were of famous patriots and founders of the United States. Unfortunately, the artist did not exist. Someone, unknown to this day, faked the 18th-century figures in the late 19th century. They first appeared at a "museum exhibit" in New York in 1892. They were not exposed as fakes until 1970 and by then had become parts of leading collections, including one at the Metropolitan Museum of Art.

Among the most celebrated of silhouette artists were Auguste Edouart (mid-19th century), William Henry Brown (1830's to 1840's) and Martha Anne Honeywell (mid-19th century). Signed examples by any of these artists automatically carry higher value. Martha Anne Honeywell was unusual in that she had no arms. She held her paper with her toes and cut it with scissors manipulated by her mouth.

Where To Find Silhouettes—The Market

Full figures silhouetted with additional details painted or drawn in also bring higher prices at dealers and at auctions. An Edouart can bring $400 to $500 with higher prices going to attractive family groupings. His "sitters" book, which covered the years 1840 to 1844, recently went at auction for $1,000. Silhouettes by anonymous artists bring lower prices and can be found at flea markets and garage sales, but they are not likely to be of the quality of those found at auctions of single and identified items of important collections.

Museums Notable for Their Collections of Silhouettes
   Essex Institute, Salem, MA 01970
   Massachusetts Historical Society, Boston, MA 02215
   National Portrait Gallery, Washington, DC 20560

Books Worthwhile for Collectors
   Carrick, Alice Van Leer, *A History of American Silhouettes, 1790–1840*, Charles E. Tuttle Co., Rutland, Vt., 1968
   Oliver, Andres, *Auguste Edouart's Silhouettes of Eminent Americans, 1839–1844*, University of Virginia Press and National Portrait Gallery, 1978

SPOONS

Spooners, or collectors of souvenir spoons, generally feed off a mania their grandfathers and grandmothers had two generations ago. That generation of collectors bought back a silver or other metal spoon from every place visited in the United States and abroad. If your grandparents were travelers, or traveled for business, you probably already have inherited some souvenir spoons.

The habit of bringing back spoons had its heyday during the thirty-year period 1890 to 1920. People expected and asked for souvenir spoons at every scenic attraction, convention, business or tourist center in the United States or when visiting foreign countries. And manufacturers obliged them by creating millions of silver spoons, some sterling, some plated, some with enameled bowls, some with enameled fiddles (handles), but all designed to recall the place visited.

As such, they were usually marked by their manufacturer and these marks included such famous names as Tiffany and Gorham. The artistry varied with the manufacturer and the more sculpted they were—rather than stamped—the more valuable they became.

Other themes were based on Christmas or religious figures such as the Apostles—thirteen themes depicting Christ attended by his twelve apostles. The practice of manufacturing special spoons was given impetus in 1880 by Daniel Low, a silversmith of Salem, Massachusetts, who traveled abroad and brought back with him souvenir spoons from several European tourist cities. He decided to do the same for his small town of Salem, founded by Puritans and made famous by its witch trials of the early 18th century. Thus was born the Salem witch spoon, which has become the most popular single item among spooners in the United States. One in good condition can bring as much as $85 at auction. Another popular single spoon is the Gorham ladle created in 1892 to benefit the Actors' Fund of America. Only 500 service spoons were created, with handles bearing the faces of famous theatrical people of the time. One of these spoons today will sell for $250 or more. Oddly enough, a new sterling silver spoon or ladle today can cost almost as much because of the price of an ounce of silver. Eventually the silver content of a souvenir spoon will affect its auction or sales price but usually the price is based on condition, artistry and rarity rather than on its sheer worth as silver. The price of silver per ounce nevertheless acts as a floor to the value of the spoon. Thus *any* silver spoon has a melt-down value, regardless of its artistry, provenance or rarity. These qualities simply add to its melt-down value.

Where To Find Spoons—The Market

Markets for spoons are usually helter-skelter. They can be found at garage sales, flea markets, and antique shows, but do not, as a rule, appear individually at the large auction houses, even the houses that regularly auction traditional sterling sets. Commemorative spoons seem to be the stepchildren of the silver artifacts family. Yet spooners love them and undoubtedly the really extensive and fine *collections* of spoons will appear more frequently now at leading auction houses and achieve fancy prices because of the collection's scope and possibly for its sheer weight in silver—if the silver shortage becomes more acute and the price per ounce of silver rises.

Museums Notable for Their Collections of Spoons
  Passaic County Historical Society, Lambert Castle, Paterson, NJ
    07503

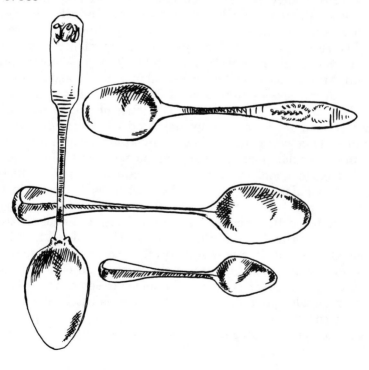

Clubs and Organizations
Souvenir Spoon Collectors of America, P.O. Box 814, Temple City, CA 91780

Magazines and Newsletters
The Spooner, Route 1, Box 49, Shullsburg, WI 53586

Books Worthwhile for Collectors
Hardt, Anton, *Adventuring Further in Souvenir Spoons, with a First Glimpse of the Tiffany Souvenir Spoons*, Greenwich Press, 1965
————, *New Discoveries in Historical Spoons: Souvenirs of the United States and Canada*, Greenwich Press, 1978
————, *Souvenir Spoons of the 90s*, Greenwich Press, 1962
————, *A Third Harvest of Souvenir Spoons*, Greenwich Press, 1969
Rainwater, Dorothy, and Felger, Donna, *American Spoons, Souvenir and Historical*, Thomas Welson, Camden, N.J., and Everybodys Press, 1968
Stutzenberger, Albert, *American Historical Spoons*, Charles E. Tuttle Co., Rutland, Vt., 1971

STAFFORDSHIRE CHINA

Known simply as Staffordshire, this china was shipped by the boatload to the United States from the potteries of Staffordshire (county) in England throughout the 19th century. It includes the famous Wedgwood ware. A whole galaxy of manufacturers or potters dug into the clay of about 12 square miles of England where there was also coal to heat the kilns for firing the potteries.

About 1820 the potteries of England began shipping to these shores "Historical Blue" with U.S. scenes. This became and remains the most popular kind of Staffordshire among U.S. collectors. Less popular is blue willowware, with an English interpretation of Chinese landscapes. Still another variant is "flow-blue," which has an image deliberately blurred during firing. Collectors with a taste for a greater variety of colors look for Staffordshire lusterware in the form of pitchers, commercial pot lids, Toby character jugs or Gaudy Dutch tea or coffee sets made during the years 1800 to 1850 for export to Pennsylvania Dutch customers. The scenes in historical blue eventually came to the market in pinks, greens and browns but they were never as popular as the blue.

With Staffordshire, the earlier the date of the piece, the more valuable it is. Some collectors prefer to collect only pieces made before 1850. Others collect complete examples from a particular pottery.

The marking system on the base of a piece was helter-skelter but there was usually a manufacturer's mark that dates the piece, at least during the years the pottery was active. Other habits of marking will give dating limits. For example, the common Staffordshire knot mark and the word "royal" were seldom used until the middle of the 19th century. "Limited" or its abbreviations did not appear until after 1860. The word "trademark" was not used until about 1875 and registry numbers first appeared in 1884. The *Encyclopedia of British Pottery and Porcelain Marks* by Geoffrey A. Godden will help you with identification by showing copious illustrations and a chart of marks used and their dates of use.

Where To Find Staffordshire— The Market

Any shop that handles collectibles is likely to have some pieces of Staffordshire, which is, of course, one of the most popular collectibles in the United States. There is plenty of it in circulation and individual pieces are in a price range that is affordable by the mass of collectors. It comes up in all manner of auctions and charity, attic, garage and rummage sales. Sophisticated dealers and shops in large cities will know its going values; for bargains you will have to find incidental pieces in the country or at estate sales where the executors do not know much (or care much) about Staffordshire. Pieces can go for a few hundred (Toby jugs, for example) to a few thousand dollars (a pair of cream-colored leopards, for example). But a 26-piece tea service in strawberry lusterware can be had for about $450. Wedgwood specialties, of course, bring the highest prices. A black basalt plaque celebrating the Death of a Roman Warrior recently was auctioned for $3,100. A black basalt teacup and saucer dating from about 1790, also recently sold at auction, brought $3,000. Figures by Ralph Wood (father or son), who produced Staffordshire in the late 18th century, can bring $400 to $500 each. Enoch Wood and Sons, of the early 19th century, produced historical blue as well as figures that can sell today for about $400 to $500. A bust of John Wesley recently sold for $400.

Museums Notable for Their Collections of Staffordshire
    Brooklyn Museum, Brooklyn, NY 11238
    Everson Museum of Art, Syracuse, NY 13202
    New York Historical Society, New York, NY 10024
    Smithsonian Institution, Washington, DC 20560

Books Worthwhile for Collectors
    Arman, David and Linda, *Historical Staffordshire: An Illustrated Checklist*, Arman Enterprises, Inc., 1974
    Camehl, Ada Walker, *The Blue China Book*, Dover Publications, New York, 1971
    Godden, Geoffrey A., *Encyclopedia of British Pottery and Porcelain Marks*, Crown Publishers, New York, 1964
    Haggar, Reginald, and Mankowitz, Wolf, *The Concise Encyclopedia of English Pottery and Porcelain*, Praeger Publishers, New York, 1968
    Mountford, Arnold R., *The Illustrated Guide to Staffordshire Salt-glazed Stoneware*, Praeger Publishers, New York, 1971
    Olive, Anthony, *The Victorian Staffordshire Figure: A Guide for Collectors*, St. Martin's Press, New York, 1971
    Turner, H. A. B., *A Collector's Guide to Staffordshire Pottery Figures*, Emerson Books, New York, 1971

STAMPS

Oddly enough, one of the most popular and rewarding collectibles today—postage stamps—is only about 140 years old. Stamps were not printed until Sir Rowland Hill, an English schoolteacher, proposed them and an Act of the British Parliament authorized them in 1839. The famous "penny black," featuring a youthful head of Queen Victoria, came out in 1840. During the next decade the practice of affixing to letters a colorful stamp worth a few pennies spread throughout the world. Legend has it that one of the very first stamp collectors in England advertised for them in 1841—she wanted to use them for wallpapering.

Prior to 1840 letters were carried and canceled with a dating stamp similar to those still used today. But in most cases the recipient was expected to pay for the letters based on the number of pages delivered. Needless to say, many recipients refused to pay. Sir Rowland Hill devised a *prepaid*, separate piece of paper with glue on its back with established rates based on weight. Despite much opposition, largely incomprehensible from today's viewpoint, the change was made official by Parliament and the practice quickly caught on *throughout the world*. A following of collectors was quickly created by the issue of more denominations and designs, and particularly in recent years, a high quality of art was used in stamp design.

Today there are an estimated 20 million collectors of one de-

gree of commitment or another in the United States, and perhaps ten times that many throughout the world. There are an estimated quarter million different stamp designs in existence and they continue to increase as events and people are commemorated. Some of the smaller nations, such as San Marino, the Vatican, Andorra, Liechtenstein and Luxembourg, and the United Nations, earn a good income from issuing stamps primarily for collectors since their small populations do not generate a large user traffic. In other words, a majority of the stamps they sell are not used; hence no postal service is provided the buyer and profits flow into the issuers' treasuries.

There is big money to be made in collecting stamps if you learn the ropes early, acquire stamps of investment quality and then persistently upgrade your collection. Collecting stamps is such a common pastime among young Americans, usually at the grade school level, that even the Boy and Girl Scouts recognize stamp collecting with a merit badge. So does the U.S. Post Office, which now offers attractive kits for young collectors and a useful booklet for beginners, *The ABCs of Stamp Collecting*.

The odd thing is that early stamp collections are usually put away (in the attic, for example) with other childish things when a youngster in the United States gets into high school and college. Then serious stamp collecting recommences in later years. Such was the pattern of Marc Haas, a New York businessman and financier all his adult life and a prominent stamp collector whose collection of about 3,200 U.S. postal covers sold in 1979 for more than $10,000,000. He began to collect as a boy of 5 but became serious when about 35 years old.

There are so many stamps from so many issuers today that a collector must specialize from the very start in a country, such as the United States or England (the only country in the world that does not put its name on its stamps). Or one can collect by subject or topic, such as flowers, sports, famous women, famous men, painters and paintings, black leaders, whatever subject seems to fit in with your interests.

You can start to save stamps from mail delivered at your house or at your office. You can ask friends and relatives who have correspondents abroad to save stamps for you. And you can barter with other collectors at the numerous stamp clubs that have sprung up all over the United States.

If you live in a major metropolitan area, your main post office is likely to have a special counter or window for philatelists and the leading newspaper is likely to run a Sunday column on stamps and coins. Stamp collecting is one of the most organized of hobbies; its market and collectors' associations give unusually fine information and authenticating services. If you follow the right procedure, you will have more protection against fakes than you will with most other collectibles.

In the world of stamp collecting everyone knows the *Scott Standard Postage Stamp Catalogue,* which identifies stamps by a Scott Catalogue number, gives used- and unused-stamp prices and gives the denomination, the common name of the stamp and its first day of issue. You will find these identification numbers indispensable for reading ads and offering lists in magazines and newspapers put out for collectors, and for deciphering the briefed-down remarks in auction catalogs.

Attending stamp auctions, which take place periodically in many major cities, as well as conferences or conventions, you will get to know the dealers who may send you stamps on approval. That is, after you outline your objectives, the dealer will send you by mail stamps you can examine and select for purchase. You send a check for the ones you want to buy and send back the rest. Of course, you cannot expect very valuable stamps, at the start, to arrive by mail. You have to establish yourself as a customer who has a good credit payment record by personal check or by credit or bank card.

Where to Find Stamps—The Market

Almost every family has a stamp album hidden away someplace; someone, when young, fell victim to the stamp collecting bug just as they had measles or mumps. That is where you should begin; take over this fledgling collection (or collections) and weed them out and give them greater focus. A dealer will usually give you a free, informal appraisal of the stamps you have in the attic album. You may then want to sell the entire collection or perhaps just prune it down, selling the excess and using the proceeds to build the value of a narrower objective. Most dealers will give you their current catalog and news of upcoming auctions, club meetings and the like, if you visit their shop. But they will make a small charge, such as a dollar or two, if you answer an advertisement and ask for a catalog by mail.

If you get to New York City, visit the Collectors Club at 22 East 35th Street. It was established in 1896 and is now located in its own Stanford White mansion for the use of stamp collectors. A visitor can make use of an unusually complete library of philatelists' handbooks from countries throughout the world as well as

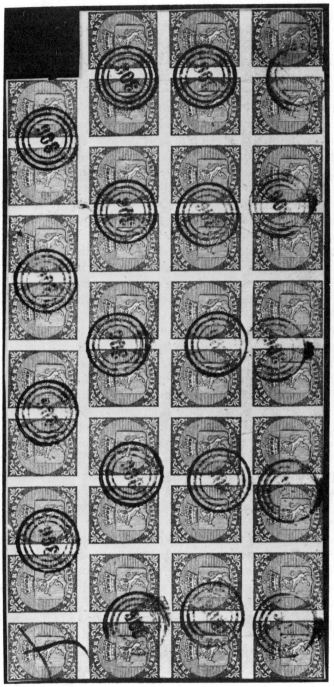

Printed Blue Paper to Some; a Small Fortune to the Stamp Collector *This block of 39 Norwegian stamps—the four skilling, which represented Norway's first issue in 1855—were put on a large envelope which a Norwegian ship was to carry to the United States. But the letter went back to the sender's post office because it missed the boat; it was lost in files for many decades. The stamps reappeared at an international exhibition in the 1920s, were bought by a U.S. collector and recently were sold for more than $210,000 (£105,000) by Phillips in London. (Photo: courtesy of Phillips.)*

auction catalogs with prices. The librarian can probably answer serious stamp collecting questions if you make an appointment for a consultation (212-683-0559). Nearby there is also the Philatelic Foundation at 270 Madison Avenue, which serves as an educational institution for stamp collectors. It helps them to determine the authenticity of rare and valuable items. Its Expert Committee will give you an opinion, though not a guarantee, as to whether or not philatelic material is genuine and whether a stamp or cover has been altered—regummed, reperforated, trimmed, falsely overprinted or repaired. A part of the foundation's library is the worldwide stamp collection, nearly priceless because of its unique scope, of the late John N. Luff, who attempted to bring together an example of every stamp listed in the Scott catalogs, which he edited for many years. The Luff and other eminent collections serve as a basis, or touchstone, for comparison in the authenticity research the foundation carries out for members as well as dealers and nonmembers on a fee basis. You can obtain an outline of these services and a directory of audiovisual educational programs by dropping a note to the Director of Education, Philatelic Foundation, 27 Madison Avenue, New York, NY 10016.

Prices for stamps have been appreciating about 22 percent annually on average over the past ten years. A rare two-cent Hawaiian missionary stamp was recently sold for $230,000 at auction. It belonged to a Japanese industrialist. A previous record for a U.S. stamp was $135,000 for a 24-cent airmail stamp with an inverted airplane. A Swedish stamp has sold for as high as $500,000. You can, with the help of a dealer or other expert, put together a beginning portfolio of investment quality in U.S. stamps for a few hundred or a few thousand dollars. Like coins, stamps have a higher value if in finer condition and collectors' organizations have established generally accepted definitions of grades, which depend on such criteria as centering, clarity of picture, and number and evenness of perforations.

As a general rule of thumb, more expensive stamps appreciate in value more rapidly than cheap ones. With highly organized collectors picking over a field of stamps for generations, there is a reason why some stamps are cheap and some are highly valuable—usually condition and rarity, which has already been established and is not likely to change over the years, even if one or two more specimens of the same quality are discovered in an attic album and suddenly come on the market.

Museums Notable for Their Collections of Stamps
  Cardinal Spellman Philatelic Museum, Weston, MA 02193
  Smithsonian Institution, National Museum of History and Technology, Washington, DC 20560
  Wineburgh Philatelic Research Library, University of Texas, Richardson, TX 75080

Clubs and Organizations
  American Philatelic Society, Box 800, State College, PA 16801
  American Topical Association, 3306 North 50th Street, Milwaukee, WI 53216
  Collectors Club, 22 East 35th Street, New York, NY 10016
  Philatelic Foundation, 270 Madison Avenue, New York, NY 10016
  Society of Philatelic Americans, Box 9041, Wilmington, DE 19809

Magazines and Newsletters
  Linn's Stamp News, Box 29, Sidney, OH 45365
  Mekeel's Weekly Stamp News, Box 1660, Portland, ME 04104
  Minkus Stamp Journal, Minkus Publications, Inc., New York, NY 10001
  Scott's Monthly Stamp Journal, Scott Publishing Co, New York, NY 10022
  Stamp Collector Newsletter, Box 10, Albany, OR 97321
  Stamp Magazine, H. L. Lindquist Publications, Inc., New York, NY 10014

Books Worthwhile for Collectors
  Cabeen, Richard McP., *Standard Handbook of Stamp Collecting*, Thomas Y. Crowell Co., New York, 1979
  Collectors Institute, Ltd., *Pictorial Treasury of U.S. Stamps*, Collectors Institute, Ltd., 1974
  MacKay, James A., *Encyclopedia of World Stamps, 1945–1975*, McGraw-Hill Book Co., New York, 1976
  Olecheski, Bill, *Beginning Stamp Collecting*, Henry Z. Walck, New York, 1976
  Scheele, Carl H., *A Short History of the Mail Service*, Smithsonian Institution Press, Washington, 1970
  Scott Standard Postage Stamp Catalogue, 4 volumes, Scott Publishing Co., 1981

STEINS

Accidents will happen; in the case of the Villeroy and Boch Company, potters and makers of steins, a fire in 1921 destroyed the documentation that held the secret behind their chromolith and cameo processes.

As a result, their steins, long considered the finest from any potter, were given an upper limit in number. After 1921 the steins were no longer the same and even modern attempts at reproducing the old steins gave a ware that is discounted in value.

Steins, mainly for beer, have been made ever since the 13th century and derive their name from the German words for earthenware (*Steingut*) and stoneware (*Steinzeug*).

The difference between a stein and a beer mug is the former's hinged lid, which often is the most decorative feature of the stein. The condition of the hinge and lid and their artistry can affect substantially the value of the stein.

The steins most prized by collectors were made in Germany during the 19th century and the best, as noted above, were made by Villeroy and Boch, located in Mettloch, Germany; because of the factory's location, they are called "mettlochs" by collectors.

Villeroy and Boch specialized in two types of ceramic processes. One was chromolith, in which a design in color was molded onto the stein. They appeared to be etched by hand and to be three-dimensional, but were neither—actually they were molded and smooth to the touch.

The other, an even more distinctive process, produced cameos or phanolithe. They featured translucent white portraits of scenes on a blue or green background. The effect was of a cameo and they were molded with the stein, rather than stuck on, and they seemed to emerge seamlessly from the rest of the stein. These steins are perhaps the most prized of all.

Few steins (though many mugs) were made in the United States but even Villeroy and Boch made steins and mugs for U.S. firms. United States makers included the Weller Pottery Company of Zanesville, Ohio. Well-known German competitors were Markelbach and Wick, Albert Jacob Thewalt, and Simon Peter Gerz. Steins dating from the 13th through the 17th centuries have higher value because of their rarity. After 1870 or so, the trade in steins picked up with colorful renditions of boisterous drinking bouts, weddings, animals, local buildings and people; there were even character steins—the skull for medical students, the regimental stein for a man in the army—and trade and professional steins, sometimes with the paraphernalia of the owner's personal interests. Occupational steins were popular in the early 1890's and manufacturers introduced hobby steins featuring such pastimes as golf, mountaineering, ballooning and bicycling.

Where To Find Steins—The Market

The marketplace for steins is largely through informal channels: flea markets and yard sales, where you find a few steins and sometimes a bargain if you can recognize value better than the seller. Auction houses and dealers are beginning to handle the most distinctive steins. Watch, too, for old bars that are going out of business and men's clubs of all kinds that may be closing down, renovating or just cleaning house. Steins can sell for a few dollars or they can go higher than $100 for a Mettloch cameo with a distinctive lid that is in good condition.

Museums Notable for Their Collection of Steins
No museum has as yet a notable stein collection. To see a good collection, you will have to visit a collector. This could be arranged through a collectors' organization.

Clubs and Organizations
Stein Collectors International, Kingston, NJ 08528

Magazines and Newsletters
Prosit, Stein Collectors International, Kingston, NJ 08528

Books Worthwhile for Collectors
Harrell, J. L., *Regimental Steins of the Bavarian and Imperial German Armies*, Old Soldier Press, 1979
Manusov, Gene, *Encyclopedia of Character Steins*, Wallace-Homestead, 1976

STEVENGRAPHS

There is a distinct challenge to collecting silk pictures known as Stevengraphs. There are but 188 different designs verified by the sample volume in the Coventry, England, city museum. It survived by chance the destruction of the Stevengraph Works during the World War II bombing of Coventry. The company had been weaving labels since 1862 but it began its popular silk pictures in 1879. They were made on a mechanical loom made possible through the improvements on such looms by Jacquard in France.

Before the creation of the silken scenes the ingenuity of the weavers went into illustrated ribbons, bookmarks and souvenir emblems. They were actually made in several European countries as well as in the United States (by Paterson, New Jersey, silk firms, for example) but oddly enough, among collectors the authentic Stevengraphs from the Coventry works, mounted in their original cardboard frames and in good condition with their bright colors retained, are the items that have the most value.

The subjects of Stevengraphs varied widely. There were portraits of the English and German royal families, of popular politicians, of boxers and of jockeys. Scenes often showed horse coaches, trains, battleships, hunting, and sports gatherings such as tennis and cricket games. Sometimes there were historical scenes such as Lady Godiva's ride through her hometown, Coventry, and famous battle scenes. United States collectors bid up prices on Stevengraphs with a U.S. theme, such as a portrait of Buffalo Bill, of boxer John L. Sullivan or of presidents such as George Washington and Grover Cleveland, or scenes of Niagara Falls or the remarkable silken picture of the Signing of the Declaration of Independence after the painting by John Trumbull.

Where To Find Stevengraphs and Silk Pictures—The Market

Stevengraphs, because of their popularity and relatively small supply as a collectible, have become sought after to the point where their value is pretty well known by dealers and auction houses throughout the world. You can occasionally find bargains at estate sales or in unmounted items at a local fair. Prices vary widely depending on date, condition of colors and the condition of the original customary cardboard mount. Stevens had a habit of advertising other available subjects on the back of the mount and included a date as well. By identifying the latest date advertised you have a good idea of the date of the Stevengraph you have in hand. The earlier it is, the more desirable. Of course, similar pictures from competitors in the United States or in France (where the quality and subtlety of the finished product is often better than in a Stevengraph) or other European countries can be collected at lower prices and may be in line for substantial appreciation as the Stevengraph market goes ever higher. Some of the rarest examples of the Stevens art sell for over $1,000 but most of the more common subjects can be bought for about $100. Faded colors and a mount in poor condition or replaced by a modern mount can drop prices drastically.

Museums Notable for Their Collections of Silk Pictures
> Huntington Library, Art Gallery and Botanical Gardens, San Marino, CA 91100
> Passaic County Historical Society, Lambert's Castle, Paterson, NJ 07503
> Paterson Museum, Paterson, NJ 07501
> Smithsonian Institution, National Museum of History and Technology, Washington, DC 20560

Clubs and Organizations
> Stevengraph Collectors' Association, Daisy Lane, Irvington-on-Hudson, NY 10533

Books Worthwhile for Collectors
> Baker, Wilma Sinclair LeVan, *Silk Pictures of Thomas Stevens*, Exposition Press, 1957
> Bunt, Cyril G. E., *The Silks of Lyons*, Dolphin Press, 1960
> Godden, Geoffrey A., *Stevengraphs*, Associated University Presses, Inc., 1971
> Sparke, Austin, and Darby, Michael, *Stevengraphs*, Chaucer Press, 1968

STONEWARE

Stoneware is the workaday, durable jug, pot, bowl or special container that was made, used and broken by the millions as the United States moved westward and expanded its borders. It even found an adaptation as sewer tile and it derives its name from the quality of the fired clay from which it is made. Stoneware is exceptionally strong and nonporous and, in the hands of a skilled potter, can be graceful, even beautiful.

In general, stoneware is prized for uncommon shapes, decorations or glazes that sealed in both incised lines and surface decoration. It is also collected by potters. The U.S. potters whose work has special value among collectors are James Morgan, active in the 1700's in Cheesequake, New Jersey, and the Remmey and Crolius families of New York City, who began during the Revolutionary period and continued their work into the 1800's. Also there were the Whites of Utica, New York, the Nortons of Bennington, Vermont, and the Hamilton and Jones families of Greensboro, Pennsylvania. In the south, there were Thomas M. Chandler and Collin B. Rhodes, near Edgefield in the western part of South Carolina.

Most potters stamped their wares with their names or insignia and some, under contract, stamped the containers with the name of a brewery or other manufacturer.

Where To Find Stoneware—The Market

You can find good stoneware at antique shops, fairs, flea markets and auctions. Look for the names of prestigious potters. Lacking such identification, buy for shape, decoration and overall condition of the specimen. You will find prices modest, a few dollars if you buy locally, but a rare prized salt-glazed jar made by Brewer, Clark & Son of Boston recently went for $3,500 at auction.

Museums Notable for Their Collections of Stoneware
  Bennington Museum, Bennington, VT 05201
  Greenfield Village/Henry Ford Museum, Dearborn, MI 48121
  Historical Society of York County, York, PA 17403
  New York Historical Society, New York, NY 10024
  Old Salem, Inc., Winston-Salem, NC 27108
  Smithsonian Institution, National Museum of History and Technology, Washington, DC 20560

Magazines and Newsletters
  Pottery Collectors Newsletter, P.O. Box 446, Asheville, NC 28802

Books Worthwhile for Collectors
  Barber, Edwin Atlee, *The Pottery and Porcelain of the United States and Marks of American Potters*, J. & J. Publishing, 1976
  Ketchum, William C., Jr., *Early Potters and Potteries of New York State*, Funk & Wagnalls, New York, 1970
  Osgood, Cornelius, *The Jug and Related Stoneware of Bennington*, Charles E. Tuttle Co., Rutland, VT , 1971
  Webster, Donald Blake, *Decorated Stoneware Pottery of North America*, Charles E. Tuttle Co., Rutland, VT , 1971

SWORDS

Swords, of all weapons with the possible exception of pistols, have perhaps the greatest appeal to collectors because so often they are beautifully crafted (as are pistols and guns) and also bear a mystique in their suggestion of the honor of the wearer. It is said that the Japanese samurai treasured his sword above his life. Magical swords, suggesting the strength and invincibility of the owner, belonged to King Arthur (Excalibur) and to Siegfried (Nothung), and many a historical corpse in its coffin or effigy on top of a tomb carries the warrior's sword, like a cross on his chest. Thus a sword has historical and mythological implications way beyond its use and meaning as a weapon.

Among U.S. collectors, American military swords are most popular although some collectors specialize in foreign swords, too. Since the sword's history goes back many millennia to the Bronze Age, and because the swords are made of highly durable material, there is still an ample quantity of swords to collect.

Most collectors specialize in types of swords based on shape: *sabers* with curved blades, *straight-edged swords*, like knives, and small swords whose cross sections were in the shape of diamonds, hexagons, ellipses or triangles.

Other collectors specialize in uses: military issue, ceremonial swords, even those worn by musicians in a military band, or swords used in specific wars. Many of the swords used during the Revolutionary War, for example, were manufactured abroad in Germany or Spain on a contract basis. They might have a Toledo (Spain), Alingenthal (France) or Soligen (Germany) blade but have an American cherrywood hilt wound about in gold wire. During the Civil War, contract swords were made for both the Union and Confederate forces. But the quantity was much less for the Confederacy and hence swords marked with the initials CS (Confederate States) or CSA (Confederate States of America) on the hilt or the blade are more highly prized than the larger quantity made for the Union forces.

Honorary, ceremonial and presentation swords can be faked fairly easily by adding an inscription that gives the sword a greater mystique. You can authenticate personal names or military titles, however, through diligent search of references available. In the case of a sword from the Revolutionary War, you can consult the Genealogical Library of the National Society of the Daughters of the American Revolution (DAR). The central reference division of the National Archives has military records for all periods prior to World War I. You will have to provide the purported owner's name, branch of service and home state, if you can decipher these from the sword itself. The Archives will give you from its files as much of the man's history as it has accumulated. You can increase the value of your sword, then, by including the authenticated "mystique" with the blade.

Where To Find Swords—The Market

Swords appear at auctions occasionally. You are more apt to find them at dealers that specialize in military paraphernalia. You probably won't find them at flea markets and fairs. They are among the prestige collectibles, not very expensive, actually, but they seem not to favor appearing among lowly things. Recent prices at auction have been $1,400 for a small sword with a Meissen porcelain grip; $300 for a short sword with silver mountings; and $150 for an English cavalry saber.

Museums Notable for Their Collections of Swords
  Fort Ticonderoga, Ticonderoga, NY 12883
  Metropolitan Museum of Art, New York, NY 10028
  Smithsonian Institution, Washington, DC 20560
  United States Naval Academy Museum, Annapolis, MD 21407
  West Point Museum, West Point, NY 10996

Clubs and Organizations
  Association of American Sword Collectors, P.O. Box 341, Delmar, DE 19940

Books Worthwhile for Collectors
  Albaugh, William A., III *Confederate Edged Weapons*, Harper Brothers, 1960
  Neumann, George C., *Swords and Blades of the American Revolution*, Promontory Press, 1973
  Peterson, Harold L., *The American Swords, 1775–1945*, Ray Riling Arms Book Co., 1965
  Wilkinson-Latham, Robert, *Swords and Other Edged Weapons*, Arco Publishing Co., New York, 1978

TINWARE OR JAPANNED WARE

The craft of painting tinware continues and contemporary products are collected almost as avidly as they have been for almost two hundred years.

In the 18th century, English innovators found a way to lacquer tin plate to resemble the lacquered wood imported from the Orient. These pioneers in tinware succeeded, by coating and baking several times, in creating a shiny black, protective surface on sheet iron that had been dipped one or more times in molten tin. The lacquering process, because it imitated an earlier Japanese process on wood, came to be known as japanning.

Once perfected by the English, tinware became popular in the United States and in France where it was known as *tole peinte* or painted sheet iron. In the U.S. and in England it was—and is—known as japanned ware or ornamented tin.

All kinds of household tinware were manufactured as early as 1720, and were japanned and ornamented as early as 1790. The trade continued until the middle of the 1800's. Peddlers from New England distributed the tinware as far west as St. Louis and New Orleans.

A variant of tinware was a plain tinware punched or pierced, or otherwise decorated by tooling the metal itself.

A premium is paid by collectors today for items that are old, rare and handmade. Also, numerous reproductions are still made by hand and by hand-turned machines, as was done in the early 1800's. This is then decorated, japanned, and varnished, but not oaked as in the earlier period.

Tinware can often go at attractive prices if signed. Older tinware can be highly valued even if anonymous, rather beat up and repaired. The quality of the original decoration (you never want to repaint tole) and rarity count a lot.

Item for item, mass produced and decorated (lithographed or stenciled) tinware brings less on the collectibles' market than the earlier, handcrafted variations.

Where To Find Tinware—The Market

Tinware, in its myriad variants, can be found at all the usual sources of collectibles. The beginning collector might profitably restrict collecting to a single shape or related shapes such as trays, coffeepots or canisters. There is a quantity of all these items still available at relatively low prices, say less than $35. But prized items can bring $600 (a gooseneck tole coffeepot with original coloring in so-so condition); $2,800 (a similar coffeepot with original coloring in exceptionally good condition); and $750 (a tinware tray) at American auctions.

Museums Notable for Their Collections of Tinware
  Abby Aldrich Rockefeller Folk Art Collection, Williamsburg, VA 23185
  Cooper-Hewitt Museum, New York, NY 10028
  Museum of the Historical Society of Early American Decoration, Inc., 19 Dove St., Albany, NY 12210
  Henry Francis du Pont Winterthur Museum, Winterthur, DE 19735
  Hershey Museum, Hershey, PA 17033
  Museum of American Folk Art, New York, NY 10019
  Old Museum Village in Orange County, Monroe, NY 10950
  Old Sturbridge Village, Sturbridge, MA 01566
  Smithsonian Institution, Washington, DC 20560

Clubs and Organizations
  Historical Society of Early American Decoration, 19 Dove St., Albany, NY, 12210

Books Worthwhile for Collectors
  Clark, Maryjane, *An Illustrated Glossary of Decorated Antiques,* Charles E. Tuttle Co., Rutland, Vt., 1972
  Coffin, Margaret, *American Country Tinware,* Thomas Nelson, Camden, N.J., 1968
  DeVoe, Shirley Spaulding, *The Tinsmiths of Connecticut,* Wesleyan University Press, Middletown, Conn., 1968
  Gould, Mary Earle, *Antique Tin and Toleware,* Charles E. Tuttle Co., Rutland, Vt., 1957
  Lea, Zilla Rider, ed., *The Ornamented Tray,* Charles E. Tuttle Co., Rutland, Vt., 1971
  ———*The Ornamented Chair;* Charles E. Tuttle Co., Rutland, Vt., 1980

TOOLS

The spirit of the self-reliant frontier in the United States inspired the builders of a new nation and created, too, a flood of tools for the task. Recently these have become collectible and it is likely the trend will spread to hand instruments in all trades and professions.

At the moment, most collectors emphasize woodworking tools: planes, saws, measuring instruments, boring tools and blades, augers and a host of variations of these.

Enthusiasm within these categories varies but value depends heavily on type, material, condition and maker if identified. In current markets there is heavy demand for planes and bit braces and they bring the best prices. If handles or bodies have particularly fine wood or brass, or have ivory inlays or are otherwise decorated, they are worth more. Great emphasis is placed on "working condition." The tool can have minor repairs but its parts should work. With signed tools, a known name can increase value, even if the item is not in the best condition. Toolmakers of New England, such as Francis or John (his son) Nicholson and their black associate, Cesar Chelor, stamped their planes with name and address. All three names are highly collectible.

Some handmade tools have makers' name stamped on them—machine-made tools of recent decades always do—and there is sometimes a date for either kind. Earlier, undated tools can sometimes be dated by their shape and obvious function to fulfill certain tasks in a building process. As construction techniques and materials changed, so did tools, or parts of tools.

Because most tools today are made by machine, handmade tools of an earlier age command premium prices. But certain machine-made tools are catching on among collectors, particularly early saws from Henry Disston's works in Philadelphia and the planes of the venerable Stanley Rule and Level Company. Both of these companies are still manufacturing tools.

Some contemporary machine-made tools, such as surgical and dental instruments, are so finely crafted that it is only a matter of time before they, too, will be prized collectibles. Beginners might consider them as unexploited territories.

Letter from Manufacturer Increases Value of Plane in Mint Condition *A unique item in a recent auction of tools was this side-by-side, double-throat, fancy molding plane in mint condition. With it went an original letter, dated 1866, quoting prices of other planes available from the manufacturer, D. P. Sanborn, whose name and "Littleton, New Hampshire" appear on the iron. The plane sold for $2,000. (Photo: courtesy of J. P. Bittner.)*

Where To Find Old Tools—The Market

You can find old tools in the most humble places. One of the most fruitful of them is the farm auction. On farms, they may have accumulated for generations, set aside in a tool room or barn loft as no longer useful for contemporary tasks. Other sources may be the closing (for demolition) of an old factory or carpentry shop. If your speciality is working tools, become friends with the cabinetmakers and handcraftspeople in your vicinity. These trades are highly susceptible to the father-son tradition and tools come down with the skills taught or inherited. Many of the tools may now be obsolete for use and the craftspeople may welcome the extra income and greater space made available by a "clean-out."

Some regional auctions are beginning to have special sales devoted to tools and the older implements appear at Americana and collector auctions. You can usually buy ordinary planes and saws from the 19th century for less than $50. Decorated tools and tools identified with known makers run higher.

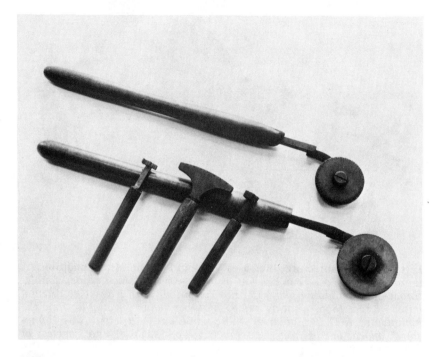

Dedicated Bookbinder Educates Others in Use of Tools *Collecting the tools of a particular trade or craft can make a fascinating hobby for an artisan in that trade. Mr. Samuel B. Ellenport, a former college teacher, bought the venerable Harcourt Bindery in Boston (which continues in business today) and sponsors a school in bookbinding. Mr. Ellenport also gives lectures at book fairs and colleges throughout New England. When he recently sold some of his collection of antique tools, he lectured and demonstrated in New York City. The tools shown in the photo are typical of those auctioned. Individual items usually sold for less than $100 each. Fillets and border rolls were illustrated in Christie's special catalog by the designer. (Photo: courtesy of Christie's.)*

Museums Notable for Their Collections of Old Tools
   Henry Francis du Pont Winterthur Museum, Winterthur, DE 19735
   Mercer Museum of the Bucks County Historical Society, Doylestown, PA 18901
   Old Sturbridge Village, Sturbridge, MA 01566
   San Joaquin County Historical Museum, Lodi, CA 95240
   Shelburne Museum, Inc., Shelburne, VT 05482

Clubs and Organizations
   Early American Industries Association, P.O. Box 2128, Empire State Plaza Station, Albany, NY 12220

Books Worthwhile for Collectors
Kebabian, Paul B., *American Woodworking Tools*, New York Graphic Society Ltd., Greenwich, Conn., 1978
Salaman, R. A., *Dictionary of Tools*, Charles Scribner's Sons, New York, 1977
Sloane, Eric, *A Museum of Early American Tools*, Funk & Wagnalls Publishing Co., New York, 1964

TOYS

Quite aside from the inevitable nostalgia they evoke for childhood, toys are moving up in popularity as a collectible because of their proven capability for increasing in value. Toys make a good item to collect because they were mass-produced for a time and then faded as their fad passed. Also techniques in manufacturing moved from metals and ceramics to plastic, from mechanical means of motion—such as wind-up—to the self-contained battery-powered electronic system based on minaturization of parts. These distinct masses of toys enable collectors to block out types and specific brands or subjects, such as wind-up animals, as a theme for a worthwhile and rewarding collection.

Collectors in the United States seem to concentrate on toys made in the United States or imported from Germany from the middle of the 19th century to the beginning of the 20th, but interest, though at a lesser intensity, continues in toys manufactured in the United States, Japan and Germany through the present day.

With collectors, working condition, in most cases, is *not* important. Collectors do not *play* with toys, they display them and talk about them. Age is a factor (the older the better) and condition tells. A cast iron or tin toy is more valuable in its original, chipped condition than if repainted. But if you find a toy with a finish "just like new" and in its original box, you have found a treasure. Wind-up toys are more valuable if they have their original key or pull-string; it does not matter if they do not work.

Fads may sweep the world of the toy collector. If Mickey Mouse and his family rise with the fortunes (and publicity) given Disneyland and Walt Disney's World, the many Disney inspired toys take off in value, the rarest at the fastest speed.

To a certain extent the manufacturer of a toy makes a difference but unfortunately only a few manufacturers, before the turn of the century, made a habit of marking their product. Catalogs, complete with pictures of a manufacturer's products, exist, however, and help in the identification and dating of individual toys and their variations over the years. You will find these datings and identifications in the catalogs of the prominent toy sales and through the dealers who specialize in old toys.

Some prominent manufacturers who once produced toys sought by collectors today are:

In the United States:

Francis, Field & Francis (tin toys with clockworks or pulls)
James Fallow & Son (tin riverboats)
Althof, Bergmann (tin horse-drawn vehicles)
George W. Brown (tin clockwork toys and carts drawn by animals)
J. E. Stevens (cast iron cap guns and cannons)
Ives, Blakeslee & Co. (cast iron firefighting toys)
Louis Marx & Co. (tin wind-up toys, often based on cartoon characters)
Francis W. Carpenter (cast iron carriages)
Pratt & Letchworth (cast iron fire fighter and artillery pieces)
Arcade Manufacturing Co. (early cast iron miniatures)
Tootsietoy (die cast miniature cars)
"Matchbox" (die cast miniature cars)
Dinky (die cast miniature cars)
Corgi (die cast miniature cars)
Lionel (electric trains)
American Flyer (electric trains)
Erector (structural toys)
Albert Schoenhut (circus figures)

From Germany; toys of the following makers are considered collectible but not quite as prized as their American counterparts:

Bebruder Bind (transportation toys)
Bebruder Marklin (transportation toys)
Georges Carette (hansoms, railways, steam engines and accessories)
Margarete Steiff GMBH (stuffed plush animals)
Richard & Carl Adam (wind-up toys)
Ernst Paul Lehmann (comic tin wind-up toys)

Where To Find Toys—The Market

Toys pop up at local flea markets and fairs as well as attic and garage sales. But the most prestigious toys turn up at the special sales of the international auction houses. At a recent Collector's Carousel at Sotheby's, for example, a tin steamboat sold for more than $20,000 to an enthusiastic (fanatical?) collector. Most prices are much lower than that but you will have to come into the 20th century and recent times to get your average toy for less than $50. An American Flyer train set of 8 pieces from about 1950 recently brought $50 but a Lionel standard gauge two-tone green set of 6 pieces in fine condition dating from about 1930 brought $8,500.

Museums Notable for Their Collections of Toys
Abby Aldrich Rockefeller Folk Art Collection, Williamsburg, VA 23185
Children's Museum of Indianapolis, Indianapolis, IN 46208
Greenfield Village and Henry Ford Museum, Dearborn, MI 48121
Henry Francis du Pont Winterthur Museum, Winterthur, DE 19735
Museum of the City of New York, NY 10029
New York Historical Society, NY 10024
Perelman Antique Toy Museum, Philadelphia, PA 19106
Raggedy Ann Antique Doll and Toy Museum, Flemington, NJ 08822
Scale Model Farm Toy Museum, Dyersville, IA 52040
Shelburne Museum, Inc., Shelburne, VT 05482
Smithsonian Institution, Washington, DC 20560
Toy Museum of Atlanta, Atlanta GA 30305
Washington Dolls' House and Toy Museum, Washington, DC 20015
Western Reserve Historical Society, Cleveland, OH 44106

Clubs and Organizations
Antique Toy Collectors of America, Route 2, Box 5A, Parkton, MD 21120
Matchbox Collectors Club, P.O. Box 119, Wood Ridge, NJ 07075

Magazines and Newsletters
Antique Toy World, 3941 Belle Plaine Avenue, Chicago, IL 60618
Miniature Tractor and Implement, R.D. 1, Box 90, East Springfield, PA 16411

Books Worthwhile for Collectors
Barenholtz, Edith F., *The George Brown Toy Sketchbook*, Pyne Press, Princeton, N.J., 1971
Bartholomew, Charles, *Mechanical Toys*, Chartwell Books, Inc., 1979
Bull, Peter, *The Teddy Bear Book*, Random House, New York, 1970

Buser, Elaine and Dan, *Guide to Shoenhut Dolls, Toys, and Circus*, Collector Books, 1976

Fritzsch, Karl Ewald, and Bachmann, Manfred, *An Illustrated History of Toys*, Hastings House, Publishers, New York, 1978

King, Constance Eileen, *The Encyclopedia of Toys*, Crown Publishers, New York 1978

Milet, Jacques, and Forbes, Robert, *Toy Boats 1870–1955*, Charles Scribner's Sons, New York, 1979

Pressland, David, *The Art of the Tin Toy*, Crown Publishers, New York, 1976

Schwartz, Marvin, *F.A.O. Schwartz Toys through the Years*, Doubleday & Co., Garden City, N.Y., 1975

Weltens, Arno, *Mechanical Tin Toys in Color*, Sterling Publishing Co., New York, 1979

Whitton, Blair, *Bliss Toys and Doll Houses*, Dover Publications, New York, 1979

Wieland, James, and Force, Edward, *Tootsietoys: World's First Diecast Models*, Motorbooks, 1980

Williams, Guy R., *The World of Model Cars*, G. P. Putnam's Sons, New York, 1976

WEATHERVANES

Weathervanes, those ubiquitous targets for .22 rifles and BB guns in rural areas, are so popular—and valuable—as collectibles that they comprise a separate category of folk art.

The earliest (and the most expensive if in good condition) were handcrafted by local smiths. If these are three-dimensional and of hammered sheet copper, they could be worth as much as $25,000 or more. Carved wooden vanes from the 18th and 19th centuries also bring top value because they are so scarce. What was left by the winds and rain is often most fragile and is often further ruined by careless handling.

In the late 19th and 20th centuries, weathervanes were factory-made by hammering copper into iron molds that shaped it. Then the two halves were soldered together and sometimes covered with gold leaf.

Some of the manufacturers who did this were Cushing & White of Waltham, Massachusetts; J. Howard Company of East Bridgewater, Massachusetts; J. W. Fisher of New York City; and E. G. Washburne & Co. of Denver, Massachusetts.

More plentiful and generally less valuable than the three-dimensional vane was the silhouette cut from sheet iron—the flat rooster, trotting horse or ornamental arrow.

A flood of reproductions from old molds and patterns of both types of vanes can easily confuse the novice collector. They are usually sold legitimately as reproductions, sometimes by the original maker such as J. W. Fisher. Counterfeits and fakes were also made and artificially aged. The experienced collector, however, by much observation and research can detect the fake and separate the authentically old item from the legitimate.

Where To Find Weathervanes— The Market

You will find weathervanes at the auction houses, usually at sales of Americana or folk art and often at top prices. The authentic old vanes, in good condition, are extremely rare and distinctive designs such as a three-dimensional copper Indian could go for more than $25,000. More common designs such as a horse or fish could run from $150 (wooden fish) to $500 (molded copper fish) or $1,000 (molded copper rooster) or $2,500 (molded copper horse).

Racing the Wind   *This U.S. weathervane of horse and sulky driver, dating from the mid-19th century, went for $4,600 at a recent Christie's auction. Had it been of a rarer subject, in better condition, and entirely of copper, it might have gone for more. (It was in fair condition.) The horse is in three-dimensional copper but with a head of lead; the driver is in lead; the sulky is of wrought iron. It is large (39" long) for a weathervane. Cast lead was sometimes used to counterweight a composition so that it would turn easily in the wind. (Photo: courtesy of Christie's.)*

You may find bargains in rural areas, particularly in the vicinity of original craftspeople and manufacturers. You may have to buy the building, usually a factory or barn, to obtain the vane but sometimes a farmer will consider your offer "found" money and simply order from Sears a contemporary vane as replacement. It pays to practice the art of gentle persuasion when you collect weathervanes—as well as to exercise your eyes (aided by binoculars) for authencity and rarity.

Museums Notable for Their Collections of Weathervanes
  Abby Aldrich Rockefeller Folk Art Collection, Williamsburg, VA 23185
  Fenimore House, New York State Historical Association, Cooperstown, NY 13326
  Greenfield Village and Henry Ford Museum, Dearborn, MI 48121
  Heritage Plantation of Sandwich, Sandwich, MA 02563
  Museum of the Concord Antiquarian Society, Concord, MA 01742

Pennsylvania Farm Museum of Landis Valley, Lancaster, PA 17601

Shelburne Museum, Inc., Shelburne, VT 05482

Smithsonian Institution, Washington, DC 20560

Books Worthwhile for Collectors

Christensen, Erwin O., *Index of American Design*, Macmillan Company, 1959

Fitzgerald, Ken, *Weathervanes and Whirligigs*, Clarkson N. Potter, New York, 1967

Kayne, Myrna, *Yankee Weathervanes*, E. P. Dutton & Co. New York, 1975

WEDGWOOD

Since 1759 when Josiah Wedgwood, a brilliant and experimental heir to five generations of potters in Staffordshire, England, began to improve on inherited pottery-making techniques, there has been a flood of ornamental and useful wares from the famous potter that has delighted collectors for several centuries.

Josiah experimented with Cornish clay and a lead glaze until he perfected an ivory-colored, light, strong earthenware that looked enough like fine porcelain to suggest elegance yet was relatively inexpensive. Because Queen Charlotte, wife of George III, ordered a tea set made of it, it became known as queensware; it is still made today along with basalt (black) ware, bone china, jasper ware, and other wares in a bewildering variety of shapes and uses—even doorknobs and bathtubs. Nearly all, fortunately for the collector, bear the manufacturer's authenticating marks. Pieces made in more recent years also bear letters and numbers that indicate date and sometimes the decorating artist.

Where To Find Wedgwood—The Market

Because of the quantity of Wedgwood and its relative sturdiness, many pieces still remain intact and available to collectors at relatively low prices. It has been a common wedding present in fairly affluent U.S. households for generations and hence it shows up in attic sales and estate clearances with regularity. Scarce pieces are usually those that proved less than a commercial success and were quickly discontinued with only a small quantity now available to collectors. They were often very distinctive, too distinctive to attract a mass market. Their flaw or fault was that they didn't make money for the company.

At auction these rarer items, or complete sets of dinner or tea services, particularly those with an interesting provenance, bring premium prices. Some examples are six plates of queensware with shells and seaweed for $400; early teacup and saucer of black basalt ware with reddish brown borders and scroll, $3,000; Pegasus vase in white and black jasper, $2,200; luster bowl with hummingbirds and a wild geese border in fine condition, $125.

Museums Notable for Their Collections of Wedgwood
   Art Institute of Chicago, Chicago, IL 60603
   Birmingham Museum of Art, Birmingham, AL 35203

Clubs and Organizations
   Wedgwood International Seminar, New York, NY 10003

Magazines and Newsletters
   The American Wedgwoodian, Wedgwood International Seminar,
   New York, NY 10003
   BMW Bulletin, Buten Museum of Wedgwood, Meriod, PA 19066

Books Worthwhile for Collectors
   Buten, David, *Wedgwood Guide to Marks and Dating,* Buten
   Museum of Wedgwood, 1976
   ———and Pelehach, Patricia, *Wedgwood and America: Wedg-
   wood Basrelief Ware,* Buten Museum of Wedgwood, 1977
   Buten, Harry, *Wedgwood Rarities,* Buten Museum of Wedgwood,
   1969
   Graham, John Meredith, II, and Wedgwood, Nehsleigh Cecil,
   Wedgwood, Arno Press, 1974
   Kelly, Alison, *The Story of Wedgwood,* Viking Press, New York,
   1975
   Klamkin, Marian, *The Collector's Book of Wedgwood,* Dodd,
   Mead & Co., New York, 1971
   Reilly, Robin, *Wedgwood Jasper,* World Publishing Co., New
   York, 1972
   ———and Savage, George, *Wedgwood: The Portrait Medallions,*
   Barrie & Jenkins, 1973

WILDLIFE PRINTS

The extreme popularity of prints (in this case hand-colored engravings) published from original oils of *Birds of America* by John James Audubon has spread to similar prints based on the work of such well-known artists as Alexander Wilson, a naturalist born in Scotland and creator of *American Ornithology*, and Mark Catesby, author of *The Natural History of Carolina, Florida, and the Bahama Islands*. After these big three come lesser figures such as Daniel Giraud Elliot, Thomas Doughty, George Edwards (a British naturalist) and John Edward Holbrook, an expert painter of snakes. In more recent years, regional painters have taken it upon themselves to preserve contemporary renditions of local wildlife. These "regional Audubons" have developed loyal followings so that each original oil or watercolor and subsequent limited editions of lithographs sell out quickly and at remarkably high prices to local enthusiasts.

In the early 18th century until the middle of the 19th, both American and European collectors absorbed an enormous number of paintings and prints from a horde of artists who regularly went to the New World wilderness to bring back their impressions of flora and fauna in as lively a way as they could for the time and circumstances. Audubon actually shot and brought home for "posing" most of the specimens he painted. Other artists painted from life, in the wild poses seen there, much as a photographer would today.

In order to make limited editions of these original works, the artist or publishers' technicians would make plates, printing them in black and white and then coloring them by hand. Sometimes a technician would carry on the work with the original as model.

Audubon's first edition of *Birds of America* went through the hands of three engravers, William H. Lizars, Robert Havell and Robert Havell, Jr. Prints from this first edition of Audubon's work bring the highest prices, although succeeding editions by others also do as well because of the artist's widespread popularity. Perhaps the most prized single Audubon print is of the wild turkey. Copies of it have recently sold for as much as $75,000 when in excellent condition.

Where To Find Wildlife Prints— The Market

Unless you know your family collected natural history books or framed wildlife prints, it is unlikely you will find examples of value in your attic or in anybody's garage sale or local flea market. The names of artists in this field are now well known and recognized, and almost all of the significant examples available come to market through dealers or auction houses.

If you choose this collectible, however, sharpen your eye and watch the credits at the bottom of a wildlife print. Something of value could be discovered among many cheaper imitations—or worse, among fakes.

Museums Notable for Their Collections of Wildlife Prints
American Museum of Natural History, New York, NY 10024

Magazines and Newsletters
Print Trader, M. Rainone, Middle Village, NY 11379

Books Worthwhile for Collectors
Elbert, John and Catherine, *Old American Prints for Collectors*, Charles Scribner's Sons, New York, 1974
Zigrosser, Carl and Gaehde, Christa M., *A Guide to the Collecting and Care of Original Prints*, Crown Publishers, New York, 1965.

Index